BOOKS BY W. S. MERWIN

POEMS

The Folding Cliffs: A Narrative   1998
The Vixen   1996
Travels   1993
Selected Poems   1988
The Rain in the Trees   1988
Opening the Hand   1983
Finding the Islands   1982
The Compass Flower   1977
Writings to an Unfinished Accompaniment   1973
The Carrier of Ladders   1970
The Lice   1967
The Moving Target   1963
The Drunk in the Furnace   1960
Green with Beasts   1956
The Dancing Bears   1954
A Mask for Janus   1952

PROSE

The Lost Upland   1992
Unframed Originals   1982
Houses and Travellers   1977
The Miner's Pale Children   1970

TRANSLATIONS

Sun at Midnight (Poems by Muso Soseki) (WITH SOIKU SHIGEMATSU)   1989
Vertical Poetry (Poems by Roberto Juarroz)   1988
From the Spanish Morning   1985
Four French Plays   1985
Selected Translations 1968–1978   1979
Euripedes' Iphigeneia at Aulis (WITH GEORGE E. DIMOCK, JR.)   1978
Osip Mandelstam, Selected Poems (WITH CLARENCE BROWN)   1974
Asian Figures   1973
Transparence of the World (Poems by Jean Follain)   1969
Voices (Poems of Antonio Porchia)   1969, 1988
Products of the Perfected Civilization (Selected Writings of Chamfort)   1969
Twenty Love Poems and a Song of Despair (Poems by Pablo Neruda)   1969
Selected Translations 1948–1968   1968
The Song of Roland   1963
Lazarillo de Tormes   1962
Spanish Ballads   1961
The Satires of Persius   1960
The Poem of the Cid   1959

ANTHOLOGY

Lament For the Makers: A Memorial Anthology   1996

THE

FOLDING

CLIFFS

THE
FOLDING
CLIFFS

A NARRATIVE

W. S. MERWIN

ALFRED A. KNOPF

NEW YORK 1998

THIS IS A BORZOI BOOK
PUBLISHED BY ALFRED A. KNOPF, INC.

www.randomhouse.com

Library of Congress Cataloging-in-Publication Data

Merwin, W. S. (William Stanley), 1927–
    The folding cliffs : a narrative / W.S. Merwin.—1st ed.
        p.   cm.
    ISBN 0-375-40148-2
        1. Hawaii—History—Poetry.   I. Title.
PS3563.E75F56   1998
811'.54—dc21   98-27434
                                                                CIP

ACKNOWLEDGMENTS: The following sections of the poem originally appeared in
THE ANTIOCH REVIEW: from "Climbing," sections 7, 14, 16, 24, 39; from
"There," section 23; from "The Valley," 40; from "The Cliffs," 40; from "The Shore,"
2, 15. DOUBLETAKE: "The Mountain," 1.

Manufactured in the United States of America
First Edition

FOR OLIVIA BREITHA

NOTE

THE CENTRAL EVENTS of the story all happened and the principal characters existed but the evidence for both is fragmentary and most of it second or third hand, refracted and remote. This is a fiction but it was not my purpose to belie such facts as have come down to us. Some of them have been moving toward legend since they occurred.

For what I have learned of them I am profoundly indebted first to Frances Frazier, whose editing and translation of Pi'ilani's account told by Sheldon was my own introduction to this story. Agnes Conrad, whose grasp of the trove of the Hawaiian State Archives approaches magic, repeatedly conjured up startling treasures that had slumbered there for a hundred years. Frederick B. Wichman has been unfailingly open with his own long-accumulated erudition on the subjects of the legends and history and names of the island of Kauai. Carol Wilcox has given me other invaluable details of the history and people of the island. Pat Boland and Anwei Skinsness have both put at my disposal their extensive work on the history of Kalaupapa and of leprosy in Hawaii.

The word "leper," of course, is offensive in any modern reference. I have used it throughout simply because it was the ordinary usage at the time of the story, part of the appalling cruelty of the history of what Hawaiians came to call "the separating sickness."

A note of any complexity about Hawaiian pronunciation would probably be ignored, and for those who are interested one can easily be found. But it might be useful here to say that if the vowels are accorded individual attention and sounds roughly resembling Spanish or Italian, and double vowels pronounced with a glottal stop between them (as in 'oh-oh') it will at least be a courteous if faltering step toward a rich, subtle, ancient and elegant language.

CONTENTS

ix

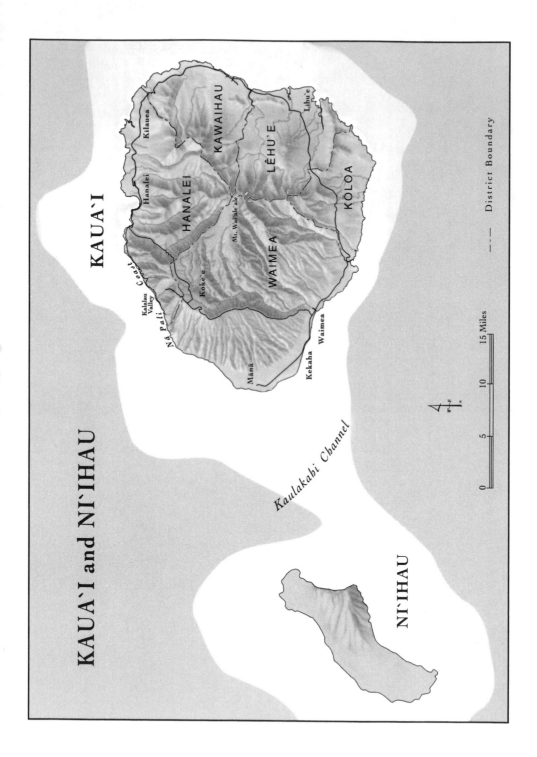

KAUA'I and NI'IHAU

KAUA'I

NI'IHAU

Kaulakahi Channel

Kilauea

Hanalei

KAWAIHAU

LĒHU'E

Līhu'e

HANALEI

KŌLOA

Mt. Wai'ale'ale

WAIMEA

Kōke'e

Na Pali Coast

Kalalau Valley

Mānā

Kekaha

Waimea

District Boundary

0   5   10   15 Miles

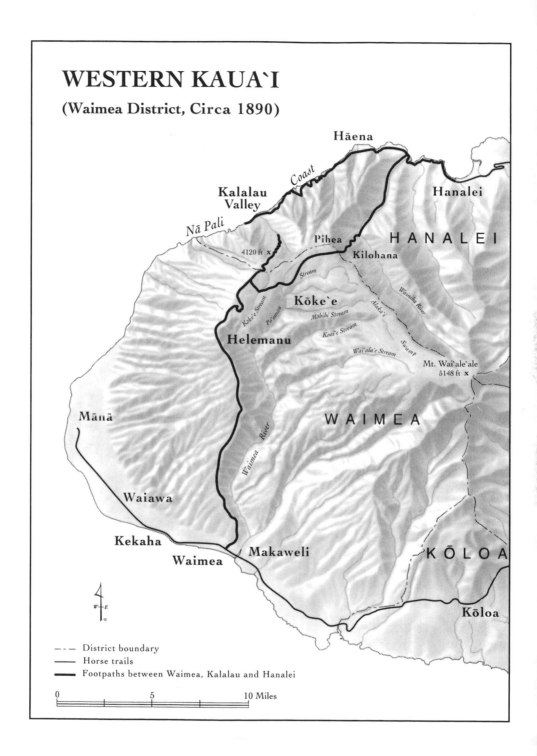

WESTERN KAUA`I
(Waimea District, Circa 1890)

Hāena

Kalalau
Valley

Coast

Nā Pali

Hanalei

Pihea

H A N A L E I

4120 ft x

Kilohana

Stream

Kōke`e

Waiauba River

Kōke`e Stream

Po`omau

Mohihi Stream

Alaka`i

Helemanu

Koai`e Stream

Wai`ala`e Stream

Swamp

Mt. Wai`ale`ale
5148 ft x

Mānā

W A I M E A

Waimea River

Waiawa

Kekaha

Makaweli

K Ō L O A

Waimea

Kōloa

W—E

- - -   District boundary
———   Horse trails
━━━   Footpaths between Waimea, Kalalau and Hanalei

0   5   10 Miles

CLIMBING

A list of characters and a glossary of Hawaiian words that occur in the text will be found following the text, beginning on page 327.

1.

Climbing in the dark she felt the small stones turn
      along the spine of the path whose color kept rising in her mind
burned-in color moment of rust dried blood color other color
      gone color by day and she knew what color was there
when she could not see it and when one of the stars was the darkness
      before any breath of daylight and the way was in her feet again
the star of Kaoʻea rushed between clouds when the dawn wind
      came toward her down across the ridges of the mountain
carrying the scent of water from the peak of Waialeale
      At a high twist of the trail far down to the left behind her
over the naked roots of the slope and the widening hollow of Waiaka
      where the folds of the mountain were still touched by the moon
she saw the sea outside the curve of coast glinting
      past Waimea beyond the dark land and the hidden houses
in one of them her father was invisible in sleep
      and past there the sea outside Kekaha where she had been born
by the shore of Oʻomano all of it barely a shadow
      from which she had set out and nobody had heard her go
even the dogs in the moonlight never barked when she went past
      looked up and watched and never barked knowing who she was
and with the next step that whole horizon was gone behind the mountain
      the blackness beginning to the right of her was the chasm of Waimea
the air running from the edge of it rustled the finer leaves of the koas
      above her the voices of the plovers stitched the night

2.

She knew the way now as something of hers a sound of the name
    that had been hers from the beginning waiting for her
when she woke into the world on the coast at Kekaha
    her night name from before anyone had seen her and from
before that always hers but more of her had answered to it
    after she had tasted what she would not taste again
infancy when the belly turns up and the echo
    of the waves rocks it and then childhood the naked rapids
then the petal pleasure of everyone's eyes on her
    telling her how beautiful she had become how
beautiful she was and then her watching him differently
    whom she had known for as long as she could remember
since they had been children there running on that same sand
    and then the feeling of him watching her and the time he first
came to her and all their early age together
    the house they lived in after the wedding when she had heard
his full name as though she had never known it although
    everyone knew it and when she heard it that time
a cold finger touched her at the top of her forehead
    and ran down the front of her over her face and her breast
to her navel and below and she had shivered and heard
    nothing for a moment until the voice of Reverend Rowell
who had taught them both to read and write turned to her and said
    her name Pi'ilani and asked her the lifelong question

3.

When she had gone up that trail for the first time they had been together
    all of them on horses Koʻolau her husband
ahead of her in the dark and Kua his friend and elder
    riding ahead of him Kua Papiohuli
who had taught Koʻolau from the beginning always an eye on him
    throwing the fishnet holding the spear the paddle
taught him the currents on the surface and the ones below
    who they were where they came from what things they had done
what it was best to expect from them in what order
    as the hours turned in the sky and Kua taught him the touch
with horses so that even as a boy Koʻolau
    was famous for his way with horses and Kua taught him
the braiding of leather the life of a sinew the spring
    of a lariat and taught him to use the lariat
so that it seemed to rise out of his hand by itself
    and fly wherever he willed it to go and drop there
like a tern fishing Kua taught him the tracks on the ridges
    and the gun the handling of the gun and Koʻolau
they would say never misses he never misses

4.

She saw it as a leaf floating under calm water
　　in the sunlight of its afternoon that was slowly ending
it was before her eyes but she could not hear it
　　could not touch it a time not yet gone they had been
getting ready all day the ones who were going
　　Koʻolau and their son Kaleimanu still a child
and sick and Kepola her mother and Ida
　　the daughter of her mother's sister Kinoulu
they had kept deciding what they would be able to carry
　　when the time came and Kukui his mother kept giving them
things to eat she kept cooking making things that they
　　would leave behind and Kinoulu kept telling Ida
what to remember and all afternoon one by one
　　the family came and tried to help or sat saying nothing
while Koʻolau's grandmother Kawaluna from whose dream
　　his name had come sat outside the door on the ground
facing the mountain humming and patting her knee
　　when they had decided that they were going she was the one
Koʻolau had asked to say what night would be good for it
　　and she had not answered for days and then had named
a night some time before the new year and the rising
　　of the Pleiades and late that day he and Kua
brought the horses to the back of the house and saddled them
　　and loaded the bags and what they were taking after all
and then they stopped and watched the sun go down past Niʻihau
　　then Koʻolau's father Kaleimanu for whom their son
had been named stood up and all at once they were silent
　　Kawaluna was humming and Koʻolau told their son
Kaleimanu to say good-bye to them each in turn
　　and they all said good-bye crying as quietly as they could
to make little noise holding each other in their arms
　　and Piʻilani's father Hoʻona said that they must pray
and he prayed like Reverend Rowell standing in church
　　but Kawaluna kept on humming she was the only one
not crying and she looked up at each face in the gray light
　　and did not speak but stood up and put her arms around them
one after the other and kissed them before they mounted
　　and Kua turned his horse toward the mountain and they followed
now as she walked they rode through her and kept appearing ahead
　　and she was riding among them a ghost among the ghosts

6

5.

She had been climbing for a long time and the moon had set
    she had passed the place where the ghost smelling of dried fish
waited by the side of the trail and she had walked on
    the night kept growing colder as the trail wound upward through trees
she stopped and bent to pull the black shawl from the bag
    she looked up through the branches to see where the stars were
she watched for them through the leaves and clouds but there was only
    darkness over her and she sat in the ferns by a trunk
not wanting to stay long and get up chilled and stiff
    she lay staring at the night above the mountain
her feet went on without moving like the sound in a shell
    she was at home in the night on the mountain and she felt
the mountain at her back the black underneath of it behind her
    going down to its dark root under the sea and the black stone
above the heart of the fire that kept turning without light
    the spring of night from which the night was coming
her head was toward the top of the mountain and she was sure
    that she was on the other side of the mountain hearing
the sound of one of the streams there and water falling
    from higher in the valley and the night rain beginning
but it was a sound the trees made and the branches
    were dripping around her and then onto her feet and her face
and she stood up listening and then she turned and went on

6.

The first shadow was beginning to surface in the darkness
  through a net of trees when she came to the swollen stream
of Halemanu the house of birds where in earlier dawns
  the birds had the forest to themselves waking there
into plumage and colors never seen anywhere
  crests and feathers heads and motions never before
entered upon voices never heard before singing out of
  a source in the yolk of their unmeasured morning
inexhaustibly beginning and beginning
  as the undisturbed trees and flowers kept beginning around them
finding in each place the morning as it was then
  in an age without numbers changing too slowly
for a single life to see it moving unperceived
  like the voyage of the mountain itself into the northwest
the eon of the birds seemed perpetual like the mountain
  long before another side of the night gave birth to humans
and for an age after that there was no sign of them
  growing closer around the unbroken horizon
the streams went on overflowing seaward taking with them
  the mountain a grain at a time and small fish and crayfish
brought their salt in from the sea and swam up the falling water
  to live in the falling before time until the first canoe
appeared in the west and only the birds saw it

7.

A light rain reached down to her face the fringe of a mist
   there was no color yet in the ghost dawn but around her
through the full consonance of the stream came here and there
   clear voices opening as she passed close to them
trills telling of water questions not continued
   some of the voices were lights flying beside her
the amakihi a yellow brilliance the olokele
   a flicker of scarlet but the light was the complete gray
before daybreak with the black bands of the trees floating
   through it then before a condensation of green seeped
into the tall reaches of the valley opening ahead of her
   the house appeared Halemanu at the end of a long rise
with the lifted shell of high trees raised above it
   the mountain palm towering behind and as her feet
brushed the wet grass she saw the four pale long uprights
   of the verandah the new wide steps leading up to it
and the dark arms of the house reaching forward toward her
   someone was there the smell of woodsmoke floated in the mist
and as she stepped forward a small light passed at a window
   she stopped and watched and a woman came out with no light
and stood at the top of the steps a tall figure in a long gown
   the hair built high on her head the same color as the hour

8.

They both stood listening and they heard the small stream nearest
      to the house the Brook of Tears Nawaimaka high
with the rains at that time of year the tall woman
      outside the door was looking into the trees and had not seen
Pi'ilani she came down the steps slowly watching
      the trees and Pi'ilani walked toward her up the slope
and without raising her voice said—Makuahine—
      and the woman turned not sure whether she had heard anything
Pi'ilani went closer and said again—Makuahine—
      and the woman said—Who is it—and then saw her but could not
make out who it was and Pi'ilani pronounced her own name
      in a voice so low she hardly heard it herself
—Can it be you Pi'ilani—and Pi'ilani stepped
      toward her and for the third time called the white woman mother
—Makuahine—and the woman said—Pi'ilani—
      and came to embrace her but Pi'ilani said
—I will make you wet—and the woman laughed and embraced her
      and then said—You are completely soaked Who is with you—
—Nobody else—Pi'ilani said and the woman said—Come in
      Come in at once there is a fire are you really
up here alone—and as they turned the rain began again

9.

As they went up the steps the white woman called—Maka'e
    Maka'e—calling again at the door and to Pi'ilani
she said—Come in come in—drawing her by the arm toward the fire
    as a Hawaiian woman appeared in the far doorway
—Maka'e I know you remember our friend Pi'ilani
    We have been out in the rain and are cold and hungry this morning—
Maka'e ran to Pi'ilani and embraced her
    —How are you—she asked—Well——Who is with you——Nobody—
Maka'e shook her head and without a word unwound
    the sodden shawl and hung it over by the fire
and the other woman picked up a blanket from a chair
    and put it around Pi'ilani and brought her to sit
in the glow of the fire while Maka'e piled on more logs
    and then was gone—I did not know you were here—Pi'ilani said
The woman nodded—We almost never come up here
    in the winter any more it is so long since I was here
at this time of the year in the rain with the streams roaring
    hard for the horses to cross how did you ever cross—
Pi'ilani said—Yes the water is high now—and she held out
    her dripping skirt in front of the fire—The first time I came—
she said—it was this time of year it was the same night
    and there was nobody here then and the children were half asleep
we tied the horses out of the rain and we ate something
    out there on the steps and rested there for a while—
—If we had been here—the older woman said—we could
    have given you something to eat that time——Maybe—
Pi'ilani said—But that time was different—

10.

At that moment the rain began to thunder down on the roof
    with the deep pounding of a waterfall and the planked room
became a sounding box with the shadows cast by the fire
    playing around it as reflections play beside water
if they had shouted they would not have heard each other
    The older woman whose name was Anne looked up at the ceiling
Anne Sinclair Knudsen born in Scotland in Stirling
    more than sixty years earlier her father a captain
in the British Navy The ceiling was a deep hollow and she felt
    the house shudder Pi'ilani looked up from the fire
to the salt-frosted boards of the walls the flowers
    trembling in a jug and she saw the silver rain
sheeting down outside the house and the shadowy trees
    waving through it she looked up into the dark rafters
two women who had lost their husbands recently
    raised their faces toward the roaring and stared upward
and the days after the deaths dissolved behind them and Anne
    saw the beams of the ceiling thirty years before
and her husband Valdemar talking of how the timbers
    were all from New Zealand she saw the men heaving them
onto oxcarts then onto mules then carrying them
    when she left the babies with the nurse and rode up with Valdemar
to the grass mountain hut before Eric was born
    she had come there with Valdemar after they were engaged
the grass hut had been here where she was sitting now
    they had built this in its place and she had cherished the thought
that the boards had come from New Zealand the first world
    that she remembered to which her parents had taken her
when she was a small child and they had built the house there
    room by room around her looking down to the bay from which
one day the news came that her father and brother were lost at sea
    and the grieving cries of the Maoris still pressed upon her
though she could not hear a sound out of all that time

11.

Looking up into the same deafening recesses
    above them at the same time Pi'ilani saw
faces in the wood and eyes and deep shadows stretching
    back into themselves through the roar and then those became
a stone overhang in a steep valley where she was lying
    looking up waiting feeling the rock tremble under her
hearing the rolling explosions echoing circling
    around the valley and the hollow crack of the cannon
starting the echoes rolling again wave after wave
    just as they began falling away and she could tell
down her back when a shell from the cannon struck the cliff face
    sending huge stones leaping and smashing down through the trees
and behind that there were the other cave roofs in the valley
    that she had stared up into and seen only darkness
as she lay awake hearing the sound of the valley
    on and on and how she had prayed up into the stone
in the first days starting with the prayers in white English
    that Reverend Rowell had taught them in Sunday School
and then the others that Kawaluna had said
    were secret the ones that Keiwi kept warning her
had to be spoken perfectly names to be said only
    from the soles of the feet words to the sleep of no return
those prayers many times under her breath with her eyes open
    then hearing the roar of the night with no sound no answer

12.

They did not hear Maka'e come in with a tray
     and set it on the table and then she was standing
in front of Anne with her hands spread out declaring
     helplessness looking up in her turn at the ceiling
to see whether there was a leak somewhere and all at once
     the rain began to let up and they listened as it
moved away through the trees dragging its sounds after it
     leaving the raised rushing voice of the Brook of Tears
in its place and Maka'e when she could be heard
     asked Anne whether she would have breakfast at the table
or by the fire and Anne said they should stay by the fire
     Maka'e set a low table in front of them
—It is an everything breakfast—she said and laughed—It is what
     was left out there I made your porridge and your tea
but all the rest is cold—Maka'e said looking
     at Anne and then at Pi'ilani whose eyes were reflecting
the fire—That will be perfect Maka'e thank you—Anne said
     and Maka'e left looking back at them sitting there
with the tea things and porridge on the tray and the cold
     bannocks a pot of jam cold purple sweet potatoes
cold taro cold pigeon dried mountain apples—Well do you drink tea—
     Anne asked Pi'ilani—If you please—Pi'ilani said
—Will you have porridge—Anne asked—If you please—and the rain
     stopped and they heard the tea being poured and the notes
of spoons on china and the fire and the stream rushing

13.

Anne said—We were together this month at Makaweli
     with Eric and Jane and Helen and the others
over from Ni'ihau and when some of them were going home
     I wanted to come up here for no reason as I thought
to begin with but then reasons came flocking to me
     we were here this last summer of course and that was the first
return after Valdemar died but this was something to do
     with wanting to be here as the century is ending
bringing all those whom I have known and have lost
     up here along with me once more in the rain and mist
often lately my cousin Isabella is in my mind
     she knew so much and was so learned and made the studies
and paintings of flowers and she worked on her book here
     we were here together years ago in the winter
she wanted to study the birds then and everything growing
     in the rainy season well I came this time with Eric
and the boys from Ni'ihau and a few to help us
     and when the others left I wanted to stay on alone
for a while I have begun to note things that I may
     not do again such as coming up here in the winter
and I am glad I came this time but before long now
     we must be going back I had thought it might be
tomorrow but we could go today if you would rather
     come down with us some time during the afternoon—
After a moment Pi'ilani said—Thank you—and shook her head

14.

She looked into the fire until Anne was wondering whether
      she had forgotten where she was but then at last she said
—They are telling me again three times now someone has said to me
      that he has been found that the grave has been discovered
and they have dug him up and have taken his bones and his gun—
      —Who told you that—Anne asked—Kekaha people—Pi'ilani said
—One of them whispered to my mother but said not to tell me—
      —Where did they hear it—Anne asked—One said he heard it
in town from somebody he had not seen there for
      a long time——What kind of person——He told me it was
nobody from here but they know all about how to
      sell things like that and who will give money for them—
—Did he tell you any names—Anne asked—No names—Pi'ilani said
      —Nobody's names ever but they talked about his gun
how his gun had been found somebody had dug it up
      and his bones——Did you talk about this with anyone else—
—No—Pi'ilani said—I never said anything
      only that nobody knows the place where I left them—

15.

Anne watched Pi'ilani looking into the flames
    —What will you do—she asked—Go there—Pi'ilani said
—Alone—Anne asked—Yes alone—she answered—By myself—
    —I am sure somebody up here with me could go with you
at least for the most dangerous part——I have been back there
    several times once Kua went with me into the valley
and came out with me and I have gone in with others
    at different times but I am going by myself this time—
—I will say prayers for you—Anne said—I was alone—
    Pi'ilani said—when I came out the first time—
—How long will you stay there in Kalalau—Anne asked—I will wait
    to see what I find there—Pi'ilani answered
—When they told you the same thing those other times
    and you went back were there signs that someone had been there—
—All my life—Pi'ilani said—I have known about it
    I heard about them trying to find where the chiefs
were buried or where any of us had been hidden
    I heard about what had been found with the bones and taken away
gold and canoes and carvings and spears thieves have been taking them
    for a long time and there were many burials in those valleys
and in the cliffs going up and many are still hidden there
    and after the soldiers took everybody out of Kalalau
and burned down the houses nobody was left to see
    who might crawl in over the rocks like crabs to steal the dead—

16.

How utterly still she sat as she was saying it all
    Anne thought and then Pi'ilani went on—There was
so much talk and talk   When I came out of the valley
    back to Kekaha the first time they had been talking
ever since we had left and they believed themselves
    each of them telling something else that meant nothing
playing cards with their own stories that they said were us
    so the bets got big and they asked me one thing or another
and I would not know what they had inside their heads
    that had been growing there while they knew nothing about us
when we were in Kalalau talking to nobody
    except each other those years while day by day there were
more things that we did not have to say or that we
    did not want to say again and what we said lasted—
—Did you see no one at all—Anne asked—After they were all taken
    out of the valley—Pi'ilani said—sometimes we heard voices
sometimes maybe voices of people we had known sometimes
    calling our names sometimes talking about us but
never seeing us they always sounded like echoes
    even when they were close to us and I have learned since
that friends came looking for us at the beginning
    bringing food for us and clothes but they did not find us
it was only our own voices that made no echoes—

17.

I remember Koʻolau's voice even now—Anne said
    —Clear and strong one time when we were outdoors singing hymns
it was shortly after you were married I heard
    one voice riding above the words and I looked sideways
and it was Koʻolau and I have heard him sing in the good days
    other songs——He always sang—Piʻilani said
—Everyone used to sing as we rode up here—Anne said—Valdemar
    always loved singing even when he had no voice left
still teaching all of us songs he remembered from Norway
    and songs from here *Oh Kaili leaf of the koa*—she hummed
—Flute words—Piʻilani said and Anne nodded—I am sure
    I was not supposed to know what all of them meant—
she smiled—But we knew—Piʻilani said and she went on
    —Kaleimanu's voice was very small from the beginning
but it travelled it knew its way he was a quiet child
    even when he was playing with all the others
he kept listening for something and he wanted to hear stories
    he was a story catcher he said and if a story
flew by him he would catch every word and keep it
    alive and later we would find that he knew it
all the way through but he wanted to hear it again
    to be told it again and he said he knew that stories
were hiding all around him in places telling themselves
    and he said that each of them knew where it was going—

18.

—We had named him for his grandfather for Koʻolau's father
    Kaleimanu who used to work for Mr Gay
on the ranch and my son wanted to know why his grandfather
    had been named Kaleimanu The Wreath of Birds
and how the name happened—And where did that name come from—
    Anne asked——Out of a dream his own mother Keawe had
She gave him that name because of something she knew
    in the dream but her son said he had to ask her
for years before she would tell him any of the dream
    and when our son asked his grandfather it was the same
for a long time he would say only that it was a dream
    of birds and I saw how our son Kaleimanu
kept his eyes on the birds running by the water the shore birds—
    Anne thought of the stilt that Valdemar shot to study
and the species had been named for him the thought made her feel
    far from everything—And staring at the stilts in the pond—
Piʻilani said—*Kyip kyip* I would hear him around
    the house so that I thought there must be a bird there
and his eyes went with the lines of birds over the sea when the sun
    was going down he could make that high sound of them as they went
that cry so thin a thread too fine to be seen not beginning there
    one day he told me that flowers and leaves in the leis
had all been picked and ended but that in bird leis
    the birds were flying only they were birds from before
and from afterward so that nobody could see them—

19.

—He said that when we hold a bird what is in our hands
    is not the bird any more and that when we look at birds
we see only a little of them——Did his grandfather tell him that—
    —I do not think so—Pi'ilani said—but I do not know
Only Keawe had been in her dream and nobody
    ever heard all of it but maybe it was a dream
that could not be told   He wanted to hear bird stories
    from back before about people from then who were birds
in that time and he kept asking all of the elders
    for stories and then when no more words came he would say
Is that all but later he knew where each of the stories
    stopped so we went on telling him stories he knew
and he would ask us about them as though the stories
    were still there even when we thought he was asleep
he might ask us about something now in the story
    and we would not have the answer and would have to say so—
Pi'ilani looked out the door to the lanai
    —We were all asleep out there that morning when we went
to the valley—she said—and when Ko'olau picked up
    Kaleimanu to go on he asked the child Do you remember
Lahi and Kaleimanu said Who ate nothing but birds
    We are going to the place on the mountain where Lahi lived
Ko'olau told him and the child said Is the giant up there
    Lahi and his uncle killed the giant Ko'olau told him
That was that time Kaleimanu said But I want to see
    We will go and see Ko'olau said and carried him half asleep—

20.

—All the way going up from here to Kilohana
      I think he was talking to Kaleimanu in front of him
on the horse and still asleep I heard Koʻolau
      at the turns of the trail telling stories in his night voice
floating over the rocks and he stopped when we rode close
      to the spring where Nawaimaka comes out of the ground
that low cave that you could pass without seeing it there
      and the clear pool that keeps moving into the Brook of Tears
he told Kaleimanu asleep in his arm about the spring
      and the child asked is this where Lahi waits for the soldiers
and Koʻolau said—No we are not there yet—and we rode on
      up the trail then all at once I heard a raw voice
above me *ʻuwaʻu ʻuwaʻu* like one bird
      crying like one sea-bird ʻuwaʻu the petrel
then I heard Kaleimanu laughing and he said—I know
      it is no ʻuwaʻu it is you then I heard it
again farther up and again Kaleimanu
      laughing and he said—I know it is you Kua you are not
ʻuwaʻu but the sound came again and Kaleimanu said
      —It is you Kua it is at night the ʻuwaʻu calls
and still Kua and Koʻolau kept making that sound
      and Kaleimanu laughed but he said—Lahi will eat you—
and he told us he was awake now and kept asking what
      bird he was hearing because birds were all around us
he sat up watching them until we came to the high edge
      at Kilohana where the trail climbs on but the whole
world falls away in front through the clouds and the valley
      of Kalalau appears to be as deep as the sky—

21.

—And on the edge I thought I was hearing nothing
      the wind kept rushing at us along the cliff face
hitting us and shaking the trees and the voices
      of the birds must have been still calling around us
but it seemed cold with silence and we came to Kilohana
      where we would separate and Kua would go back
with the horses so we all dismounted there and Kua
      walked to a place on the edge hanging out over the clouds
so bright they were hard to look at and the rusty cliffs
      rising around them and he pointed to one rock
out on a cliff fold where there was another like it
      close to it and he said—Kaleimanu see
that one there That one is Kua——It is not—Kaleimanu said
      —You are Kua I know you—But Kua said—That is spirit Kua
Do you remember the story of the two spirit children
      the boy and the girl whose father was lazy and sent them
to the spring every night for water—and Kaleimanu said
      —That was Naiwi The Bones and one night at the spring
children like us who die found those spirit children and they
      stay playing all night because they forget and the day starts
to come so that it is too late for them to get back
      before the sunlight turns them to stone——There they are—Kua said
—Do you remember their names—The girl's name has leis in it
      so I remember she is Hikimaunalei
and the boy is Kua——And so now—Kua said—you will
      look up at that rock some time and say that is Kua—
but the boy kept looking at Kua without answering—

22.

Pi'ilani remembered them all saying good-bye then
    on the mountain and she looked out the doorway at the morning
with its sunlight glittering on the green dripping branches
    and she said—Makuahine down there in Kekaha
they tell me now that I never talk to a soul
    they tell my mother I never say anything any more
and it may be true but see how I have been talking
    up here—Anne said—I am happy you will tell me
these things that must be in your mind all the time now
    I have known what happened only as most people do
in parts and all of them hearsay and then for a long time
    I heard nothing whatever and you had gone back to Kekaha
and had been there for a while before I was told of it—
    Pi'ilani said—At first I would not go out at all
Only the family in the house knew I was there
    I was still hiding but everyone let me alone
Now they do not ask me anything they move farther away
    from asking anything—Then she saw that Maka'e
had been standing in the doorway behind her listening
    and she stood up and Maka'e came over to her
her voice choked with crying and said to her I would never
    have asked you anything that I wanted to know about that time
but when I heard you talking I could not go away
    do not be angry with me Pi'ilani—and she put
her arms around Pi'ilani and stood with her eyes
    shut and tears running and Pi'ilani embraced her
and after a moment said to her—It is a little thing—

23.

She stood with her arms around the older woman
  rocking her as though she were reassuring a child
until Maka'e turned to Anne and said—Forgive me
  Makuahine—and she went out with the tray
Pi'ilani said to Anne—It is so long since I saw you
  I know you lost your husband and it is late to say it
but I was sad to learn of it——Thank you I remember
  what admiration he had for Ko'olau in the days
when your husband worked at the ranch he would boast about
  Ko'olau this Ko'olau that Ko'olau was
the best he had ever seen Ko'olau could do
  anything—Pi'ilani said nothing—They came up here
together I cannot say how often with Kua
  and maybe Kapahu and some of the others looking for
wild cattle they said but he always hoped to discover
  a new wild flower for the museum Almost every trip
he brought back something new—Pi'ilani nodded—Sometimes
  Kua or Ko'olau or one of them would have told him
a name for a plant and what sickness it might be good for—
  Pi'ilani said—Ko'olau told me about
a spear at the doorway of your house—Anne said—That was
  a present from long ago——He told me about that
before Kaleimanu's first birthday—Pi'ilani said
  —And that was a long time ago and now I am glad
to have seen you Makuahine and thank you
  and I ask you to excuse me it is time to go—

24.

—You walked all night—Anne said—There is still a long way to go—
    Pi'ilani answered—I want to be down there
in the valley before it gets dark—She took off
    the borrowed shawl folded it on the bench and lifted
her old black steaming wrap from in front of the fire
    and slung it around her shoulders Maka'e came in
and embraced her again and then Pi'ilani
    turned to Anne—Good-bye—she said and they kissed near the cheeks
with the distance in place between them like a pane of glass
    that had always been there and Pi'ilani stepped out
into the sunlight that changed her into the color
    of a shadow and she went down the nine steps like a shadow
and up the trail among the old trees and was gone and there were
    only the trees as Anne stood looking and she could almost
see what she had known there and would not see again
    faces and garments in the sunlight of the early days
husband children friends certain that it was all theirs
    the certainty swelling their voices as they sang
their hymns under those trees on the mountain repeating
    their claim to the wilderness she kept holding off
memories of Valdemar who knew so much Vally
    so much older than she was showing her the skulls
he had dug up at Manaulepu many years
    before he had known her it had all been for science
she recited a psalm Blessed is the man she said
    stiffening slightly as she stood there becoming the severe
bony old woman her grandchildren would not like
    she heard a step on the boards and nobody was there
and she remembered the time soon after they were married
    when he was away from home at the legislature
and she heard footsteps that the servants told her
    were the sound of a spirit but she had gone out
with a lantern and seen the night heron fly off over
    the garden and she smiled because she took no stock in such things

25.

Pi'ilani had never meant to stay so long
    at the bird house fluttering in words in the net of words
she had planned to be farther up the mountain by the time
    the rays of the sun were leaning at this angle in the mist
through the gray 'ohias here the net was the braided
    tracks of wild cattle leading away into ravines
a few of them freshly churned in the black mud of the forest
    and more recently used than the trail she was remembering as
she came to it the hoof-prints frayed out full of sky
    into thickets and concealed clefts and she was careful
of her way that looked different each time with branches fallen
    low growth taller she hurried listening for the sound
of cattle in the woods it was along through here
    that she had heard Ko'olau telling Kaleimanu
to be listening for wild cattle and Kaleimanu's high voice
    asking why they were wild and Ko'olau saying that all
the cattle came with the haoles and some of them ran loose
    on the other face of the island from the beginning
But they got around here to the west of the mountain
    in my own lifetime he said in the year I was born—
—How wild are they—Kaleimanu asked—Oh they are wild
    as lightning—Ko'olau answered—How big are they—
—They are bigger than any bulls you saw down below there
    They can pick up a horse and rider and throw them both
over their shoulders——How did they get there—the child asked

26.

Then Kua who had been old enough to be riding
     with hands from Valdemar Knudsen's ranch at Waiawa
at the time it all happened joined in the story and told
     Kaleimanu how Makua Valdemar Knudsen
had been able to lease all the land from Waiawa westward
     to the wide plains beyond Mānā and first he ran
what they called Texas Longhorns and goats on that whole pasture
     and later because it was the tallow and hides
that made money he put in a number of Durham Bulls
     to get weight on them and that made an easy strain
grazing wherever it suited them along the hills there
     and into those dry valleys but not very far
so at round-ups it was no trouble to herd them down
     into the pens—I can remember that time and then
they tell me one day this young Englishman turned up
     rode all the way around the island from Hanalei
where he had some kind of ranch set up and as I heard it
     a letter had come from his brother in Australia
with bad news and he had to go as soon as he could
     but he had this hundred head of cattle and nobody
he could trust with them and he wanted Makua Knudsen
     to pasture them for a year at Waiawa and offered
a hundred dollars well Knudsen told him he did not
     want his cattle but he would do it and he sent a few hands
half way to Hanalei for them and we met them
     up almost to Kilauea they were miserable
half dead worn out starving we could hardly get them
     to move at all and the Hanalei hands helped us
bring them across the Wailua River the ones
     that did not lie right down in the water and die
and there were a lot of those floating toward the sand bar
     it happened at each of the rivers we had to cross
and we crept so slowly that they sent Kapahu along
     to see what had become of us and we all doubted
whether any of them would make it to Waiawa
     I think in the end there were twenty-five that did
and it was all they could do to stand up but Makua Knudsen
     said turn them into the grasslands so that is what we did
they walked out like that as though they would simply die
     but when some from the ranch went out to round up cattle

a few months later they found the red Hanalei ones
     in with the good ones but when they tried to round them up
the Hanalei ones stuck up their tails and headed
     up into the valleys and knew their way onto the mountain
later we heard that those cattle had been wild to begin with
     and were caught and fenced up but they could only be herded
when they were starved half dead and we never knew more than that—

27.

Pi'ilani thought of riders coming back from the mountain
    when she was a child the horses suddenly there
with leaves in their manes and the raw meat slung
    behind the saddles the polished horns swinging and a vast
blackening crater dripping in her mind the red cliff
    where the neck had been and the hacked off bull's head riding
upside-down with its tongue dangling and its eyes staring
    at the ground and then after the trips how they sat
late eating and chewing over the whole story
    and then the old stories again the surprised meetings
the bulls charging on unchecked by bullets that barely
    dented their skulls the huge hearts driving them on even
with holes torn in them and always Me'eawa
    saying he knew that those wild cattle had been crossed
with the same power on the mountain that made the giant
    men of the cliffs with the one red eye it all lit up in her
again for a moment each time she started through these woods
    listening knowing that there were almost none of them
left on the mountain any longer but she listened for them
    without thinking more about them watching the trail
ahead of her always following that first time
    startled when she looked up to see that now there was
nobody in front of her and the sun was already high

28.

She came to hills of bright cloud rolling up out of the valley
    and before noon she had arrived at Kilohana
where they had all dismounted that first time and had stood
    in silence looking around them at the stream slipping
toward the edge and at the falling away and away of the cliffs
    fin after fin drifting among clouds the great bay in the air
as deep as the mountain the valley of Kalalau
    its measureless hollow Kalalau The Straying
they could see through white clouds threads of surf unrolling
    slowly into shadow the cliffs hung steep as blankets
on a fence she could see that Kepola her mother
    was frightened looking over past the edge and Kua
said he would say good-bye now and Kaleimanu
    went to him and embraced him laying his head against
Kua's stomach and then asked him if this was the stream now
    where it happened—Where what happened—Kua asked him
—Where they met the soldiers—Kaleimanu said—This is
    the stream—Kua told him—but this is not the place—
Kaleimanu said—Will you tell me the story once more
    right here—and they stood in a ring in the wind listening
to Kua tell of Lahi the boy who ate birds
    and his uncle who was Kanealohi Slow Man

29.

He said—After they came up here to eat the ‘uwa‘u
    that live in the cliffs first there was the giant who tried
to kill them and Kanealohi told Lahi When the giant
    comes you hold out a bird to him but when he reaches
to take it you back up into the tunnel and he will
    follow you and since you are smaller than he is
he will get stuck in the rocks and then I will kill him
    so they did it that way and then the great chief heard about them
up here eating birds and he said Those birds are mine
    and he called together four hundred of his soldiers
to come up here and kill Lahi and Kanealohi
    but those two moved up this stream to a smaller one
that runs into it and if anybody steps
    in the stream anywhere along it even far below here
the surface away up there begins to ripple and they would know
    there was somebody coming and one day it began
to ripple so they came out and could see the whole army
    climbing up to kill them and Kanealohi was frightened
but Lahi went to where the rocks almost come together
    with the top of the trail between them and there only
one man could climb through at a time and he killed them as they came
    one by one and they fell all the way down from the cliff
and the last one was the chief himself and they say that
    he recognized that Lahi was his own son and he said so
and asked Lahi to spare him and the boy let him pass
    and it was Lahi who became the chief later in the story

30.

It was then that Kua had led Kaleimanu
    to the edge of the cliff where the light rose from the valley
and had showed him those two rocks that were the children
    of Naiwi and said to him—That is where the right trail
goes down—and he pointed to a thread like a goat track
    following the knife edge of one of the fins out in the clouds
—That is the one that goes all the way—he said—The others
    end in nothing—And he hugged the child and told him
—But it is not good to look back—Then he went to help them
    load themselves with the few things they would be carrying
Pi'ilani stood looking down at the clear water
    gliding in front of her toward the fall its surface
not appearing to move she knelt in the wet moss
    to put her mouth to the cold pane and drink from it
with her eyes open at first and then she closed them
    and plunged her head and hands into the unseen current
for a long breath overhearing the voices in the water
    talking and then she sat up and ate a few pieces
of taro and drank again and lifted her head to stare
    at the face below her in the stream with the sky
under it and the eyes burning from their dark places
    she looked at it feeling that she knew nothing about it
and then stood up in the day and walked to where the right trail
    disappeared over the edge into Kalalau

31.

At first there were small trees rooted in the crevices
 above the shallow groove descending the flank of the cliff
groping the folds and strung around the ribs of rock
 and there were the tops of bushes reaching up just below
the faint path that plainly was little used now and was blurred by
 rains and by the wind that struck at her the moment she stepped
down and it came at her again around every corner
 but there was nothing to hold onto bare rock on one side
and on the other beyond the tops of the bushes
 empty air and her eyes crept along the snaking path
that twisted downward ahead of her she set her feet to it
 like hands she did not look up to see nobody there
she pulled her mind back even from that first time when
 Koʻolau had been in front with Kaleimanu
slung over his shoulder and she kept hearing him
 saying Hold still Keep your eyes closed Keep your eyes closed
Lie still and every part of the path seemed longer
 than she remembered it then the bushes were behind and there was
only the drop of the cliff beside her and after
 Koʻolau there had been Kinoulu her mother's
sister and the little girl Ida who had wanted
 to come to be with Kaleimanu and then Kepola
Piʻilani's mother who gasped at the corners
 to begin with but the wind took away the sound
most times and Piʻilani pulled her mind back to the path
 in front of her and the wind rose as she followed it
out onto the top of the long fin like a crooked
 log with the drop disappearing on both sides into
shadows and out in the margins of her vision
 white flecks came and went small as dust in a sunbeam
tropic birds the size of gulls soaring in circles that far
 below her then almost at the end of the fin the path
tightened around a corner to double back downward
 so that the curtain of rock hung again beside her

32.

The wind had lashed at them here as it lashed at her this time
    the sky had filled with dark cloud and the rain had found them
they had leaned against the cliff wall in the racing fog
    the water spilling over them as they crept forward
scarcely able to move but afraid of being caught there
    when the light went so they inched ahead until the rain
let up and at last it stopped and the clouds tore apart
    over the drop and they could see the gaunt buttresses
towering around them out of the depths of the valley
    and she had tried for a moment and had not been able
then or ever to conceive of what Koʻolau
    had told her about them carrying Judge Kauai
into Kalalau some time earlier taking him
    down that same path when the old man was already
too sick to walk and too heavy to stand on his feet
    so that it took four of them just to lift him she could
not see how four of them with him slung between them
    could have found footing on this draped hair of trail and the Judge
had been dressed up for the journey in his town clothes
    wrapped in his robe and wearing his blue spectacles
and the broad hat with the peacock feathers around it
    and she had come to know all the men who had carried him
one of them Kilohana who went back to the top
    again and again by himself to carry down others
whose feet were gone or withered and no use to them

33.

She had been sure before she set out that nobody
     had found where he was buried and she had been sure of it
all the way up the mountain through the night and she had kept
     seeing the grave as she went the fur of moss around the black
branches above it in the deep shade back among
     broken rocks with the cliff looming far overhead and the stream
leaping across the stones below it a place from which you could see
     anyone coming and never be seen and it appeared to her
to be untouched the ferns and bushes grown over it
     unbroken undisturbed unnoticed how could it
be taken away from him when it was what he had
     always been it was where the cold touch had come from
that ran down between her breasts at their wedding when
     Reverend Rowell carefully pronounced Koʻolau's whole name
—Do you—he had said—Kalua i Koʻolau
     Do you The Grave at Koʻolau Do you The Grave
on the Windward Side take this woman Piʻilani
     Climbing Heaven to be your lawful wedded wife
from this day forth—and the rest that he had sworn to
     and that she had sworn to with that cold still running on her
Only once near the end she had asked him about his name
     and he had told her what she had already known about it
how Kawaluna his grandmother Kawaluna
     The Age Above had been there when he was born and she
herself had delivered him and when she held him up
     she had announced—He is Kalua i Koʻolau—
and if anyone dared to ask her later she always
     answered the same way saying that she had known it in the night

34.

And it was in the night that he had died just as
    the Iʻa The Fish The Milky Way was turning
and Piʻilani after his breath had stopped when his pulse
    was no longer there had put her head down on his chest
with her hair across his body and had listened
    to the darkness below her and the darkness above her
while the last embers of the small fire among the rocks
    at their feet went out and the cold of his hands deepened
and her tears kept turning cold when they ran down onto him
    she heard the darkness of the mountain under her
all the way to the underside of the sea floor
    and through her hair she heard the night winds high in the valley
rising and leaving and she heard *ʻuwaʻu ʻuwaʻu*
    the cry of the petrels echoing in the cliffs
the stream whispering over the rocks and the faint sounds
    some said were crickets and others said were land snails
singing and they were spirits and when the wind was quiet
    she could hear the sea far below her where all the waves ended
she sat up in the dark and saw where the stars had come
    she picked up a shell and started to pat it rocking
slowly forward and back chanting under her breath
    first she chanted to him by name by the name that she
had called him all her life and already she could hear
    the difference—Koʻolau Koʻolau you are going
you are going now you are still here you are going
    you are not sick any more you are not dying now
but if you want to come back Koʻolau come back come back—

35.

She had chanted the same words until she heard them
    go out like the fire and she patted the shell rocking
without words and then began again—Ko'olau
    it is the time of your going I hear the sound of it
but I go on trying to think of something to give you
    where you are on the mountain that keeps turning away
and all that is left here now is that you are gone—
    She chanted until the stars at the top of the cliff
began to grow faint in the ghost dawn and she stood up then
    and slowly climbed down to the stream and washed her face and hands
When they had been sure that he would not live many more days
    they had moved for the last time together back to the hollow
where they had taken Kaleimanu when the child
    was dying and where they had buried him in the low cave
at the foot of the cliff and when it began to be day
    she pushed farther back in the narrow among the rocks and found
a place deep among them not far from Kaleimanu's grave
    and there she knelt chanting her husband's full name—Kalua
i Ko'olau Kalua i Ko'olau—and as she chanted
    she began to pull back the ferns and pry up the stones
but she had only the stones and sticks and the kitchen knife
    to dig with and she dug all day but at sundown
it was not deep enough and she slept that night beside him
    and all the next day she dug the grave knowing nothing
but what she was doing until late in the day she thought
    it must be deep enough and she lined it with ferns
and hauled Ko'olau's body to it and settled his gun
    on his chest and then filled the grave and rolled stones
onto it and closed the bushes back over it

36.

Then it had been dark and once more she had chanted to him
 —Koʻolau now it is night for me and it is night for you
now we are in the night Koʻolau there is only night where we are—
 When the chant had ebbed in her breath she had got to her feet
and gone down to the stream again stepping like a stranger
 as though she were feeling her route through a rolling cloud
she had come to the water running cold from the cliff
 she had heard it come up to her talking to itself
not to her not to her even then not to her yet
 she had stepped down into it and knelt among the big stones
slipping between them she had lain down among them letting
 the breathless touch glide over her until she could feel it
no longer while the colorless syllables still
 hurried past her she had got to her feet and followed
the stream through the dark knowing her way down the valley
 It had been years since she had spoken to anyone
except him and in an earlier time Kaleimanu
 but some who had lived in the valley had come back
people they had known once had come back a few of them
 at a time she had seen one or two of them approaching
the floors of ashes that had been their houses
 had seen new grass roofs later and backs in the taro ponds
she had heard the voices and slipped close to listen
 and that night she could see small fires down in the valley
near the east headland and she had wanted to be with people
 but she had gone past the fires to where the current rattled
across the shingle she had felt the canoes drawn up there
 she had walked slowly along the rocks to the white streamer
unfurling on the tops of the low breakers and she had sunk down
 into the night surf to be washed clean in the darkness

37.

As she came down the dry cliff in the heat of the afternoon
     into the smells of rock dust and lantana that rose
like a breath out of the gorge she thought of standing
     in the sea that night in the cold of Kanaloa
the hand of the dark pulling her pushing her she had felt
     what it was taking away and what it was leaving
what it was leaving her darkness darkness and she came
     to the top of the side valley and the smell of ginger
where the thin cries of the tropic birds were no longer
     far below her she began to hear water and she went on
and here was the lap of ferns where they had rested
     that first time and then farther down where the dim path
wound among rocks at the foot of a high wall of stone
     she stepped away from it into the shade of kopikos
she was sure that nobody had found the grave as she
     opened her way through the branches in the narrow cleft
she was sure as she had been sure each time the rumor
     had reached her and she had gone just the same to tell
Kawaluna what she had heard and ask what Kawaluna
     thought of it and each time the answer had been the same
there had been the day when Ida had brought her the page
     of the Commercial Advertiser where it said
that Deputy Sheriff Coney and Police Officer
     John I had dug into a mound in the upper valley
and found a couple of rough boards and then a body
     wrapped in a coarse gray blanket with a raincoat around its head
buttoned in the back the hands folded over a rifle
     a Mauser with a woman's satchel full of cartridges for it
and the brigand's revolver since they were certain
     that the body which they estimated to have been
four or five months in the ground had once been Koʻolau

38.

Everything on the torn tongue of paper had told her
    that they were wrong and she had been sure of that to begin with
all of it she said to herself reading it over
    nobody had found him but just the same she had gone
to Kawaluna to read her the scrap of paper
    and that massive woman sat looking down at it
without moving and then Pi'ilani had seen
    that she was shaking and when she looked up she was laughing
she said—You know that nobody has found Kalua
    i Ko'olau—and she held up the paper as though
it had mud on it and Pi'ilani began
    to wonder whose grave they might have found she kept
thinking it might be Mamala it might be Mamala
    who had got away into Wainiha when the soldiers
had rounded up everyone they could find in the valley
    and who had lived back there taking wild cattle and goats
after Ko'olau had stopped using the rifle
    Mamala she thought but then who would have buried him
whatever he died of a friend must have buried him
    to have left him his Mauser and the revolver
and ammunition and wrapped him so carefully
    and brought the boards from some ruin there had been others too
living in the other valleys they had known there were others
    but as she thought of it she wanted to be able
to say that she had been back to the grave and had seen
    that no one had found it and she decided that this time
she would go over by herself into Kalalau

39.

She was sure now as she lifted the tangle of branches
    guava and then 'ohia and kopiko remembering
Kawaluna looking at her steadily each time
    and then shaking her head and saying—You know that nobody
has found him—and yet Pi'ilani had come each time
    to see what she knew the litter of moss and brittle twigs
undisturbed the russet fur along the fern fronds
    untouched the sunlight floating on patches beyond
reach she saw it all in her mind as she came up
    between the rocks and there was no path there were no
footprints or broken shoots and then the hollow in the crag
    and the corner into it and she saw the place before her
almost as she had seen it in her mind only
    a little changed in itself a little estranged
giving off no sign that it knew she was standing there
    the shadows whispering among themselves the cliffs
with their backs to her the new growth on all sides not
    knowing her it was what she had known and been sure of
she stood watching the ragged light scattered across the leaves
    tears were running down her face and under her breath
from the center of her body she chanted to the place
    Kalua i Ko'olau nobody knows where you are
nobody has found you nobody has found you

40.

She moved cautiously to the grave breaking nothing
    making scarcely a sound until she could kneel beside
the flat stone in the shadow of ferns and touch the green
    moss just above ground there she waited birds were speaking
in branches close to her elepaios curious
    not singing and she waited and then she lay down
breaking nothing and put her ear to the ground and listened
    as she did each time she came and in one ear she heard
the leaves and the birds in the branches and in the other ear
    the one note of the mountain of Kane the silence
under the forty forms the darkness under the day
    it had not changed and she closed her eyes and was filled
with it and at last she stood up slowly and with the same care
    went along to the cleft in the rock wall and the bushes
of 'ulei that had grown over the mouth of the low cave
    at the foot of the cliff where they had buried Kaleimanu
the small green leaves were shining like eyes and the white flowers
    were hiding among them and slender branches were swaying
slowly out over them into empty air and she
    put her ear to the warm stone and stood listening there
then sat against the rock wall beside the 'ulei
    and saw the shadow rising on the cliff and heard
the birds that were not the ones Kaleimanu had listened to
    telling their day and its passing and when she felt the shadow
she unwrapped the last of the cold taro and ate
    and then she lay down and heard the sleep of the mountain

THE MOUNTAIN

1.

The mountain rises by itself out of the turning night
      out of the floor of the sea and is the whole of an island
alone in the one horizon alone in the entire day
      as a word is alone in the moment it is spoken
meaning what it means only then and meaning it only
      once with the same syllables that have arisen
and have formed and been uttered before again and again
      somewhere in the past to mean something of the same nature
but different something continuing and transmitted
      but with refractions something recognized in its changes
something remembered from what is no longer there
      and behind it something forgotten as the beginning
is forgotten and as the dream vanishes the present
      mountain is moving at its own pace at the end
of its radius it is sailing in its own time
      with the earth turning away under it as the day
turns under a word and it came late as a word comes late
      with a whole language behind it by the time it is spoken
its fire came late among the fires in the dark of space
      its burning plume rose late through the plated shell of the globe
it formed late at the end of the old plume unfurling into
      the black depth of the sea and it burst up at last into
the air higher and higher collapsing sliding away
      and pressing anew from beneath splitting open lifting
and finally moving away from the fire-plume and cooling
      almost twice as high in its youth as the scored peak
in the story and setting out in that giant time
      following its elders the earlier usages
already invisible beyond the late day

2.

There it towered where each of its antecedents
    had stood in a cloud–hidden unremembered past
barren and farther from land except for each other
    than any coast in the sea that circled the globe
and already there had been ages when the engendering
    plume of fire had fallen back into its own darkness
for so long that the earliest craggy intimations
    looming and cloaked with clouds and commanding the currents
of the ocean had washed crumbled and subsided
    and had sunk in succession under the breakers
until none was left rising above the water
    and beyond the most ancient surviving reef that scarcely
showed through the waves a submerged convoy was continuing
    the voyage consonants of an archaic language
all their high sayings returned to sand and each of them
    had once faced the rain and wind the sun and the night sky with
bare rock and the shining black drapery and jagged
    stone salients of lava and across them the weather had broken
measureless all through the time before time and before
    the first waifs of life had found their way to those surfaces
solitary travellers lifted by storms and long swells
    to a naked place where one day they found company

3.

Some came from the invisible islands sinking
  already far ahead into the past some had become
what they were only there on one island in the waning
  course of its age and then had been carried backward
into the future on an island from afterward
  where they went on to become what they would be only there
and then were ferried in turn to this mountain to continue
  themselves some from the sea cast up on the surprising shore
some from the air in a dream of roots so from one branched
  coral polyp waving far off in the unanswering
night before the gods the family of coral and its white choirs
  came into being so from one star in the shallows
the constellations of starfish moved outward so
  from the mussel its child the hermit crab emerged
at the foot of the mountain so from the fronds floating in
  on the waves the ferns were formed that woke on the mountain
after the night ran through the narrows of changing
  in the darkness without eyes and some were born in the sea
some in fresh water or on land so in the caves were born
  the crickets of each cave ground crickets and when there were trees
tree crickets swordtail crickets and the sound they made
  that in time would be called singing ran through the mountain
born only there were flowering trees and lobelias
  and birds that discovered them and were changed when they tasted them
born was the plover into flight born were the birds
  each from the wingbeats of the others born were the guardians
the noddy at sea guarded by the owl on the mountain
  birds passed the peak in high streams that blacked out the sun
and at daybreak the wet hollows of the earth opened wings
  and flew up in answer into the light and the infant
shoots of the taro uncurled and reached for the morning

4.

It had all come late to the first age still without measure
    except for the turning in which it was turning
the longest age the age of origin the aeon
    through which processions of islands rose and were washed away
without names the aeon before the gods which the gods
    who came in time to take all the names of the light
and of what appeared in the light for themselves would call the age
    of unbroken darkness and empty night but the whole
day of the world had hung there in a drop of rain on a leaf
    with no need to fall and the mountain had been sailing
away from its source through sunlight and starlight far longer
    than the age of all the gods that were yet to come
the next mountain had risen into its following
    tree of smoke behind the horizon and it was as long
again before the next and the next and still the gods
    knew nothing of the light and the waifs of life drifted
back into the future and again into the past
    coming to be made by where they woke so that the offspring
of seeds of shrubs here and there grew into tall trees
    and so little menace and pursuit was there
that toxins and thorns were given up and generations
    of insects and birds forgot flight and the use of their wings
then came the day when fear found the edge and fell into
    the age of night fear and day fear and the hiding and crawling fears
the time of the hairless ones and of blood on the leaves
    and of standing figures arriving from their distance
from the night the time of people coming the time of time

5.

They came on a wide cloud with three separate floors
    they appeared on an island that turned as it flew
so it was told later when there was no one alive
    who could remember any longer the way it had happened
and it was all true in a way only the way kept changing
    they had become their journey which was the tale they repeated
they told where they thought they had been and thought they remembered
    they told of the faces of death they thought they had left
one after another so that their own shadows
    were its shadow now and they claimed that they were the heirs
of the root of the earth the source of the earth they had it
    with them wherever they went it was the fire they were carrying
before which there had been nothing and their own footprints were names
    which they had given to the stars they had followed
out of the night of Asia into the islands new names
    for the sky as they went from Newe and Kauana lipo
under Haku po kano to Hoku pa‘a and their wake
    was what they had almost forgotten broken shells on a house floor
a bed pile in a dark corner and bones of a half-eaten child
    they came from beneath the stars of the south that brought
the bad weather they came in the fever of a sick wind
    on the hot flailing air some called themselves Take
and the islands from which they had sailed they called Hiva
    but when they saw the mountain they said it was theirs

6.

It looked to them like the world they had come from
    or like the way that world might have been there were steep valleys
formed like the ones they had seen inhabited crowded
    tended and fought over foot by foot but here they found no one
at first except big birds that could not fly away
    and feared them so little that it was easy to catch them
so they feasted on them until there were none of them left
    and they set up houses and others came and joined them
it was a land of crags and rocks and slopes veined with water
    where they moved immense stones into vast masonry
giant walls and waterways platforms causeways that would be
    their monuments rising out of silence when they themselves
had become legends after they had been overrun
    by others in waves among them those from Tahiti
called Manahunes who had been invaded and had sailed
    north to pass on their defeated name to those they conquered
who withdrew into the cliffs or sailed into the northwest
    to the old islands taking with them the old tongue
and all certain knowledge of themselves and they grew
    small in the distance and were belittled in stories
where they appeared as dwarves knee-high with arts of their own
    great powers the strength of giants the cunning of sorcerers
and were still claimed as forbears long after they had vanished

7.

And from the southwest in that age came the goddess of fire
     Pele following the source of fire to make her home there
some said she was born in Tahiti some said she was born
     in Kaui helani a land floating like a cloud
some say she was driven away by her stern sister
     the sea goddess Namaka who predicted that Pele
would set fire to everything and they say that when Pele left
     she had with her in the canoe her brothers the gods
and under her arm her small sister Hi‘iaka
     they sailed to the ancient syllables the line of faded atolls
in the northwest and then journeyed back to the mountain
     which the inhabitants by then had named Kauai
and since that was the way she came her prow grounded
     on the shingle near Hanalei and Haena and she
found everyone dancing there and Pele fell in love
     others say she had travelled the length of the islands digging
for the well of fire and was settled at Kilauea
     on Hawai‘i when she heard in a dream the sound
of the nose flute coming from somewhere on the mountain
     on Kauai and first she thought it was old Pohaku
her grandfather but when she followed the sound she found it was
     coming from Haena beside Kalalau where they were
all dancing and she fell in love as a fire would
     fall in love and she loved a young chief named Lohiau
and she emerged into the firelight and the chanting
     with her back like a cliff and her breasts proud so that everyone
thought her the most beautiful woman they had ever seen

8.

The story was so old that everyone dancing
    there at Haena that night had always known it
it was the same story that they were dancing and it led
    into holding and losing into absence and rage and ashes
and into returning and it was rising out of Pele's dream
    far away on the island of Hawaii and in her dream
with her eyes on Lohiau she chanted *Hanalei*
    is overcome by the great rain as the flame leapt
between them and it told of her biting his hand
    as she turned to go home and of his sister finding him
when he had hanged himself from the roof-tree after Pele went
    and of his dog refusing to leave his grave and of Pele
waking and persuading her sister Hi'iaka
    to bring Lohiau to her and of Hi'iaka
coming at last to the coast below Kalalau
    and seeing in a cave high in the cliff the ghost
of Lohiau and of her bringing him back to life
    and of love waking between them in turn and the barriers
their love came to one after the other and triumphed over
    and then of Pele's own fires burning up Lohiau
and his return to life one more time and reunion
    with Hi'iaka it was all there in the chanting
in the sound of the drumming at the base of the mountain

9.

With Pele had come her brother the Chief of the Sharks
    and the shark rock was there at the headland of Kalalau
the dragon had arrived from the birthplace of Pele
    the owl of the mountain commanded from the cliff
people had settled in all the long valleys running
    in from the sea on the steep north slope of the mountain
they had terraced the green gorge of Nualolo
    with its broad table high above the surf they had taro growing
in Wainiha that narrowed climbing toward Kilohana
    and while they were dancing the darkness went on wheeling
so that they came to nights in which the stars over them
    burned in places where a few hours earlier
they had been seen higher above the horizon
    by Arthur sailing for Iceland and by Merlin
versed in the turnings of western islands and by Brendan
    and the animals with him in the small ark of his summer
and then by Charlemagne's veterans in the dark of Europe
    still furred in its forests that harked back to the ice
with their roots in amber worn faces had looked up through woods
    that they had been given for the felling and later
far north where the nights were blank the Norse followed secrets
    in search of somewhere it seemed they must remember
with a name like time and in time farther west they cheated
    the Skraelings for furs a first touch of a flayed new world

10.

Farther west and later past currents and tracts of ocean
     so crowded with fish that in some places a hull
might have trouble forcing its way among the braided backs of them
     beyond the coast of the continent and inland through forests
of spruce hemlock and birch there were eyes at night watching
     those same figures glittering between the auroras
others were watching from farther south by the low tones
     of rivers in a land full of the lives of animals
beaver in the streams bear in the forests wolves deer and moose
     their ways forming the fabric through which the colors
and charactery of the human lives were continued
     season by season and in that wholeness remained whole
believing that they might draw from the life around them
     from the senses and quickening of the animals
what they truly needed and no more and that in return
     for their restraint and compunction the creatures around them
who they knew were their elders and were spirits and powers
     would protect them from the evils of sickness and pestilence
it was an understanding that sustained them until
     fishermen out of England came upon that coast with
diseases carried from Europe and with offers of iron
     for furs and then epidemics in waves erased villages
and the survivors believed the animals had betrayed them
     and they took the guns and cloth and treatment they were given
and set out into the three centuries of screams
     and dismemberment the piled scalps parades of zeros gross fortunes
far away and the bleeding across the continent from the constant
     skinning familiarly known as the fur trade that finally
arrived at the sea which by then was called the Pacific

11.

It had been a long time since anyone on the island
     remembered some name from the south for a bay or a narrow
fold in the Hivas that the ancients had once clung to
     and then had sailed from and later the Spaniards came to those
steep coasts but finding no gold there they christened
     the constellation of peaks the Marquesas and sailed on
leaving little except the diseases they happened to have
     and some of them vanished in those seas and planks from their
wreckage rode the currents northward and from time to time
     beached on the island and someone picking shellfish from the rocks
at Lawai or Kapa'a or even at Kalalau
     might find them and take them home and they would be
passed around and touched and the shapes and surfaces
     discussed and the red and black on the iron spikes
hammered in Spain with ends that could cut would become
     treasures and were indeed prophets generations after
anyone had arrived from Tahiti or had sailed there
     and come back to tell and the name had come to suggest
mirages and clouds or another life before
     or after and by then stars had dropped out of their knowledge
below the southern horizon Hokuloa and Ka'awela
     and other lights had never been known as beacons
only the ancients had told of the stars of Kuanalipo
     that were leading the floating forests to Tahiti
directing strange sails to the islands of the ancients

12.

An age of passing with nothing appearing to change
    a succession of comings and goings of the moon
a history of tides generations of calendars
    families seeing themselves pass in running water
an aeon when the chiefs had divided the round island
    among themselves and agreed that it would remain
under a spell set apart from the other islands
    a cradling a kind of calm that ripened around the mountain
days for planting returned and they planted by the lower streams
    nights for fishing returned and the nets came up full
more than once they were invaded by chiefs from other islands
    and drove them off and were left at last unmolested
though drawn step by step into the bloodlines woven
    through the island chain but still the horizon was their own
as in their eyes it had always been and would be
    for that long again and then one morning in the season
of rains the time of Lono the days when the Pleiades
    had risen and the year had become new again
when the high chiefs of Kauai were Kaneone
    and Keawe in the gray moment of the ghost dawn
at Waimea on the shore by the canoes Kauiana
    thought he saw parts of a forest out on the ocean
which had not been there the evening before when the sun
    had gone down and these were like no forests he had ever seen
so that for a moment he was not sure they were there
    then the others with him saw where he was looking
and caught sight of the same things and one of them shouted with fear

13.

For three days the sick wind had been reeling into them
     from the south bringing these things closer to Waimea
Kuimana the chief had heard the shout from the shore
     he came down with Aimaku both of them with spears
and saw the black shapes out past the surf there was more light then
     and the low parts were rocking like canoes in the water
the trees on them rocking with the rest and gray things like dead rays
     were swinging in the branches Kuimana stood watching
while the others talked without knowing and then he said Take out
     the canoes and see what they are and Aimaku
went out with seven canoes at first but people
     kept coming down to the shore when they saw those things
and the canoes kept going out and by that time
     there was daylight so they could see that the things were
part island and part canoe and could see pieces of iron
     all over them on the outside many shapes of iron
of different sizes some very large and they said
     to each other that the iron that they had been sharpening
into knives must have come from islands like these and they saw
     creatures on them with three-cornered heads and white faces
like human faces their skin dark blue and white hands like real hands
     which they kept raising and voices like voices calling out
something that sounded like the word iron so the people
     called back going closer until they saw steps being lowered
from the canoes to the water so that they could climb
     up the black sides and see the iron waiting everywhere

14.

These creatures had long hair tied back so that at first
    they appeared to be women and there was smoke blowing
out of the mouths of some of them they had wrinkled skin
    with treasure holes in it that went far inside them
and they could reach into those and bring out knives and nails
    beads and a kind of white tapa and many other things
and they talked the way people talk but what they said
    was like pebbles going around in a gourd they babbled
noises *blither blather jabble jumble rumble*
    berry love Tahiti love baby love woman
Moku saw a roll of rope with an iron club on it
    lying in front of him and picked it up and when they
pulled him by the arm he broke loose and jumped over the side
    and Kaleo was looking into everything
like an eel and he came out of a doorway laughing
    holding up a big knife with a square blade and they
tried to catch him but he stood up on the wall laughing
    and as they reached for him he jumped too and Aimaku
said it was time to go and they left and went back
    to tell the chiefs and others about all this
they kept telling it over and over talking about
    what to do and by then people who had seen those things
out to sea from Kekaha and Makaweli were coming
    until there were many sitting watching along the shore
by the time the sun went down and they saw a row
    of fires all at once jump from one of those black islands
all the fires the same like fish and in a moment they heard
    thunder coming from there and then it happened again
and then it was dark and they sat trying to see

15.

Some stayed there all night watching and others sat
     beside fires talking some said they were sure the strangers
must be gods and insisted that the fires jumping from the island
     and the thunder afterward proved it but others
did not believe it and some said they needed to see
     whether the strangers would bleed and they went on talking
until the fires sank and the voices came more slowly
     then the woman chief Kemalia who was very old
reached over to a drum that a friend was holding
     and patted it with one finger like a heart beating
until that and the thin wave spinning out along the sand
     were the only sounds and then she said as though
she were sitting there alone—No they are not gods
     One time after Umi had died on the island
of Hawai'i and while his son Keali'iokaloa
     was chief in his place a thing like one of these came there
and we thought it was an island and called it an island
     but they are not islands they are only a big kind
of canoe and that one was named Konaliloha
     and it broke into pieces on the rocks at Palemanō
we were told and many died there but one man and one woman
     reached the shore alive and they stayed on the sand a long time
on their knees so the place is called Kneeling even now
     everyone wanted to help them and people brought them
into their houses and gave them food and the man's name
     as they remembered it was Kukanaloa
and they thought the woman was his sister people asked what they
     ate where they came from they ate fruit and everything
no one could understand them but they lived there after that
     and were people and had children and died like anyone—

16.

By then the sick wind had come to an end and they let
    the fires go out and slept or sat watching the darkness
in the darkness out to sea listening hearing
    over the low brushed syllables of the water
the calling of plovers across the night the two notes
    leaping up and then from out on the water a hollow
knocking and at times other notes in pairs not rising
    echoes of a pebble on a beach or a bird voice
but not a sound of a living person and then for a long time
    they would not hear it and suddenly it would be there again
clear and thin but so faint that they would ask each other
    whether they had heard it they sat watching the flying stars
and each of them there began at some point to remember
    sitting beside someone who had died and watching listening
to what was not there and to what still seemed to be there
    in the last night some remembered that the death had been
heralded by a ringing in the ears and they found
    themselves trying to tell whether the night was still breathing
and not knowing what they were groping to remember
    and now they would not know it until they themselves were gone
but everything else was still the same the night sky
    constellations in their places the sea stroking the sand
the shore onto which they had been born and where they had
    been who they were then the stars began to leave them
growing smaller disappearing and a breeze woke
    just as it used to and they no longer heard anything
from out to sea but as the darkness faded those dark
    spider shapes of it remained and as they went on watching
into bare day they saw from one of those islands
    a smaller darkness born a canoe coming toward them

17.

Black prow broad in the water paddles far to the sides
 like the wings of a chicken they could not tell as they watched
whether it was scarcely moving or was approaching them
 like a thrown spear and for a moment when they looked
it hung still in the gray light like the thread of white
 water suspended in the high falls at Moeloa
far up in the gorge of Waimea at that hour of the morning
 after the months of rain that late in the winter
while the shout of the water was echoing in the cliffs far
 behind them out of their hearing as they edged down
along the sand saying again the same things they had said
 in the night and some of them were holding offerings
standing in the water with pigs in their arms chickens
 dogs bananas taro such gifts as might be offered
to any stranger a few were carrying spears
 they talked faster louder as the canoe came closer
and they could see the black heads and blue skins of the strangers
 who were paddling backwards they were coming backwards
they must be coming from afterwards or from somewhere
 that was already gone and people started to laugh
girls were laughing arranging the flowers on themselves
 Kapupu'u who had come back with the big knife
was laughing and said—I am somebody who will pick up
 what I can—until Kemalia heard him and told him
—That could be stealing and you know what happens to you
 if you steal from people—He said—Maybe they are not people
at all not people—and he laughed and went on laughing
 as the canoe came closer and they all crowded toward it
and caught hold of paddles a stranger was standing
 in the prow holding a pole with an iron hook
and Kapupu'u snatched the pole and the other
 would not let it go so they both pulled back and forth
and another one standing in the canoe pointed
 an iron rod at Kapupu'u and it flashed
and roared and Kapupu'u fell back in the water
 kicking and from a hole in his chest his blood began
to flow around the canoe until it was all around it

18.

The soundless white thread had not moved in the waterfall
  everything had stopped but nothing was stopped they let the canoe
go and saw that it was something else it was not a canoe
  and the figures with blue skins looked to them like things moving
under clear water they heard the voices coming from them
  echoing echoing while the echo from the iron stick
still circled in their ears they heard in the sharp rattling
  syllables of the strangers the habit of seizure
and the rush of fear and the paddles rose all together
  from the sides of the canoe and then fell together
into the red water but now the strangers were paddling
  forward and away and Kapupu‘u was floating
face up with his eyes looking at the sky but he was dead
  some of them picked him up feeling the warmth of him
and carried him up the sand with the blood dripping
  all the way to his house and the wailing going with them
and some stayed to watch the strangers turn at a distance
  of several spear throws when their voices and the hollow knock
and creaking of the paddles could still be heard as they moved
  saw them paddling on toward the left following the shore
to the river mouth and across it and on past
  Makaweli and Koloa and a few of the men
followed to see where they would go and the rest gathered
  in the shade at Waimea where they could watch the islands
of the strangers out in the dazzling sea with the crying
  and the chanting for Kapupu‘u close upon them
some wanted to face the strangers now as enemies
  and recalled the alien armies that their ancestors
had driven off and how many of the invaders
  had been left dead along the shore at Kekaha and Mānā
and they shouted but then some spoke of the thunder
  and the fire at night from those black islands and said maybe
the strangers were gods after all and at last Aimaku
  stood up and they were silent and the wailing seemed louder
He said—It is not in my mind that they are gods but for now
  we should act as though they were gods and had taken
their sacrifice and we will watch everything they do

19.

So it was still their day their light their shore with those trees
    they knew and the same birds running in lines along it
like shadows of threads lifting off and alighting
    it was still they who said who were gods and who were not
and the spirit of Kapupu'u was still somewhere
    not far away perhaps listening to the wailing for him
and shuffling softly among the old leaves then from the sea
    a sound came to them like rocks rolling in a stream bed
and one by one they stood up shading their eyes watching
    those black islands turning slowly in their places
and three more canoes appeared and were coming toward them
    the paddles out to the sides flashing too slowly for wings
and again they went with offerings the same ones
    they had been holding the first time and they stood along the sand
waiting pointing out things to each other and they saw
    in one of the canoes strangers with brighter colors
and one of them kept telling the others what to do
    then when the prows were near shore strangers jumped out and began
pulling the canoes to land and still the people stood watching
    until the stranger who seemed to be the high chief
swung his white legs over the side of his canoe
    and set his black feet down beside the water's edge
then they all knelt down and lay on their faces touching
    the hot day in the sand and heard the stranger say
something that sounded far and calm and Aimaku stood up
    and saw the stranger slightly below him hold out
his empty hand and repeat what sounded like a greeting
    and Aimaku swept his own hand toward the shore behind him
and turning to the stranger said—You have a house here—

20.

If the stranger were a god he would understand
    Aimaku was sure of that and it was clear to him
in a moment that the stranger did not understand
    Aimaku waved to the people with offerings
and they came forward holding out the gifts they had brought
    reaching out to the strangers and staring at them
both the men and the women watching them as intently
    as a heron with its eye on the water but the men
and the women were watching them differently and the strangers
    kept looking at the women's breasts as they took the gifts
and turned to pile them in the canoes and they turned back
    to look at the women and go on looking and then their chief
said something to them and facing Aimaku he made
    a gesture as though he were drinking and the strangers
rolled out a round wooden box with iron circling it
    and raised it so that water dripped out and it was empty
as water gourds are empty after any trip
    and Aimaku had the men help unload more of those boxes
and he and Kanalu led the strangers' chief to the pool
    of good water and he directed the men to help
fill the containers with water while he took the chief
    and the chief's companions up the valley to the place
of the gods with many of the people following them
    and everyone lying face down as they passed by
there Aimaku showed the strangers the enclosure and altar
    and images watching them all and listening to them
and he could tell that they thought they understood what was there

21.

Three times during those days the small canoes came ashore
　　from the tall ones that kept turning and moving closer
in the daytime and farther out at night and the men filled
　　many of the round boxes with water and handed the strangers
more and more pigs to carry away and sweet potatoes
　　often giving them for nothing or exchanging them
for the pointed sticks of iron that the strangers had with them
　　the strangers wanted to touch the women and many
of the women wanted to find out what the strangers
　　would be like to lie with and they managed to slip away
into houses or through the bushes and the women
　　found out how the strangers hid in their skins and they gave
themselves to discover it and for the pleasure and for
　　nothing at first and then they learned to ask for those
sticks of iron and to bargain sometimes for more than one
　　so that many of them had handfuls of iron by the morning
when the black islands had vanished from the horizon
　　and they shared the iron with their fathers and brothers
but after a number of days some of the women had red
　　swellings where they had welcomed the pleasure and then sores
opened discharging yellow rot and the smell of dead things
　　and pain spread through their limbs and on some the flesh around
the sores began to die and drop away and the men
　　with whom they had lain since they had been with the strangers
began to show sores of the same kind on their bodies
　　and on some of the men and women growths emerged in the shapes
of fruit or fish while the sores spread to their faces
　　into their mouths and throats and along their bodies
many of them had pain passing water yet they felt
　　a need to do it all the time and little water came
but occasionally a green fluid and there were rottings
　　of the face bit by bit the nose falling into itself
and a stabbing in the bones a fire burning in the bones
　　all day and hotter at night and the same troubles kept touching
others one by one and they would begin their dying

22.

While some were dying the heat was rising around them
    as it does from stones on a shore after the sun has gone down
but some were shivering and twitching the way a fish
    shudders at the moment of death while the chief of the strangers
whose name as they knew then was Tapena Tute
    or Kapena Kuke was eating a part of a pig
from a family garden by the river at Waimea
    having guided the two black islands northward into a winter
that did not retreat before them when the calendar
    said it was time to be planting peas in England
they had sailed up blue canyons between towering forests
    deep in snow the silence ripped by the swirling screams
of eagles and along cliffs of ice with their own radiance
    while echoes from the crags creaked and thundered around them
the hollow thump and scrape of floes crowded up to them
    never leaving through the fog halls and the frozen nights
when they could not see the stars or the black water
    mornings when they could see nothing and never
the passage that they thought they had glimpsed again and again
    believed they had come to and had found it and it was a ghost
in the future that word before language that northwest
    passage that did not exist ice hung in the rigging
solid with the sails he was rheumatic from the waist down
    he turned back south toward the islands to which they had given
the name of a person of position and influence
    on the other side of the world an earl named Sandwich
and Cook sailed to the island of Hawaii and the bay
    named the Road of the God where he found the diseases
that his crews had brought had travelled ahead through the islands
    and were waiting for them there and there he was killed trying
to recover something that had been taken from them

23.

Late in the month of tangled waves a little more than a year
　　after the first appearance one morning off Waimea
the black islands were there again and no one was
　　surprised and no one was happy to see them the surf
was high it was dangerous getting in and they wanted
　　everything again as they had wanted it before
a welcome and every provision and comfort
　　at that moment and for the time to come and all of it
for nothing or almost nothing as a kind of tribute
　　but the chiefs had been talking about it in the meantime
and the greeting was stolid and the prices were prices
　　that grew with discussion and Kuke was not there with them
where was Kuke but his successor in the command
　　Clarke spitting blood by then with consumption had cleared out
the women they had on board from the other island
　　to keep the news of Cook's death from travelling with them
the people showed the strangers the sores and deformities
　　on their persons urging the strangers to take away
what they had brought a few parted with pigs or salt but the chiefs
　　bargained for firesticks indicating with gestures
that they required those for conflicts on the island
　　and a single musket was worth the days of many pigs
and though the strangers were not gods they had powers
　　known and unknown and racks full of strange possessions
glinting with the suggestion that even their touch
　　would relay some of their hidden substance and the women
gathered the strangers as before and a few of them stayed out
　　on the black islands and were gone when those islands were gone

24.

In his heart Cook had known there was no such passage
    but it was the kind of knowledge that is not a thing for words
and since that was what they had been sent for Clarke continued
    the commission sailing northwest the way of succession
coughing his orders keeping more and more to his cabin
    arriving at Kamchatka and there as he considered it
unlikely that his vessels could survive the voyage
    and was certain that he himself would not he confided
Cook's journal to a Russian major who had become
    his friend asking him to dispatch it across Russia
to the British Admiralty and so the Imperial
    Academy in St Petersburg knew of Cook's
landfalls and his death before anyone did in England
    and Clarke turned once more to the search along the walls
of ice and found only a route to extend
    the peeling enterprise that by then had crossed the continent
marked by mounds of rotting animals born into fur
    considered only as skin trapped for it and screaming
into a time of contagions until they were all but gone
    from the lakes and rivers from the forests and the forests
in turn were going and even in dreams the animals
    were harder to see and by the time Clarke was groping
along the Aleutians island by island the sea cows
    the Russians had found there thirty-odd years before
already were nearly extinct the meat was like beef
    the fat of the calves could hardly be told from fresh pork fat
they fed upon seaweed they had no fear of humans
    a hunter could walk to them in shallow water and lay
a hand on them large hooks were put in them and rope parties
    of thirty dragged them ashore with those in the boats
beating on them to exhaust them while they groaned
    and the blood shot up in fountains and the others
would come to try to help by unhooking or breaking the ropes
    floundering after them and staying near them even when
they had died and all with no voice but the breath they groaned with

25.

It had been said that they were there merely for the taking
     so they had been taken but Clarke's crews came upon
sea otters sitting in the waves and families of seals
     easy to kill and they kept the furs and recorded
the locations to come back to though Clarke on the way south
     died before they reached Cathay the goal which the Genoese
had sailed for the true China they anchored in the crowded
     harbor of Macao and found that the furs they had with them
were treasures commanding prices they could scarcely credit
     because those in power in that country and those with wealth
dreamed of draping their persons their families their
     concubines beds saddles all that betokened them
with furs of other animals and the English officers
     Portlock and Dixon could see the fur trade crossing
the Pacific by way of the Sandwich Islands
     where ships could stop for provisions of food and water
salt and firewood and in Macao they smelled wood dust burning
     with a fragrance they thought familiar and then they remembered
a similar fragrance from the fires beside houses
     in Waimea and the merchants in Macao inquired
whether the English could bring them wood of that kind
     which they valued highly its name proved to be sandalwood
so that when they came back to Kauai with their first cargo
     of furs they let the chiefs know that they were looking
for the fragrant wood and the payment could be in guns

26.

Along the river above Waimea the English
    admired the family gardens laid out with great skill
and judgment the trenches bringing fresh water to the fields
    the taro ponds intersected by embankments
stands of bananas fences of sugar cane the houses
    set among mulberry trees with a designing sense
the English said was almost scientific and all tended
    with care and diligence that would have reflected credit
on even a British husbandman and the cane
    was fine and equally cheap the taro the finest
obtainable anywhere superb roots for an eight or a tenpenny
    nail their industry in supplying us with everything
in their power was beyond example their eagerness
    to do acts of kindness and their hospitality
were unbounded But each visit seemed to leave new
    sickenings invisible spells against which they had
no defences epidemics that overtook them
    like flood waters each one arriving with its own
alien heat its cold shakings aches and eruptions
    smells discharges scales constant incontinence
unexampled discolorations and deformities
    starings wild speech chokings and blackenings before
death and still the people flocked to the shore welcoming
    each visit and paddled out to the vessels to hold up
offerings wanting to go with them to see that Britain
    where it was coming from and one who left with them was a chief
Taiana taller than the English a handsome man
    and shrewd who went with the furs to Canton where the English
colony made much of him dressing him like one
    of themselves having his portrait painted he found there
a Hawaiian woman Waineʻe who had sailed
    from another island as a servant to a captain's
wife but had taken sick and stayed and he remained there
    for some time to the great pleasure of the English
and bought knives axes saws carpets cloth iron entire sets
    of china and guns and ammunition to take home

27.

The English supplied him besides with whatever might be
    useful to his country such as bulls cows sheep goats rabbits
and when in his time on a later vessel and with
    a different captain Taiana attired and cheered by
His Majesty's subjects in Canton sailed east for the islands
    he insisted on taking with him that sick woman
Waineʻe having promised that he would see her home
    but she died at sea and they wrapped her in a sailcloth
that had seen the world turn and dropped her over the side
    and the captain told Taiana that he would repeat
a prayer to the true god in English and Taiana
    looked at the clouds and the horizon and from the depths
of his voice called softly to Kanaloa older
    than all the names he had survived Kanaloa from whom
all worship and all forms had washed away Kanaloa
    the beginning and the end death and the west and the sea
the rays of the octopus the sleep inside the shell
    of the coconut riding the currents of himself
—You Kanaloa Kanaloa—he called under his breath
    —I have returned your fish to the ocean and said go back
take her back to Ulukaʻa to the island turning
    out of sight in the night sky where there are women waiting—
Then once again he was the only one with his words
    and since when he had left there had been threats from other
chiefs his enemies he feared they might be in power at home
    and when they arrived at the island of Hawaiʻi
he learned that it was so but a young chief of that island
    named Kamehameha who was already a favorite
of the war god welcomed Taiana's knowledge daring
    and all those possessions and weapons into his own ambition

28.

When a sorcerer is projecting harm in secret
    small fires are seen at night sometimes flying across the sky
as Taiana knew and he knew that it is not fortunate
    to see them but even more dangerous are those fires
whose flight cannot be seen like trains of powder smoldering
    he had been troubled in Canton when first he saw beggars
he had wanted to feed them all and he was shocked by the deformities
    and mutilations among them and at Macao
around the fringes of the marketplaces he was looking
    at one of the hidden fires burning there among the Chinese
some of whom were taken as crew carpenters shipwrights
    even purchased by the head from India to sail
to Alaska for furs and among them they carried another
    disease to Hawai'i that would bloom like blood in a stream
he had seen that fire and not known it but now he kept
    close watch on the way of Kamehameha who tried first
to procure from the same captain who had taken Taiana
    two Chinese carpenters to build him a warship
and failing that he had them construct on his double canoe
    a platform and mount on it a small swivel gun
which he would use in the coming invasion and conquest
    of Maui and all that time the women were kind to
the carpenters wherever the ships went but as for Taiana
    before long he had had enough of Kamehameha
and left him and joined the forces gathered against him
    but the swivel gun followed him and Taiana was killed
at Nu'uanu when they were all driven over the cliff

29.

In a time of blood fountains when the chiefs were at war
      on all the main islands Taiana with his imposing
presence evident gifts and knowledge of the world
      and an audacity that had frightened Vancouver
into thinking that the young chief might seize the Discovery
      perhaps was hoping through alliance and strategy
to make himself ruler of his own disputed Kauai
      where the rightful high chief was scarcely more than a boy
whose regent after repeated struggles had many
      enemies but the cliff battle left Kamehameha
and the small reverently sequestered carving
      of his war god in dark red kauila wood in command
of all the main islands except Kauai and he was hungry
      to invade at once despite the exhausted state
of his own army the wreckage and the starvation his wars
      had left everywhere and the reluctance of his own chiefs
and he brought together the largest army and fleet
      there had ever been in the islands and he offered
human sacrifices on the altars of Kū
      before that midnight in late spring when they pushed off
to attack Kauai and its young chief Kaumuali'i
      his superior in birth and in every grace
but the night wind struck the invading fleet in mid-channel
      sinking so many canoes and drowning so many
that Kamehameha in bitterness gave the order
      for the remnants to turn back and that was the first time
and then for years he gathered forces and wrung the islands
      to provide a still larger fleet for another attempt
and as they were about to embark from Oahu
      they were hit by a sickness that would kill a man in the time
it took to go and fetch water and the bodies turned black
      his army was dropping all around him and he was sick
almost to death and lay thinking of Kaumuali'i's
      mother who was known to have a prayer of such power
that it was spoken of in a whisper all through the islands
      and he knew in his fever that it was she who had done this

30.

Whatever allowed him to recover did not leave him
　　the same ever afterward and he would not again
attempt an invasion although the armed men who might
　　have opposed him on Kauai could not have withstood him
but he could not rest without Kauai numbered among
　　his holdings and he fell back on ruses and offers
made with one hand and on promises he whose name was
　　The Lonely One he of whom no one could be certain
whom no one could trust he who on his own island
　　of Hawai'i had invited his last rival there
Keona to a meeting to talk about ruling
　　the island in peace and as Keona landed
he was speared and then all his companions speared except one
　　and Kamehameha had soon married the daughter
of the man who had speared him and that was Ka'ahumanu
　　and so Kaumuali'i had neglected to answer
Kamehameha's proposals for him to rule
　　Kauai as an untroubled island tributary
of The Lonely One and when the invitations came
　　from Kamehameha he had replied by sending
emissaries with gifts and garlands of fine words
　　but had stayed home with his faithful friends and felt the looming
of that Other with the islands lined up behind him
　　and the nature of a moray waiting and it took
two brothers from New England named Winship a brace
　　of sea captains to bring Kaumuali'i to meet
Kamehameha in Honolulu and set foot ashore
　　after both chiefs had performed a duet of accord
but an Englishman in that place warned Kaumuali'i
　　of a plot to poison him and he left for home at once
and they poisoned the Englishman yet the brothers Winship
　　had arranged enough peace for their own purposes
which involved cornering the traffic in sandalwood

31.

Most of twenty years it had taken to assemble
  that fragrant pyre from which there would be no returning
it had been hard to deal with the chiefs during the fighting
  when they needed men for raids and were unreliable
about schedules and contracts with one eye all the time
  on the next step in the match and the first sandalwood
sent to China from the islands had been of a kind they did not
  esteem there so the price had been low and the merchants
in Canton kept it down by insisting that all the wood
  that came from what their shipwrights already were calling
The Sandalwood Islands was of poor quality
  but of some ten species of santalum found from eastern
India through the Pacific four distinct kinds
  were native to Hawai'i in the drier forests and once
they were common varying in shape from tough bushes
  and in some places vines to trees fifty feet tall
always occurring in symbiotic relation
  to a host tree often the Hawaiian acacia koa
and of the kind prized for commerce it takes forty years
  for a tree to acquire down near the root a core of heart wood
where the sweet smell is housed and the whole tree must be cut
  at or below the ground to obtain a short length of it
all the rest for the most part they left where it fell
  and as long as Kamehameha lived he and Kaumuali'i
enjoyed the profits thus taken from the islands under them
  while the ruin went before them and climbed the mountains

32.

The chiefs bought on credit to be paid in sandalwood
    and the chiefs' collectors dug the commoners out of their
family gardens and sent them farther all the time
    into the steep forests with axes to fill the quotas
of sandalwood notching tallies but even the records
    lasted no longer than smoke although in some places
a unit of measure remains a hole in the mountain
    that the men were told to dig there at the beginning
its shape and dimensions those of the hold of a ship
    which they would fill with heartwood for the next cargo
the men were given little or nothing to eat
    and they ate whatever they could find in the forest
they were given nothing to wear on the mountain
    nothing to cover them when they lay down after dark
on the ground in the cold some were weak with the new
    sicknesses and their farms went to ruin while they were gone
famines followed in waves named for the bitter roots
    they learned to eat each time near starvation and when the cut logs
carefully stacked filled the holes the wood was loaded
    onto their backs held in place by a rope that ran
across the shoulders and under the arms each load
    weighed one picul a Chinese measure of one hundred
thirty-five pounds and the scars from the rope and the bark
    remained on the men's backs for the rest of their lives
but some died there among the trees some on the trails some reached
    home for a while as the demand for the wood quickened
and the debts mounted and it is legend that the cutters
    pulled up every sandalwood seedling they could find
but Kamehameha bought sailing vessels and cannons
    and assorted merchandise Kaumuali'i bought a brig
sets of china uniforms more things than he could keep track of

33.

Even so there were those who lived to look back upon
    that time as a last moment in their own bodies
a familiar face falling away far below them
    no one could have measured how much waited upon the life
of the opaque Kamehameha with his heart
    of kauila wood until all at once he was not there
and Liholiho his son the heir to his imperium
    at twenty-two had his father's demanding manner
without his authority whereas Ka'ahumanu
    the dead chief's favorite of his twenty-one wives
had will enough for any deed and made for herself
    the post of prime minister enlisting others
among the widows to play Liholiho like a fish
    in the shallows until he sat and ate with them
and with that one meal ripped irrevocably
    the merciless web of caste and ceremony
of ritual and dread and sacrifice and coherence
    the kapus that maintained the power of the war god
and of the chiefs themselves a fabric that had been
    decaying for longer than anyone could remember
but much faster since the foreigners had first breathed on it
    and the widows may have imagined that the rending
of this fretwork of fear and distinction would allow
    women access to further power but the power
even as they held it turned into a ghost and escaped them
    appearing out of reach while the god of the powerful
foreigners appeared to many in the strangers' wealth
    and their impunity long before the year when the chief died
and the grip of the kapus was broken and many were
    curious about this stranger god by the time the first
boatload of missionaries embarked from New England
    summoned late in time to save unknown souls from their lives

34.

They were allowed to stay for the time being at least
     perhaps they would be permitted to set up permanent roofs
for teaching their lessons in righteousness and reading
     though nothing in their gray probity pleased the widow-in-chief
and on Kauai Kaumuali'i welcomed two of them
     mainly because they brought back his son George who had been
sent to school in New England as a boy though the money
     for his schooling had vanished along the way and the heir
to Kauai had apprenticed as a carpenter
     worked on a farm joined the US Navy held a job
in the Boston Navy Yard acquired a reputation
     for outlandish behavior but was homesick and ready
for the ride back with the bearers of glad tidings
     and the missionaries to Kauai raised their tabernacles
and George who of course had been named for the King of England
     moved up a valley with a random following
of hopefuls to pursue a good time and then one morning
     two years later an open boat appeared offshore
bearing the young chief Liholiho and his retinue
     and he and Kaumuali'i exchanged fulsome assurances
and after Liholiho came his sumptuous brigantine
     with its own history as Cleopatra's Barge bringing
his five wives and the two chiefs sailed around the island
     sightseeing and feasting for forty-two days and nights
until one evening at Waimea after more than two months together
     at the end of a feast on Liholiho's yacht
the anchor was quietly weighed and without a word
     the vessel set sail for Oahu with Kaumuali'i
given no answers all night as they crossed the channel

35.

In Honolulu he was treated as a guest of state
    he assured those who asked that he was returning a visit
but this time he could not leave and the abduction
    apparently had been planned by the ruling widow
Ka‘ahumanu who put the island of Kauai
    into the custody of her brother and forced
Kaumuali‘i four days after his arrival
    to marry her then soon afterwards made his son
by his royal wife become a husband of hers also
    and having thus tied up the family line she toured
the islands showing off all her pets on their strings
    taking with her a retinue of a thousand or so
her vast self borne on occasion in a whaleboat held high
    on a grid of spears in the fists of seventy warriors
but when she fell sick the missionaries ministered to her
    with a certain success which they nursed without sleeping until
her conversion whereupon she kept Kaumuali‘i
    as her only husband and he then sickened and grew weak
he was dying and delirious and the will taken down
    in his last days left what he owned and what he owed
to Ka‘ahumanu and Liholiho and then he died
    to be buried in the uniform of a British hussar
with foreigners saying that he had been handsome courteous
    dignified honorable and beloved and on Kauai
the news of his death released a ground swell of disaster
    there was wild mourning and the succession was dubious
nobody could be certain about keeping the land they lived on
    some feared the chiefs from the other islands the cabinet
of Ka‘ahumanu and some hoped that Kauai
    might be left to itself again as it used to be
after the summer solstice that year came an eclipse of the sun
    and the missionaries kept saying that it meant nothing

36.

Kaumuali'i's son George after he had returned
     with the missionaries from his hand–to–mouth education
was a disappointment to his father from the beginning
     a shiftless abusive arrogant drunkard who burned down
a whole building in Waimea when the shopkeeper declined
     to give him a bottle of gin but he soon acquired
a large like-minded following of those who had nothing
     after the diseases and the sandalwood ordeal
had torn up families and left the terraces untended
     and they listened as George ranted after the kidnapping
of Kaumuali'i and more of the disaffected
     of the island more of the uncertain and the covetous
the gamblers and holdouts gathered around him and made him
     their figurehead although George himself had no great
mind of his own and when the first governor came
     from Ka'ahumanu George would have been willing
to get along with the fellow but his own followers
     talked him out of it and a week later at first light
a party of them attacked the company from Oahu
     quartered in the fort near Waimea and they called upon
the whole island to rise—It is ours—they shouted and then
     retired to sit in the shade some miles away leaving ten
of their own and six from Oahu dead and they did
     nothing more as the reprisals began and schooners
brought troops and volunteers in growing numbers to rub out
     what they called the rebellion and after a single skirmish
they began a slaughter that did not spare women or children
     shot bayoneted speared mutilated left to rot
and they caught George drunk and shipped him to Oahu to die
     and went on with a meticulous hunt for the families
of the chiefs of Kauai to root them out entirely

37.

It was not an impromptu havoc but an ancient
     rancor whose moment had been heating for a long time
children of the chiefs on the other islands had grown up
     hating the chiefs of Kauai who had once claimed
the entire chain except Hawai'i itself and they all knew
     that the genealogy of the chiefs of Kauai was older
and loftier than that of the recent leaders
     of the younger islands to the east and the latter were never
allowed to forget it even the legends often
     began on Kauai and ended there and Kamehameha
was one of the later chiefs with whom the others
     had aligned their fates so that the failure of two
giant invasions of Kauai was beyond forgiving
     and besides Kauai for generations had given refuge
to those running from battles or feuds or shifts of power
     on other islands and the pursuers remembered and went on
caressing their weapons and waiting for the day
     to cut down Kauai and so it was accomplished
and afterward the island was carved up and given
     to the kin and followers of Kamehameha and some of them
drew the income in absence and some moved to Kauai
     and established themselves as the missionaries
had been doing and other alert and enterprising
     foreigners merchants ship chandlers in the early days
of the whalers and one of the missionaries began
     to make sugar and molasses at Waimea
and encouraged the Hawaiians to grow sugar for their own good
     and thus the sugar business became part of the Lord's work

38.

Since the missionaries on O‘ahu had managed
    to coax the widow-in-chief Ka‘ahumanu
into the fold before Kaumuali‘i died
    at his funeral everyone sang The Dying Christian
in Hawaiian and a flock followed after her
    into the faith so that the day of righteousness seemed
to be breaking upon the heathen or what was left of them
    after four decades and more of falling like leaves
of being carried off by new sicknesses that kept coming
    from the horizon first the venereal that began
in welcome and grew like gossip mutilating
    and repulsive then the varying succession
of fevers poxes boils and of running at every
    orifice the swellings sores coughing breathlessness
blackening and emaciation and the constant pain
    and foulness the bewildered burials when everything known
in heaven and earth every cause and expectation
    and the gods themselves were suddenly insubstantial
like smoke or the air clutched in falling a time when those
    who still had strength for growing taro and mending terraces
and sluices and cleaning the channels were compelled to travel
    far into the mountains for the receding sandalwood
nothing to them but costing their lives and when the land
    that had been theirs without ever belonging to them
seemed to be slipping away through their hands like water
    and on Kauai the chiefs of the island whose word
had been the way the world was and whose ancestry led back
    into the nights before creation had all of them been cut down
even their infants dismembered and the hacked pieces
    desecrated so that nothing was left of the past
or of the future and they had come to where they had nothing
    this was the moment into which the missionaries
translated their promises of lands beyond death
    and in this life the substance of the island began to pass
into the keeping and plans of strangers whom the Lord
    had led there to make something out of the waste places

39.

Not all the new landholders from the islands to windward
    were retainers of Kamehameha's who had shared
his long coveting of Kauai the ancient the aloof
    the island apart there were those among them who were mere
fringes on the skirts of the reigning widow watchful
    idlers happy to join in the hunt when the cry went up
and to flail in the battue of the chiefs and carve up
    first the limbs then the spoils among themselves but later
when the destruction had unstrung the common survivors
    around the island and weeds wrapped up the taro terraces
famine followed sickness and the lands themselves rendered
    grudging return to the alien claimants some of whom
moved in among the ruins and tried to resume
    a semblance of the old life and it came to be part of them
others listened to foreigners and picked up the parlance
    of leasing while the hungry who could do a day's work
were taught to labor and be paid in credit and the streams
    were turned out of their former veins into alien
enterprises there were plantations of coffee
    wide marshes of rice and the irresistible poison
and imperial promises of sugar with the volcanic
    sounds and smells of its mills the lands around them flowed into them
all that had lived in those places flowed into them and the taste
    was sweet nothing and meanwhile on the mountain the cattle
that the first captains had brought as presents for the chiefs
    ran wild trampled and multiplied and the horses
that had come in those early years grew in numbers
    and the ranches of the foreigners spread like a change of climate

40.

While the sandalwood trade was shrinking during the years
    after the death of Kamehameha the debts
of the chiefs continued and they climbed like the stakes
    of hapless gamblers until foreign warships arrived
insisting upon collection and the government
    assumed the debts and levied taxes to pay them
then the landed chiefs' sole remaining wealth was the land
    which no one but they could own but they could allow
the use of it as they had always done for payment
    of some kind agreed upon verbally at first
and the enterprises of the foreigners were based
    upon such agreements at the beginning but as more
was invested in them greater security
    was demanded by the speculators there were contracts
in writing of course and for lengthening terms and then
    no more than a single lifetime after the masts
of Cook's vessels had appeared off the coast at Waimea
    a commission was appointed at the insistence
of foreigners to determine the real ownership
    of all the lands in the kingdom which thereafter
foreigners would be able to purchase outright
    on the same terms as Hawaiians but it was a manner
of thinking about the land which only the foreigners
    understood and after ten years when the commission's
Great Division went into effect the control
    of the lands of Hawai'i was in the hands of foreigners
who had title to the greater part of them allowing
    a portion for the chiefs and their overseers though that might be
further reduced upon claim and then there remained
    fragments for the people still living in the valleys
whose ancestors had built the walls of the terraces
    and who had been lucky and had been told what they
had to do and what building they had to go to
    what room to find what table to stand in front of and there
had said what their names were and described the stones and marks
    by which you would know the places where they had been born

BORN

1.

Born in a dark wave the fragrance of red seaweed
    born on the land the shore grass hissing while the night slips
through a narrow place a man is born for the narrows
    a woman is born for where the waters open
the passage is for a god it is not for a human
    the god is a gourd full of water and vines climbing from it
there the forest rises to stand in the current of night
    with time moving through it and the branches reach out
into darkness the blue darkness at the sea's root
    it reaches up through the current of time and holds
the night sky in its place while in the sea the child
    of the hilu fish is born in the night under the tides
the child floats through the seven currents it is already
    someone to bow to in awe born is the sandalwood tree
on land the guardian of the whale in the ocean
    born Kanemahuka to remember the sound
of the stream at Poki'i and voices by the low fire
    talking about a killing born is Keawe in the valley
of Waiaka whom he would hold in his arms Keawe
    to remember crying above the rushing water
the burials along the valley the mourning from doorways
    born to them both Kaleimanu to remember
the smell of oxen and of crushed sugar cane in the mud
    born is Nakaula to remember spears stacked by the door
and whispers about canoes at night born Kawaluna
    to remember the cave her grandfather showed her alone
where he had hidden the sacred images and to remember
    the sound of guns close by and shouts of strangers and screams
and blood on bodies under the trees born is Ho'ona
    to remember the island of Hawai'i the sea cliffs
at Onomea and the donkey trail to the landing born is Kukui
    to remember drums and her mother dancing born is Kepola
to remember the shadow of smoke born is Ko'olau
    to Kaleimanu and Kukui in a new year
a month of long waves born is Pi'ilani to Ho'ona
    and Kepola in the spring in the time of the flying fish

2.

When the stream from the falls at Waipao wound among rocks
    all the way to the sands at Kekaha there were still
a few thatched roofs beside banana trees half a lifetime
    after the chiefs of Kauai had been hunted down
and after the age of murders and dying from hunger
    and from unknown sicknesses and the going for sandalwood
and after the great distributing of the lands
    for the sake of the foreigners a few of the old
terrace walls were still in repair along the watercourse
    with the sluices cleared and taro at different stages
as though everything were the way it used to be
    and the children thought that was how it had always been
but it was all made out of pieces salvaged from ruins
    hauled out wept over huddled among for years shored up
with the old knowledge but not the old assurance
    families still fished when the nights and the seasons were right
and when the first ranchers tried sheep on the plains toward Mānā
    Kanemahuku and Nakaula and their sons all went
as shepherds rather than work in the cane fields or the mill
    Kukui's first child was born in those days a daughter
they named her Kamaile but she lived only one day
    then in a few years Kukui was in labor again
and it seemed she was dying the midwife was her mother
    Kawaluna who kept massaging her moving with her
telling her to think of red seaweed and that the child
    would come when the tide turned and as she was saying it
the preacher Rowell was riding past on his way
    to a house where someone had died and he heard the moaning
as he passed the door and he stopped to ask whether
    he could help and Kukui thought he had called her by name
he said a prayer over her and left and when the tide turned
    she gave birth to a second daughter Niuli
and Kukui was sure she owed both lives to his prayer

3.

Kawaluna was of an older mind than her daughter's
    but she said nothing and she watched over Niuli
with unwavering tenderness from the day she was born
    the child's name came from Kukui who said she had heard it
during the red hours in labor and she told everyone
    about the preacher appearing in the doorway
with his black clothes and white hair and saying her name
    she talked about him with friends of hers who knew him
he had lived in Waimea since she had been a child
    she remembered the times she had seen him at burials
and people in Kekaha whom she had known all her life
    had gone to his church but she had never spoken with him
she decided she wanted to take Niuli
    to his church in Waimea for him to put a blessing
on the child as he had done for some of the others
    in the village and one morning they put on
their best clothes Kukui with the baby and her husband
    Kaleimanu and her father Nakaula
and her mother Kawaluna and family and friends
    they walked along the cart road with the sun in their faces
toward Waimea hearing the terns toss their grace notes
    over the surf and then the note of the church bell
and they stood in the shade outside the building and greeted
    people they knew and showed them the baby and went in
to stand up and sit down when the others did and they heard
    the loud singing and went up for the blessing when they were called
and Kawaluna watched it all like an owl in daylight

4.

It was the new church that had just been finished the one
    they all called the foreign church although there had been
a foreign church at Waimea since Kukui's parents
    were young and they had told her of the missionaries
first arriving and bringing the high chief Kaumuali'i's son
    home to him and they had told her of the house the chiefs
had them build for the foreigners and of the white faces praying
    toward their feet that was long before Kukui was born
Nakaula and Kanemahuku had guided ox carts
    that brought the cut coral limestone to build the first church
and the big house for the missionaries that seemed to be one
    house on top of another and they had driven other oxen
when their hair was white to bring the stone for the new church
    and the broken coral to burn for plaster and whitewash
and the church walls still smelled of lime with the procession
    of sunlight squares moving over them slipping down to the sounds
of the voices but none of the family had been
    inside the church since it was finished Nakaula
pointed out to them down there in front Valdemar Knudsen
    who they knew had the big ranch at Waiawa now
and near him the new Judge Kauai whom they had all heard of
    a Hawaiian with his wife beside him and their clothes
looked so beautiful to Kukui that she thought they were
    shining people and after the service when they all went out
and stood under the trees talking to friends the Judge
    and his wife came over to them to see the baby
and how handsome the Judge was the women thought and how lovely
    his Hawaiian wife was they agreed and on the way back
Nakaula said there was land above Makaweli
    that was hers from her father who had been given it
by Ka'ahumanu herself and that was good land he said
    and Kukui smiled without thinking about anything

5.

That evening they set out a feast and the village gathered
    bringing food and they sat looking across the terraces
toward the sea after the sun went down and the wind dropped
    they recalled building the church and the oxen the mules
mule stories and the way Nakaula talked all the time
    to animals—Oh yes—he said—you have to keep them
listening to you and they listen in different ways
    so you speak to them differently as you speak to
foreigners differently—then they considered Kauhiahiwa
    the old man in Waimea who had been there when the first
goats and pigs that Kuke brought had been put ashore
    on Ni'ihau and when the first cows and horses
had been brought to Kauai for the chiefs and Nakaula
    showed how Kauhiahiwa imitated the animals
coming from the ship onto this strange land where there had been
    only dogs and little pigs and rats until then
so when the new animals came people were glad to see them
    and Kauhiahiwa had followed them watching them
he was the one who looked after Reverend Rowell's
    cows and horses and talked them down to the river
in the mornings and told them to swim across to the pasture
    and called them back in the evening and Nakaula
said that as a child he had followed Kauhiahiwa
    and listened to him and learned to speak with the animals
which he would rather do than hoe in the fields toward Mānā
    when the tobacco was there or bend in the cane fields
or work in the mills and they sat late around Niuli
    talking about what had gone on before she was born

6.

Then they talked about the new Judge Kauai and how old
    he might be for he had not been born on the island
and he was still a young man and they considered the story
    that he was descended from the high chief Kaeo
the old ruler of Kauai and half-brother of Kahekili
    and Nakaula turned to his father Kekiele
who kept the times straight in his mind the time when they
    hunted the chiefs of the island in the valleys
above Koloa the time when they built the fort
    the time when they erected the gallows at Waimea
and hanged three men and one woman north south east and west
    and buried them beside the platform while old Father
Whitney stood by the graves reading prayers from his book
    the time when the coughing came over them and Kekiele
repeated to them how Kaeo and Kahekili
    had ruled before Kamehameha and how Kaeo
had ruled Kauai until the death of Kahekili
    and how Kaeo on his way home from Maui
had been attacked by Kahekili's son on Oahu
    and the foreign ships had joined in and killed Kaeo
he told of the mourning when they had learned that the chief was dead
    Kekiele had been a young man then and he had seen
the sky turn dark and then they considered the Judge's
    kin on the island and what lands each of them had
and the Judge's wife Kaenaku and her lands
    at Makaweli and then the lands at Mānā
that the Norwegian Knudsen had come to take over
    a few years back after the tobacco failed there
and of the cattle he had and the horses he had brought in
    they talked about Knudsen and about his horses

7.

Nolewai Nolewai some of them had heard him say
   Norway the land he came from wherever that place was
somewhere in the great cold and different from Scotland
   or England or America which people from the island
had sailed to Norway was farther than any of them
   and colder and Valdemar Knudsen laughed much more
than the missionaries and he sang songs from Nolewai
   that were not like the hymns and Eleao who had been working
for Knudsen planting foreign fruit trees and diverting water
   through Waiawa said they all liked Knudsen who asked them
what the name was for everything and older men came
   to see Knudsen and stay at his house and they picked flowers
not to wear nor for medicine but to talk about
   and draw pictures of and pull apart and write about
they shot birds not to eat but to measure and draw
   and count the feathers and they asked their names and Knudsen
rode out with some of his guests to the shore and to caves
   where they dug up bones and whatever else they found there
they asked about them in Hawaiian and talked about them
   in other languages and took them away and the people
at Mānā had told him they did not want him to dig there
   for the bones of their ancestors but old Puako
took Knudsen to Keoneloa and other sands
   where there were bones to dig and he told long stories
about fleets and battles and Knudsen wrote all that down
   and not a word of it was true and they wondered how Knudsen
could believe Puako who had always been happy
   to lie to anyone who would listen to him
one more reason they said why Knudsen needed a wife

8.

One of the sounds that Niuli would remember
>from her childhood when that time had vanished behind her
a sound that she could not name when first she recalled it
>and could not be sure she had heard while she was
awake and could not tell when it had come to her
>for the last time before it was only remembered
was the light hollow patter of small hooves running on stones
>and the crying of sheep the same few cracked notes making
question and answer somewhere between bird and child
>and she remembered hearing them talk about sheep
and the smell of sheep and the sight of them like pale shadows
>shifting in the glare out toward Waiawa and the cliffs
and then they were not there and had not been there a long time
>and nobody spoke of them and the one time she asked
her father Kaleimanu about them he said only
>that they were gone and it was just the cattle now
out there and the horses and the talk was of cattle and horses
>and of work in the sugar mill at Kekaha and she thought
the sheep must have been in a time before Koʻolau
>was born and that sound like water on its way over pebbles
they told her that she was three almost four when he was born
>she remembered the rain drumming at night and her mother's moans
and the baby crying and Koʻolau as a small face
>in Kawaluna's lap and the sounds of horses then
and a crowd of people standing out under big trees
>then Koʻolau's voice later when he was a child

9.

Through those years Kukui always spoke of the Reverend
    George Rowell as a kind of guardian spirit
partial to her in particular though he never again
    rode past their door and she had been back to church only
when a friend of theirs took a child to be baptized
    and one time for a wedding but her mother
clearly went there with reluctance and her husband Kaleimanu
    explained that the foreigners in the congregation
disapproved of the natives calling The Reverend
    Father Rowell the way the men who worked for Knudsen
called him Father Knudsen the foreigners were afraid
    that with a minister it might be mistaken
for the way the Catholics at Koloa who were Christians
    but the wrong kind of Christians called their priests Father
but the natives at Waimea went on calling Rowell
    Father he was George Berkeley Rowell who had come
from Cornish New Hampshire and Andover Seminary
    sailing in the Tenth Company of Missionaries
with his wife Malvina Jerusha and his brother
    Edwin on the brig Sarah Abigail a voyage
of one hundred forty-three days and had watched his brother
    die almost at once upon their arrival and when
they had settled on Kauai had listened while his wife
    gave birth to seven living children he was something
of a doctor and helped with the deliveries
    something of a carpenter and oversaw the building
of the big church at Waimea something of a farmer
    and kept cattle and a mixture of stock and he
had a big garden up the river at a place named Kakalae
    where he grew mangos and loquats oranges bananas
even peaches by the bucket and for an outing
    the family rode up the valley to the garden

10.

After Koʻolau was born Kukui wanted
      to take him to the church in Waimea to be baptized
but her father Nakaula who drove mules most days
      into Waimea and back told her it might not be
as easy as she imagined because he had heard
      angry talk from members of that congregation
about the pastor's behavior Nakaula
      was a close listener and he said there were many
who would hear no complaints against Father Rowell
      and grew heated in his defense but there were others
who insisted that the pastor was breaking the church laws
      they said he was neglecting his duty to perform
the ceremonies including The Lord's Supper
      that he welcomed as members of the church anyone
who wanted to come without examining their belief
      and kept no church records and had said in public
that too much reliance had been placed upon matters
      that were formalities and that he saw no reason
to question his congregation about their faith
      or to insist on church ceremonies but thought it enough
sometimes to play to them on the melodeon
      and let them sing if they wanted to so the trustees
with Judge Kauai and Valdemar Knudsen among them
      were announcing that Rowell was not fit to be called
a minister of the faith and Nakaula
      told Kukui he would have to ask whether the pastor
was still performing baptism and he seemed surprised
      some days later to inform them that Father Rowell
had said he would not refuse baptism to anyone

11.

By then there had been a church at Waimea for most
      of four decades and long before Kukui was born
first there was the grass shelter by the beach standing open
      toward the sea and then the wooden room with its echoes
dwarfing the sounds that made them and its hollow darkness
      and odor of mortality then the stone upon a stone
set in sand in the salt smells of sweat and mules and unkindness
      world without end as they sang at the time and then
what they called the great stone church that was more of the same
      but its name was still the Foreign Church and it represented
somewhere else it was a long walk from the Kekaha house
      that Nakaula and Kaleimanu had built
from boards they had fished out of the harbor for Knudsen
      that had come from New Zealand as ballast and glittered
with salt where the sun bleached the top ones on the loaded
      mule cart that dripped half way up the mountain toward the house
Knudsen kept adding to and he gave them enough
      for the two rooms and roof and porches near the shore
where Koʻolau was born it was too far for Niuli
      to walk or to be carried and they took the mules
and the wagon and some of them rode and some walked behind
      with friends and when they got to the church this time they were
all watching somebody some were watching Father Rowell
      to see what they could see some watching Judge Kauai
and Knudsen and the ones that Nakaula pointed out
      as the trustees and when the pastors announced the sacrament
of baptism they all stood up and walked to the front
      with two other families and Kawaluna answered
first when Father Rowell asked the name of the child
      to be baptized and she watched his face as she told him
the whole name beginning with the grave and he looked up
      and asked—Is it a night name—and she said—It is his name—

12.

When she turned to the rows of faces she looked directly
     at Judge Kauai and his eyes were on Koʻolau
awake in Kukui's arms and gazing up at the sunbeam
     that crossed the room and when they filed out of the church
to the playing of the melodeon and stood talking
     with friends who had gathered to see the child Judge Kauai
and his wife Kaenaku came over as they had done before
     both of them tall and stately in their beautiful clothes
and Kukui was sure the great chiefs must have looked like that
     moving the way clouds move and they paused in front of Kukui
to admire the baby and Kawaluna listened
     to the Judge's voice asking Kukui—What do you
call him yourself—and she watched his face as Kukui smiled
     and said—Koʻolau—and then the Judge said—Koʻolau
Aloha Koʻolau—then the melodeon
     stopped and they heard the leaves stir at the end of it
and the terns calling out past the sand and the Judge waved
     good-bye to his friends all around them and was gone
and they were on the wagon bench going back to Kekaha
     and they caught up with Kepola whom Kukui had played with
when they were children and Kepola was with a stranger
     they were going along more slowly than the mules so they
fell behind and Nakaula said over his shoulder
     that the man was Hoʻona who had come from Papaikou
on the island of Hawaiʻi something to do with sugar
     but whether it was the sugar or Kepola
that was keeping him on Kauai nobody seemed to know

13.

Niuli looked after Ko'olau from the beginning
          and they all said it was Niuli who taught him to walk
she put his clothes on him and she took them off and they talked
          to each other when no one else understood the sounds he made
they splashed in the shallow lagoon where the stilts waded
          and she washed him and dried him as her mother had done
they touched and clung to each other and he followed her
          wherever she went and Kaleimanu watched them
play with the dogs and he taught her to be careful
          around the mules but he caught them both up on the oldest
mule and took them riding in the summer evening
          friends calling to him from the end of the day and the first
owls gliding out from the ravines over past Waiawa
          where he worked most days for Knudsen and later when
he could understand what both the children were saying
          and they wanted to ride the mule by themselves he settled them
astride the warm withers and for an instant that was gone
          before he could grasp it he breathed the day of the mule
with no age to it no story no reward and he led them
          along the sand toward Mānā where old friends he seemed
not to recognize with the late day shining on their shoulders
          were casting their nets in silence and drawing them back
intent and moving like waves with sometimes a call coming
          across the water and the gulls flashing and shrieking
Ko'olau shrieking to the gulls and smoke climbing far behind them
          from the sugar mill and fading upward and Ni'ihau
its own shadow on the horizon he came to wish
          those evenings had been every evening and when he came
home from one of them after Ko'olau began to talk
          Kukui told him that Kepola had come to visit her
to let her know that she was going to have a baby

14.

And they stood smiling in spite of everything they knew
    and could not know and Kaleimanu asked her—Is it
the one from the sugar mill from Papaikou there
    from Hawai'i the one with the clothes—because they had
noticed the way he was dressed that day on the way home
    from church those clothes that looked as though they had never been
worn before and had nothing to do with a place like this
    the dust and the midday glare that bleached the colors
out of the day on all sides like a white shadow
    in which those clothes remained bright as a fire and stayed
in everyone's minds when they had ridden on out of sight
    and afterwards whenever they had seen him he was
dressed that way like somebody with news and maybe
    he had been going each time to visit Kepola she had
been a quiet one when they were children Kukui said
    not wild with the boys like the others and she laughed
—His name is Ho'ona—she reminded them for
    the future and Kepola had said that he wanted
to marry her in the church and he had been taking her
    to church every Sunday and Kepola said she liked it
—I like it too—Kukui said laughing and Nakaula
    and Kaleimanu were sitting listening as she
told them all that Kepola had said Ho'ona
    was important—No—she said—not important I mean
he is serious—and she pronounced the word slowly
    like a new thing to admire—Well—Nakaula said
—I suppose that is all right maybe he will take care of her—

15.

Nakaula wondered whether Father Rowell
    was performing weddings now and Kukui said
she was sure he was because he had married Keoniki
    only a few months back—And it is important—she said
and Nakaula said—I remember Keoniki's baby
    was nearly born then——Maybe Kepola's will be too—
Kukui said—Just as long as they are married in time
    that is what matters——Two eyes and a nose—Kawaluna said
—and one mouth—and they let it rest there until some weeks later
    when Kukui announced that they were all invited
to the wedding which she said Hoʻona himself
    had arranged with Father Rowell and they took the mule wagon
to Waimea on the eleventh day of the moon
    called Huna or hidden because the horns then are hidden
it was the day Kepola's mother Nahola had chosen
    and it was clear that Hoʻona was well acquainted
with Father Rowell and with Mrs Rowell who played
    the melodeon for the service—There was none of that
when we were married—Kukui said to Kaleimanu
    —We just stood there and said what he told us and held the pen
while he pushed our hands on the book and that was that—
    —This is more like his clothes—Nakaula answered
and afterward on the beach when they were all eating
    pig and fish Kepola told them that Father Rowell
had made Hoʻona a member of the church and one
    of his close assistants—When is it coming—Kukui asked
looking at Kepola's waist—In two months maybe—
    Kepola answered and it was a night in spring
the night of Hua the egg the moon almost full
    when she went into labor and Hoʻona wanted
Father Rowell to be there because he was a doctor
    but Nahola sent for Kawaluna to deliver
the baby a girl whose name would be Piʻilani

16.

—You hear the owl just when the baby was coming—
    Kepola's father Kapahu asked Kawaluna
—I did—Kawaluna answered looking at his eyes
    which she had known at every stage of his life—Good thing maybe—
Kapahu said and she nodded and gave him the baby
    —She is a good thing—Kawaluna said—Look after her—
and she took away the umbilical cord and as
    the stars were fading she hid it in a hole in the rocks
then she walked down to the sea and in the light before sunrise
    she stood in the water chanting as the waves broke
—You mountain of Kane island of the ancestors
    I have washed away the blood now you wash away the blood
it is for the spirit to watch over her it is time
    for the spirit to come with wings and watch over her—
Then in a few days they brought Niuli to see the baby
    and Niuli began right away to take care of her
as she had taken care of Koʻolau and the three
    children grew up together and when they were playing
with the other children they stayed together it was less
    than ten years since the last wave of sickness the fever
and weakness the skin breaking out in pustules they called
    smallpox had killed so many of them and had taken
it seemed all of the children then and Kaleimanu kept thinking
    of that time as he watched them playing and he felt
that he was holding his breath as he saw them rolling
    in the edge of the sea and as he looked at Koʻolau sitting
up high on the old mule and felt the reins in his hands

17.

Nakaula and Kaleimanu picked up threads
    of news from Knudsen's ranch at Waiawa and Hofgaard's
store in Waimea and from friends coming and going
    and they followed the game of land trading between
Knudsen and Judge Kauai who had his family
    out Makaweli way and up toward the mountain
not a convenient location for his work at the courthouse
    he owned land here and there on the island some of it
through his wife Kaenaku and some that he had acquired
    in his days as tax assessor and the way that he
and Knudsen worked it out Knudsen got the land up toward
    Makaweli which was where he finally settled
and Kauai got the stone building and the land surrounding it
    at Kekiaola in the middle of Waimea
not far from the church and he moved his family into town
    Knudsen and the Judge remained friends and both attended
the church where they got along worse and worse with the Reverend
    Rowell who managed to have Judge Kauai removed
from the Board of Trustees and publicly demanded
    the return of the church keys which the Judge refused
arguing that Rowell's proceedings were in violation
    of the laws of the church which he quoted as the voices
rose into the koa rafters and the congregation
    took sides some with Dr Smith but most of the natives
whom the pastor had admitted without examination
    siding with Rowell and the pastor put new locks
on the front and back doors of the church and denied entrance
    to Judge Kauai and his party which included
several foreigners and many who were members
    of the congregation in good standing first he shut
the door in their faces and they heard the new locks close
    and the next time they came they found the doors boarded over
and the pastor standing there holding a hammer and nails

18.

And then there was the matter of the melodeon
     which the pastor had ordered to be sent out from Boston
some years before and Ho‘ona had learned the details
     from Pastor Rowell himself one day when Ho‘ona
was whitewashing the walls inside and the pastor explained
     that the melodeon was his own property purchased
upon his order by a congregation in South Hadley
     Massachusetts which had recently installed one
of the same make in their own church the price of the organ
     was two hundred and fifty dollars and the dealer
in Boston deducted the sum of twenty dollars
     because it was being bought for the mission field
and the gentleman who selected it a Mr
     W R Wright of North Hampton waived his commission
and a Mr Harford collected fifteen dollars
     to contribute to it and a Mr Smith another ten
and a further three seventy-five for the insurance
     and the pastor had sent a hundred and fifty
of his own money and the balance later which sums
     were never repaid him so it was his melodeon
but Judge Kauai et al sued him on the question
     of who owned the church itself and who was entitled
to lock up the property and Pastor Rowell
     lost the case and appealed and the supreme court then ruled
that he had neglected church ordinances and The Lord's Supper
     and had regarded baptism as unnecessary
the covenants as useless and for aught that appeared
     had disregarded even a declaration
of belief in the Holy Scriptures and he therefore
     had forfeited his relation to the church altogether
as had those whom he had encouraged and who sustained him
     the church was not his nor was the melodeon
and the doors were opened but by then Pastor Rowell
     had resigned and he and his own congregation
were building themselves a church nearby independent
     of the Board of Foreign Missions and there he started his school

19.

Nakaula and Kaleimanu had been using
      Knudsen's mules and their own to move Judge Kauai's household
to the stone house in Waimea on the days when the rains
      that year allowed them to make the journey through the mud
and the swollen Waimea River and they were hauling
      loads for Pastor Rowell for the new church the sandstone
foundation blocks cut with axes each stone the length
      of the yardstick and half as wide and a span thick
they drove the wagons up near the smoking lime pit
      and they took the mules without the wagons up the mountain
to drag back the tie-beams and rafters and they and the children
      were present for the Judge's house-warming and again
when Pastor Rowell held his opening service in the new church
      the foreigners were divided over that but Knudsen
the Gays the Robinsons of Waimea and Dr Smith
      of Koloa had stayed with the pastor in the end
and Ho'ona had heard them agreeing that Pastor Rowell
      had views far ahead of his time and they spoke with approval
of the new school for native children which Mrs Rowell
      was planning to teach and Ho'ona said he wanted
Pi'ilani to go to that school and he asked
      Kaleimanu about Niuli and Ko'olau
but they were all too young and Mrs Rowell could not
      manage the rough children so that Pastor Rowell himself
was the teacher by the time they were old enough to attend
      Niuli liked the company Ko'olau hated the school
Pi'ilani did her lessons without a word

20.

Whatever the pastor pronounced to them in that voice
    that was not the one he talked in and not the one
he spoke in when he stood up during the church service
    and not the one he used for English with other foreigners
whatever words the pastor uttered from the moment
    they walked through the door onto the dead wood each syllable
of their own language articulated so carefully
    that it did not sound like their own language at all
not only because every sound that he uttered
    with that round deliberation was always wrong in his
particular way but because it was coming from those
    particular clothes that face mouth regard that way of turning
and staring at them and because those words although they
    were like the words of their own were really arriving
out of some distance that existed for him but not
    for them and they could hear it echoed in his children
who went to Dr Dole's school in Koloa with
    the rest of the foreign children and who were never
allowed to play with the little natives as they
    had heard themselves called but who spoke the language without
that foreign wrongness and even so they were only
    partly in what they were saying and the rest somewhere
out of sight like hands making shadows the air in the room
    was hard to see through like water but they repeated
the names of the solitary letters that they
    said every day the threads of a seamless garment
and he showed them what each letter looked like it was
    white whether large small straight or flowing and it was
in itself silent in a black sky where his hand drew it
    and it stayed there meaning a sound that it did not have

21.

They learned to draw the white lines themselves and repeat
　　their names in the order the pastor said was the real one
they learned to pray with their eyes closed and say together
　　that they believed in the only god and his son who was killed
back when nobody remembered and he taught them
　　that the old gods had never been and he taught them names
of numbers and how numbers behaved with each other
　　Niuli stared at him but she saw the white dog lying
under the back step when they left for school and they
　　were laughing about something as they were going past
the wet canoe dripping onto the sand and she smiled
　　trying to remember why they had been laughing
and Pastor Rowell asked her to answer his last
　　question and she said—I believe in one god and I
believe in my father—and she stopped with the pastor
　　looking at her pebble to pebble and he told them all
that other foreigners would not be so patient with them
　　as they would find out if they had not yet learned it
then he pronounced the word Indolence in English
　　three times very slowly and then molowa molowa
molowa and told them that is the source of vice
　　and of misery and death it is the mother of disease
he said improvidence brings on decay and is rotting
　　your people you must learn to want more than you have
it will elevate your characters I have seen your beds
　　on the damp ground in the dirt the dirt Koʻolau had stopped
thinking about punching Makuale with whom
　　he had been having fights on the way home from school
and he was thinking about disease and what he had heard
　　from the boys in Waimea about a sickness
as close as Koloa that was different from the others
　　it had got into a man whom one of them knew who lived
down by the harbor and if they said you had this sickness
　　they arrested you no matter what you told them
and they put you on a boat and you never came back

22.

He forgot about Makuale on the way home
    and when they were almost there he saw his father
Kaleimanu down by the canoes with somebody
    he had never seen and he thought they were going fishing
and he wanted to go out with them and when he got there
    —This is Kua—his father told them—You remember
me talking to you about Kua Papiohule
    who works with me at Father Knudsen's at Waiawa
and trains the horses for Father Knudsen—they looked
    up at a tall thin man who smiled and repeated
each of their names in his quiet voice taking his time
    Kua said—You are going to school can you read books yet—
and Niuli looked at her feet—What are you learning—he asked
    and Pi'ilani wrote an A in the sand and stood up
pointing to it and said A and he nodded—You are
    teaching me now—he said—And I would like that—and turning
to Ko'olau he said—Your father tells me you like horses—
    —I like horses—Ko'olau said—But mostly I know mules—
Kua said—Maybe some day we can all go out
    to Waiawa and you can see what you think of the horses—
Kaleimanu said—We have been talking about the news
    from Waiawa Father Knudsen is going to be
married at last it took him a long time to find
    the right one and we used to wonder whether he
would ever do it—and the men laughed—Who is she—Niuli asked
    —Miss Anne Sinclair—he said to her—And her mother
is Mrs Sinclair who owns the island of Ni'ihau
    and two years ago bought most of the land division
of Makaweli from Victoria Kamamalu—
    and Kaleimanu said—It appears that Father Knudsen
had Miss Sinclair picked out years ago and all those trips
    to Ni'ihau in the whaleboat looking for birds
and eggs and flowers he had Miss Sinclair in his mind
    and all through those land arrangements with Judge Kauai
out toward Makaweli he had his eye on her—

23.

—The right one—Niuli said—What does she look like—
　　—Oh she is a beautiful young woman—Kua told her
—and plenty of men have been hoping to marry her
　　　and she loves horses she is good on a horse she rides
like a cloud——Is that why he wanted to marry her—
　　Niuli asked and Kua said—I think there may have been
some things besides that although the sight of her
　　　at a gallop out there on the sands would not be
soon forgotten but there were some who were trying
　　　to catch her who I think have no eye for horses
there was more than one of those studying men who visited
　　Knudsen and went over to Niʻihau with him
looking into books and drawing pictures of the plants
　　　growing over the rocks who were watching her their voices
would change when they talked to her and they say that when
　　　she first came with her mother from New Zealand and they
sailed into Honolulu in their own vessel—
　　Kua spoke to Niuli as though he were telling her
a story in which anything was possible
　　　and he said—they had sailed all the way to Vancouver looking
for land enough for themselves and had found nothing
　　　to their liking but wherever they went the young men
all wanted to marry Miss Anne from the time they stopped
　　　in Tahiti at the beginning and the British Consul
begged her to marry him and in Honolulu
　　　the King and Queen Emma invited them to all
the banquets and dances and she could have married
　　　just as she pleased and her mother could have had
the lands at Kahuku or Ewa with the island
　　　in the harbor but she chose the island of Niʻihau
and Miss Anne gave her hand to Valdemar Knudsen
　　　though he is older than the others and they talk about that
but Knudsen says they can talk if they like for the choice
　　　was hers all along and that is how it looks to me—

24.

—When can we go and see the horses—Ko'olau asked him
    —I will come and tell you—Kua said to him and they all
walked with him to the shade of the milo tree two horses
    stood there one a handsome bay with saddle and bridle
gleaming and Ko'olau stood staring at that one—Is he
    yours—he asked Kua and Kua said—Yes—lifting his hand
to the black mane—Knudsen gave him to me when he was born—
    Kaleimanu said—And the saddle Kua made himself—
—Could I learn to do that—Ko'olau asked Kua
    —You could if you want to—Kua answered—I want to—
Ko'olau said and Kua told him—When we go to Waiawa
    we can talk about that and we will see what your father says—
Then he said good-bye and mounted leaving the other horse
    under the tree behind him it was a fine chestnut mare
—Whose horse is this—Ko'olau asked—Mine now—his father said
    —Kua brought her down from Knudsen's where I was riding her
when I worked up there and Knudsen says I am going
    to be working there most of the time so I should have her—
—And keep her here—Ko'olau asked—In the family—
    Kaleimanu told him and he unhitched the reins and said
to Ko'olau—Go on then—and nodded toward the horse
    and Ko'olau got his bare foot up into the stirrup
and scrambled into the saddle with his feet swinging
    and his father led the horse on home but Niuli
stood watching Kua riding out toward Waiawa
    and then Pi'ilani started home and Niuli went with her
they kept asking each other questions about getting married

25.

Niuli questioned her mother quietly about Kua
      where did he come from and grow up where was he living
did he have any family any sisters a woman
      —Ask your father—Kukui said looking sideways
at Niuli—He knows more about Kua than I do—
      but it was Niuli's grandfather Kanemahuka who said
—I knew his family out there by Kaumakani
      his grandfather was with the chiefs of Kauai
he was along with Deborah Kapule at the time
      of the slaughters at Hanapepe and he was killed then
by mistake they said some kind of mistake——And his
      parents—Kaleimanu told Niuli—both of them are dead
they died in one of the foreign sicknesses long ago
      and he had an older sister die at the same time and then
he was alone when he was younger I think than you are
      and he was out at Hanapepe down near the harbor
trying to help when they were fishing and help with the horses
      that is how he managed then with the fishing and taking care
of the new horses and that was his school he picked up
      as he went he knew old Kauhiahewa who calls
the animals for Father Rowell he seems to know
      everybody on the long road he has been to the house
of the chief Deborah Kapule he can sing
      a song he has heard once Archer had him looking
after his horses and then Knudsen kept those horses
      and Kua with them when Knudsen was just beginning
and now the Waiawa horses and the horses at Makaweli
      there are so many you will never see all of them
and Kua knows them—Kaleimanu said and Kukui
      was smiling at Niuli—He is too old for you—she said
Niuli looked at her feet—Father Knudsen is older
      than all the others who wanted to marry Miss Anne—
—she said—But he is the one she wanted to marry—

26.

Koʻolau was doing badly at school the fighting
        was more interesting than the learning and he listened
from farther and farther away when Reverend Rowell
        started over the numbers or the words of the Bible
Piʻilani and Niuli were doing better but he
        wanted to leave though now it was Kaleimanu
his father who wanted him to stay—What will you do then—
        he asked Koʻolau—If you stop school—and Koʻolau said
—I want to work with the horses and make saddles
        and Kua will teach me——What have you learned in school—
Kaleimanu asked him—You have not learned how to learn
        Can you read yet can you write yet—and Koʻolau answered
—I can read and write now—and Kaleimanu asked him
        —What can you read now——A little—Koʻolau said—That is not
enough—his father said and when he was next at Waiawa
        he talked about it with Kua—The boy should be able
to read and write—Kua said—He is going to ask me
        whether you can read and write—Kaleimanu said
—I learned what I could here and there—Kua said—and I can read
        a little but it is not enough and I can write my name
and a few words but not easily and it is not
        enough tell him and so when he can read and write
so that Father Rowell says it is good then I will
        teach him other things—and when Koʻolau heard that
he astonished Reverend Rowell with his attention
        and before long he was reading and writing
better than most of the others at school and the pastor
        said to him—That is good that is good—and Koʻolau waited
until Reverend Rowell was saying it without
        surprise as something that he expected and then
he said to Kaleimanu—Go and ask Father Rowell—

27.

It was when the still days of summer were gone and the light
     at every hour held the reflection of something never
visible as the glaze does in the eyes of someone
     remembering a time not there the good winds were back
the trades out of the northeast coasting along the ridges
     cool and lifting the heart and it had been raining
at night as it does most years during the autumn
     in the time named Hilinama a season returning
to an old happy way of doing things that had been
     forgotten for some reason now vanished at last
and in the clear sky of morning bright clouds were racing
     westward across the mountain where at every turn
of the climb streams were splashing down among the black rocks
     though the trail was not yet muddy with the long rains
of winter and as they wound through the woods and along
     the edge of the canyon picking their way on the path
threads of voices a phrase here and there flicked past them
     like the flutter of wings in the trees and they were caught up
without seeing that it was happening to all of them
     in a moment of beginnings unrepeatable
and brief as when a number of planets seem to burn
     in the same place though the depth of the sky is around each one
so the beginnings were with them unnoticed as their breathing
     Anne Sinclair was seeing the vast cloven green-towered
mountain that she would soon love as fiercely as any place
     on earth and would summon up as she lay dying
in the dry light of a distant continent but as she
     rode there at the start of her life with this inquisitive
viking she had chosen for a husband she was gazing
     again down at the bay at Craigforth in New Zealand through woods
on the hill before they had been cut all the way to the sea
     and Knudsen whose youth seemed to have returned entire
saw himself climbing through the high fjords as a boy
     in Norway hearing the glacier streams and the birds of a short
far summer and Kua who could sense a new time arriving
     in the life around him felt the light hands of those he had
watched dying one after the other when he was a child
     and pain rose up without faces and at moments the faces
without the pain and Koʻolau to whom the day

the mountain the horse under him the presence of Kua
the occasion the company the forest were a complete
world was surprised to catch sight of himself sitting
in Father Rowell's schoolroom and what startled him most
was the feeling he had of watching a fish escape him

28.

He talked of it afterward as though it were what he
    had grown up to do and to know the riding and the sound
of the forest the learning from Kua the kindness
    of Knudsen and of Miss Sinclair her face and her voice
that made English sound new and easy and the gun
    that Kua taught him to hold when they hunted the wild bull calf
the fire beside the cabin at Halemanu and after the hymns
    that Knudsen got them all to sing there then the other songs
they went on singing in the dark of the trees he told
    Niuli and Pi'ilani about it the echoes
followed him into the winter when he rode to Waiawa
    with Kua and Kaleimanu to work with cattle
and with horses and to hunt goats and to go with Knudsen
    and sometimes with Knudsen's guests and Miss Sinclair riding
far up on the mountain looking for birds that Knudsen
    and his guests wrote about in notebooks and for flowers
that they picked and shut into the books and he saw what Kua
    meant about Miss Sinclair riding like a cloud and he
taught Niuli and Pi'ilani small as they were
    to ride and when the date was set to announce the engagement
between Miss Sinclair and Valdemar Knudsen Kua told them
    that they were all invited to Waiaiwa to the party
and they all took the wagon up there on the day before
    and helped get things ready and they slept there in a cabin
and sang after dark again and Knudsen had been planning
    a parade on horses in the morning and when he learned
from Kua that Ko'olau had taught Niuli and Pi'ilani
    to ride he came over to them to invite them
to ride in the parade and he told them he would find
    beautiful cloaks for them and they looked at each other
—Say you will—Ko'olau said to them and first Pi'ilani
    and then Niuli nodded but they lay awake most of the night

29.

Koʻolau kept to himself like a secret Kua's telling him
    that he looked as though he had been born on a horse
and that what he had to hold in his head was to stay with it
    stay with it and Kua let him ride more of the new
horses and then help with the patient training
    of the colts even though he was still a child and always
small for his age and the boy learned to handle the lariat
    until it seemed to rise into the air by itself
and wait there for him to let it come down and he treasured
    the old Harper's Ferry rifle that Kua had let him
take care of telling him that it had been through a war
    showing him how to empty it and clean the bright tunnel
touching the long cold of the barrel and smelling
    the oil the hard scent of the metal the old fragrance
of burnt powder coming through itself like a small wave
    along the sand with the whole ocean behind it
that winter Kua let him shoot goats twice on the ridges
    back from the edge of the canyon where they would be able
to get to the bodies to take them home and Koʻolau
    was learning the trails webbing the mountain the hidden
entrances and after the wedding on Niʻihau
    there were processions from Waiawa and Makaweli
and a service at Pastor Rowell's new church at Waimea
    it was too small for everyone but they could all hear
the new melodeon that had come from Boston
    bought by the congregation and they joined in the singing
and Koʻolau helped Kaleimanu and Kua keeping
    an eye on everyone's horses and on the carriage
that Eliza Sinclair had brought from Makaweli
    and on Judge Kauai's carriage and after the service
when they rode up to Waiawa for the banquet
    Koʻolau listened to Kua and the Judge talking
like old friends and later at the ranch they were standing
    together and Kua saw Koʻolau watching them
and he pointed the boy out to the Judge who nodded
    and Kua told him good things about Koʻolau
and when the Judge spoke to Koʻolau the boy told him
    how his mother remembered the Judge at Koʻolau's christening
—Maybe I saw something good from the start—the Judge said

30.

Niuli and Pi'ilani were helping Kukui
     over by the kitchen and Ko'olau saw the children
of the foreigners the Dole children from Koloa
     Dr Smith's older children and Reverend Rowell's and others
he did not recognize talking on the far side of the house
     they all appeared to be in white clothes moving there
in the sunlight but when he looked at them one by one
     he saw that was partly a trick of the light and he caught
Reverend Rowell's eye watching him and the pastor nodded
     —Are you one of Reverend Rowell's students—the Judge asked him
—I used to be—Ko'olau answered—and I learned to read there—
     —A very good thing—the Judge said—I learned to read
from a missionary on Maui when I was a boy there
     it is good that Pastor Rowell started that school of his
so you know how to read and I hope you go on reading—
     —I am working now with my father for Father Knudsen—
Ko'olau told him—You can still go on reading—
     the Judge told him——Have you ever read a newspaper—
—All we read there was the Holy Bible—Ko'olau told him
     —You should know that of course—the Judge said—but you must not
stop there I will give Kua things for you to read
     if you will read them but will you read them——I promise—
Ko'olau told him and saw that the Judge was looking
     at Reverend Rowell—Are those Reverend Rowell's children
over there—he asked Ko'olau who told him that they were
     —Do you know them—the Judge asked—They are older—Ko'olau said
—Do they go to Reverend Dole's foreign school in Koloa—
     —Some do—Ko'olau said—They have to wear shoes there—
the Judge said and he laughed—Did you and the pastor's
     children ever play together—the Judge asked—We used to—
Ko'olau said—But they were not allowed to and he gave them
     beatings when he caught them and he will not let them speak
Hawaiian because they speak it better than he does—
     —Do you think that is the reason—the Judge asked—Keep reading—

31.

In a while they would look back wondering where that
    time had gone which seemed to be theirs and to be staying
the children growing up the Knudsens at home at Waiawa
    then the big new house at Makaweli where the Knudsens
moved and their children were born and Koʻolau listening
    to the men talking in Hofgaard's store in Waimea
where he went first with Kua and Kaleimanu
    and Father Knudsen at the time when Mrs Knudsen
was expecting their first child and Koʻolau listened
    to every word there about sugar and about changing
the courses where the streams ran and about cattle and horses
    and the King and debts the place was a second school for him
and the Judge came in there and Koʻolau heard him talking
    about reducing the King's salary and about postage
and the legislature and he heard them arguing
    about whether the Chinese disease had come from China
or whether the Hawaiians had carried it all the way
    from India if they had come from India
where the disease had always been a fact of life
    and this was the same sickness Koʻolau had heard of
there at school in Waimea and the thought of it had been
    like a stain in daylight the sickness that was
a crime and if someone was accused of it that person
    would be arrested and taken somebody had been taken
from Kauai lately put on the schooner at Koloa
    in a stall with a bucket and cup to go to be judged
on Oahu and then to Kalaupapa on the island
    of Molokaʻi at the foot of the high cliffs by the sea
the place they never came back from it was the Hawaiians
    who had the disease the men said in Hofgaard's store
the Hawaiians mostly and the men more than the women
    and then they talked about whether there was ever a cure
and whether removal was the only thing to be done

32.

At Kekaha the children had outgrown playing
    together at the edge of the water although they supposed
that they had simply been busy for a while with other things
    Niuli had always been quiet serious affectionate
helping her mother with everything and Kukui
    needed her because she suffered from shortness of breath
which left her exhausted and all at once everyone was agreeing
    that Pi'ilani would be beautiful that she was
already beautiful and Ko'olau heard them say the word
    and it echoed through him like a bell and he recognized
the name for part of what he had been staring at
    and he had known something of it even before they started
school when they ran naked with the other children
    and rolled in the small waves and touched each other everywhere
he had liked to touch Pi'ilani more than the others
    and when they were older they would meet after dark
and lie down between the canoes then Pi'ilani's father
    Ho'ona was away more and more of the time
at work at the sugar mill and in Waimea helping
    Reverend Rowell with the church work he seemed to be
wearing new clothes each time Ko'olau saw him and he brought
    clothes home for Pi'ilani's mother Kepola
and for Pi'ilani and sometimes they were new clothes
    sometimes they had belonged to somebody else and her father
said Reverend Rowell had given them to him
    but sometimes at night he did not come home from Waimea
and said Reverend Rowell had let him sleep there but people
    in Kekaha knew he had a woman in Waimea
and they told each other what they had heard about her

33.

At the mill Kaleimanu had heard the men laughing
    with Hoʻona about women and about what they had learned
of him when he was over at Papaikou on the Big Island
    of Hawaiʻi before he found his way to Kauai
women at Onomea women all the way
    from Hilo to Waipio wherever his errands
directed him and his good reasons for leaving
    that island just in time like the old chiefs in flight
and Kaleimanu heard it at Hofgaard's store when Hoʻona
    rode by one day in a new hat and Koʻolau heard it
in Waimea from boys he had known at school it was
    what Hoʻona was known for the usher in church on Sundays
and dressed for it Koʻolau never mentioned her father
    to Piʻilani but whenever he went to her house
he watched her mother who seldom spoke and her grandmother
    and grandfather and helped them and Piʻilani
saw what he was doing and she understood why
    and she could see that her family was proud of Koʻolau
and that they liked the two of them being together
    and wanted them to stay together she looked at other boys
all of them watching for any hint of welcome
    and she thought they were all missing something that she
had always known in Koʻolau it was already so
    when they both found themselves lifted up as when a wave
arches itself under a canoe and the whispering hull
    pauses like a caught breath and then is flung forward racing
down the blue slope that keeps curling out from in front of it
    they felt themselves hurtling in a single rush with no thought
of anything else no sense of before or after
    yet it seemed to them that they were not moving at all
and everyone around them could see what was happening

34.

Then whatever they were doing they found that they were
    singing and Pi'ilani remembered the words
of the songs her grandmother kept starting again
    as she worked around the house and Ko'olau kept up
with the songs the men sang at Waiawa as they were riding
    or sitting with guitars in the evening and when they
spread out feasts at Kekaha for birthdays there would be
    a moment when they all began singing whatever
came to their minds there were chants from the old stories
    with somebody's hand beating on a hollow gourd
there were chants that were addressed to the gods there were songs
    about lovers in the rain and the wind in the cliffs
and the names of places and songs about places and the love
    that had once been there and they sang the foreigners' hymns
and songs of foreigners who had come with the cattle
    and had brought guitars Pi'ilani and Ko'olau had been
hearing that singing all their lives but not as they were
    beginning to hear it on the wave that was running with them
and around Kekaha and even at the ranch those who knew
    Pi'ilani and Ko'olau were overtaken by pleasure
at the thought of them and a sense that something was turning out
    right at last and that all of them were reflected in it
and when they repeated the stories they thought of Pi'ilani
    the face and presence of Pi'ilani and of Ko'olau
who could have been a chief they thought and one of their own
    they gathered more often as they said they used to do
in other times and in spite of all that had happened
    for a while they imagined they believed their own stories

35.

At the ranch at Waiawa and at Hofgaard's store
    and wherever else Koʻolau went they would be talking
sooner or later about the Chinese sickness
    sometimes they called it the chiefs' sickness and Kua explained
that as a child he had heard of a sickness before his time
    among some of the soldiers in the King's bodyguard
and it was said that carpenters had brought it from China
    when they came to build ships for the chiefs but no one was sure
and the talk would turn to the law now and how many
    had been arrested so far on Kauai and taken away
there was no way of being certain of that either
    for sometimes the signs of that sickness had been found
by Dr Smith or the doctor in Hanalei
    when they had been examining some other complaint
and there were those in Hofgaard's store who insisted
    that all the natives should be examined without wasting time
and they longed for the means to do it but no one wanted
    to be sent away and those who feared they might have
the disease stayed out of sight of the constables
    both native and foreign who prowled through the villages
and around the edges of towns and there were rumors
    of someone or other having been seized somewhere
on the island and carried off by the constables
    with no one to stop them and of others who had
disappeared when they had been left alone in their houses
    Kaleimanu knew one of the constables who haunted
all the settlements from Koloa to Mānā
    who said that his name was Nali but they all knew him
as Iole the rat and even when they could not see him
    they could tell when he was around by the way the dogs barked

36.

Kaleimanu had heard that this Iole came
    from the valley above Hanapepe and Kua told him
that the rat was someone like Kua who had no family
    but this one had been living by stealing before they
made him a constable and then Kawaluna began
    to talk about the people called Mū who had been there
on the island before the first Menehune arrived
    maybe it was the Mū people who set the rock at the top
of the mountain to be the altar of Kane long ago
    when they were as tall as trees and lived in the forest
and the Menehune fought with them and believed
    that they had killed them all but the Mū people lived on
and from time to time someone would go into the forest
    and disappear because the Mū people had caught them
and then in the time of the war chiefs it was Mū people
    who watched for those whose faces were not on the ground
when the chiefs passed or whose shadow touched the shadow
    of the chiefs or whose arm dropped when it should have been held up
the Mū people saw them and laid hold of them and dragged them off
    to be sacrificed and Kawaluna said that those
people could disappear or turn themselves into shadows
    but they were still there and this rat might be one of them
Kua told them that at Makaweli Eliza Sinclair
    who owned the island of Niʻihau had let it be known
that the constables would not be welcome there and that she would
    not send from her island anyone who had leprosy
but would keep them clean and bathe them and nurse their sores herself

37.

When Koʻolau heard the men in Hofgaard's store talking
    about the Chinese sickness he tried to listen
without being noticed and he saw that the subject stopped
    if Judge Kauai came in as he did many days
unless he was busy in the courthouse or away
    in Honolulu at the legislature and Kua
told Koʻolau that Judge Kauai made no secret
    of his opposition to the government's policy
of seizing victims of leprosy or those suspected
    of having it and sending them away from their families
for the rest of their lives and he said that the judge
    had been trying to learn what happened to those people
at the leprosy station in Honolulu
    and at the settlement on Kalaupapa from which
they never returned and Kua said that Knudsen himself
    had spoken against the government's way of dealing
with leprosy and had told Kua that he had seen
    that sickness in Norway when he was a young man and that he
had been angry in his own country at the way the lepers
    were treated and he said the sickness was dying out there
but not because of separating the sick ones
    and hiding them away to rot and Father Knudsen
had told him that some of the best doctors now believed
    that sending the sick ones away did no good at all
Koʻolau noticed that it was the foreigners
    whom the sickness almost never attacked who feared it most
and what the Hawaiians dreaded most was being taken
    away from their families he thought of that while he rode
to Piʻilani's house as the sun was going down
    beyond Niʻihau and he remembered his father
in that same light setting him on the mule when he was a child
    he could still feel the mule's warm shoulders and the bones moving
and then he walked with Piʻilani down to the canoes
    and she told him that she was going to have a child

38.

Pi'ilani said that her mother had understood
    what was happening long before she did and her family
all knew before she knew and she laughed and they lay down
    on the sand laughing and watched the light go out of the sky
she said—Now I want to tell Niuli—and when she did
    Niuli cried and said it was because she was happy
and Kukui when she heard it threw her hands up and shouted
    and Kawaluna sat watching Ko'olau and smiling
then Kaleimanu began to talk about where the children
    could live and whether they could build another room
and he was smiling and they all began to say
    good things they were thinking about Pi'ilani
Niuli was cleaning a fish and said she remembered
    Pi'ilani as a baby and Kawaluna said
—Your finger is bleeding—and Niuli said—Yes it is—
    and put it in her mouth—Is it bad—Kukui asked her
—I do not even feel it—Niuli said—I was thinking
    about that time then and remembering how we were all
round and small—and she stood there with her finger in her mouth
    looking at them as though she had just been asleep
then Kukui asked when they had known about it
    over at Pi'ilani's house and when the baby
was supposed to come and she started counting on her
    fingers and started over and they laughed at her
—I am trying to see when would be good for the wedding—
    she said and she asked Kawaluna when it should be
and Kawaluna asked—Have you decided where it will be—
    —In Waimea—Kukui said—at Reverend Rowell's church—
—What about Pi'ilani's family—Kawaluna asked
    —Do you know what they want to do and does Pi'ilani
want to get married at all—and she looked at Ko'olau
    —A wedding—Ko'olau said—We never talked about that—

39.

Koʻolau thought Judge Kauai had forgotten saying
    that he would give him things to read and when he saw
the Judge now and then at the store in Waimea
    the Judge never mentioned it so that Koʻolau
had forgotten it himself when he saw the Judge one day
    near the courthouse and the Judge said to him—Come
to my office by and by—and Koʻolau found his way
    to the right door which was open—Close it behind you—
the Judge said and he took from his desk a bundle
    of papers with a string around them—You can read
Hawaiian I know—he said—Can you read English too—
    —If I have to—Koʻolau said—You have something
to thank Reverend Rowell for—the Judge told him—I have been
    saving these for you from the papers in both languages
and a few things from the legislature but I preferred
    not to pass them to you at the store and when you have
read them we can talk about them somewhere in private
    maybe here if you find my door open and now I am told
that you are going to be married——How did you know that—
    Koʻolau asked and the Judge smiled—You are a little bit
famous around here—he said—You and your beautiful
    Piʻilani that is good that is good——If you please come
to the wedding—Koʻolau said and the Judge answered—I will—
    and on the day when they came in by horse and by wagon
from Kekaha the Judge joined them in front of the church
    and they were still more surprised when Kua pointed
to Father Knudsen and Mrs Knudsen by the church door
    there had been a meeting of church officers that morning
and the Knudsens had stayed for the wedding and Doctor
    Smith of Koloa had been standing with them and was
at the door of the church as the shy faces filed in

40.

After the wedding the Judge and his wife Kaenaku
    came to the feast in Kekaha and when the singing
began they sang with the others and they stayed a while
    when the old dances started though some hesitated
at first to dance the hula in front of the Judge
    but when the Judge learned of that he laughed and clapped his hands
and waved them on to dance and Kaenaku sat talking
    with Pi'ilani and with Niuli and Kukui
and then a few days later when Ko'olau was working
    with a young horse at the ranch at Waiawa he turned
to see his friend Ka'aka from Kekaha ride up to him
    at a gallop shouting—Ko'olau Come Hurry Come—
and he rode on to Kaleimanu and Kua shouting—Come—
    and as they mounted he kept calling out—Sister Sister
they are taking her to the doctor—and as they were riding
    they tried to understand what he was telling them
the sheriff's deputy had come to Kekaha to the house
    to take Niuli away to the doctor in Koloa
and they had cried but he said she had to go with him
    the men galloped to Kekaha where Kukui and Kawaluna
were still at the house and friends had gathered there crying
    but Niuli was gone and Kaleimanu got the wagon
to drive them all to Koloa and Ko'olau and Kua
    rode on ahead and arrived at Dr Smith's house
and knocked and the deputy sheriff opened the door
    and told them that the doctor was with a patient
Ko'olau said—I want my sister—and the deputy said
    —If you create a disturbance I will put you in jail—
—We will wait here—Ko'olau said and they all stood on the steps
    until the doctor came out and they heard Niuli crying
as the wagon drove up and then the doctor told them all
    that Niuli had leprosy and that his duty forced him
to send her away on the schooner—Let her come out—
    Ko'olau said and the doctor went in and led her
out through the door she was holding her hands over her face
    then she stopped and stood looking at them while they were there

THERE

1.

There was very little there was probably nothing
    that he could promise them the Judge said there was probably
nothing that he could do once the doctor had decided
    and he explained that he was opposed to the way the problem
was being dealt with but that he could not alter the law
    and Father Knudsen told Koʻolau and Kaleimanu
much the same thing he said most of the foreigners
    in the legislature and most of the Board of Health
believed in having the lepers taken away
    from everyone else by force if need be and he told them
that their one hope for Niuli was that the doctors
    in Honolulu might disagree with the judgment
of Dr Smith or might say that she had the sickness
    in a mild and curable form and send her back
when they believed she was better perhaps in a year or so
    you can write to her he told them you can send her things
the schooner had not yet sailed but she was on it
    and as he rode from the ranch Koʻolau looked at the horizon
that he had always seen and he knew nothing there
    at the house in Kekaha they put Niuli's things
in a box and took it to Koloa to the schooner
    where she had been locked in a cabin and a constable
was talking with some men on the wharf and stopped them
    they told him the box was for Niuli and he said
—I will take it—but Koʻolau would not give it to him
    —We will give it to the doctor—he said but Dr Smith
was not at home and they found no one they could trust
    with the box for Niuli by the time the schooner
was ready to sail and Dr Smith did not come down
    to the wharf and when they called Niuli there was no answer
and then they could hear her crying coming from inside
    as the lines were cast off and the schooner began to move

2.

Twice after that Ko'olau rode to Koloa
     to Dr Smith's with the box but once the doctor
was somewhere else and once he was with a patient
     and sent the woman who was doing the housework to tell him
to leave the box there but he carried it back to Waimea
     and to the Judge's office where the Judge told him
that he himself was not the best person to arrange matters
     with Dr Smith and the Judge advised Ko'olau
to take the box to Reverend Rowell since the doctor
     was an important member of the pastor's congregation
and Niuli had been a pupil of his—But be sure
     not to tell him you came to me first—the Judge said
and Ko'olau watched his smile pass like a breath of the trades
     over the lagoon and it was Kua who reminded
Ko'olau later of the time when the pastor
     had nailed up the church doors and locked the trustees out
the Judge among them and then the melodeon business
     in the years when Ko'olau was a child and those things
are still awake in their faces Kua told him
     and you should recognize what you are seeing there
Ko'olau was thinking of that as he knocked at the Rowells'
     big house with the deep lanais and railings around
the two floors and he stood waiting holding the box
     it was Mary the Rowells' youngest daughter who
opened the door she was older than he was
     and had always seemed to him to be one of the grown-ups
even before she went away to school and now since she
     had come back he saw her sometimes at Makaweli
where she looked after the Knudsens' children
     he could tell from her face that she did not recognize him
and she told him that Reverend Rowell was not there

3.

He set the box on the horse again and rode around
    to the church and tried the front door and the latch opened
he walked in and saw Hoʻona arranging flowers
    in a milk jug in front of the church and Hoʻona
turned and saw him and waved and said his name and the empty room
    echoed stirring the smell of dying and Koʻolau
wanted not to be there but he walked up to Hoʻona
    hearing the soles of his bare feet and he tried to keep
his voice small because of the echoes as he asked
    where the pastor was and Hoʻona as though he were
confiding kept his voice low too as he told Koʻolau
    that Reverend Rowell had gone up to his garden
and then he said—Your sister how terrible terrible—
    Koʻolau answered nothing and finally nodded
—I have to see the pastor—he said and turned to go
    —What is in the box—Hoʻona asked—Niuli's things—
Koʻolau told him—For the pastor to send to her—
    Hoʻona said—You can leave them here and I will give him
the box when he comes—but Koʻolau said—I will take it
    thank you—and he turned and walked back through the echoes
and rode up along the river bank beyond the village
    to the terrace walls and plots of the old days and the garden
in the place called Kakalae where the pastor grew his
    mangos and loquats bananas oranges even peaches
the pastor was alone there hoeing when Koʻolau
    rode up and he straightened at once and came over and said
—I was shocked and grieved to hear about your sister
    something so painful it is hard to understand it
but Dr Smith tells me that this has to be done
    for the sake of everyone and there is no other way
and I do not know what I can do but pray and I pray
    I pray for your sister——These are her things here—Koʻolau said
—They took her away without them and I have brought them
    to you to ask you to give them to the doctor
to send to her we do not even know where they have put her—

4.

—I will give it to him—Reverend Rowell said—and we will
   make sure that it reaches her—and he walked to the shed
under a mango tree and put away the hoe
   and picked up his black coat and hat—Will you follow me
to the church—he asked as he mounted and they rode
   in file down the path along the river where Koʻolau's eyes
kept returning to the black coat moving ahead of him
   under the black hat and he saw nobody inside them
while they passed the broken terraces and the tethered goats
   on the way to the lane in Waimea where they turned
toward the church and he saw the pastor's thin face again
   white foreign old and remote from him and he hitched his horse
beside the pastor's and carried the box once more
   into the church hoping that Hoʻona had gone home
but his father-in-law was still there and Koʻolau stood
   by the door as the pastor walked on and talked with Hoʻona
he could not hear their words until the pastor turned and said
   —Come come—and Koʻolau carried the box toward him
feeling that now he did not want to give it up
   —Have you put a letter inside for her—the pastor asked him
Koʻolau shook his head—Would you like to write something
   to send to her—the pastor asked and Koʻolau stood
silent for a moment and then nodded—You can write
   to her here—the pastor said and went to a table
behind the pulpit and took out a sheet of paper
   and a pencil—Sit there and write—he said to Koʻolau
and Koʻolau was thinking that he did not want
   to untie the rope and open the box in front of
Hoʻona or the pastor either but he sat with it
   on the bench beside him and laid the paper on top
and wrote slowly—Niuli we were all there in
   Koloa we heard you on the boat we were calling you
we are all sad sad and you are here in our minds
   we love you Niuli write to us tell us what
we can send to you with the love of your brother Koʻolau—

5.

—You must fold it and put her name on the outside—
    the pastor said—Write Niuli from Kekaha
and is her name on the box—Koʻolau shook his head
      —It should be—Pastor Rowell said—It should bear her name
in large letters and not just in pencil—Koʻolau sat
    looking at him and then drew his knife from his sheath
and began to carve her name on the box in capitals
    Hoʻona watched him for a while and then said to him
in that same low voice—I will be going out to Kekaha
    some time later and I want to see Piʻilani
tonight or tomorrow if you wait we can go out
     together—but Koʻolau said—I want to go home early—
and Hoʻona said—Until I see you then—and Koʻolau
    stood up to embrace him and said goodbye and then went on
with the carving while the afternoon sunbeams crept toward him
    across the benches—I am going over to the house now—
the pastor said—You can bring the box when you have finished—
    then he went to the front door and Koʻolau heard the lock turn
—Come out by the back door—the pastor said—and lock it
    after you and bring me the key—and he held it up
and laid it on the table and then Koʻolau heard the door close
    and after that only the sound of the knife in the wood
the same wood that Knudsen had let them have for building
    the house even the whisper of the carving echoed
in the empty room and her name when he mumbled it
    under his breath and then it was finished and he scraped off
the shavings and put them in his pocket and untied
    the rope and lifted off the lid and a kind of darkness
rose over him like a wave as he opened the box
    and let the light touch the worn folded clothes that he knew
and nothing else there for her to hold and remember
    he creased the paper and set it on top and then he tried
to think of something he could put in to send to her
    but he could think of nothing else and he closed the lid

6.

Then he was at the door on the Rowells' lanai again
        women's voices from the back of the house and the smells
of cooking and when he knocked he could tell that no one
        heard him so he knocked louder and heard feet coming and the door
opened and he recognized Lali who worked there
        but she did not know him—Who is it—she asked him
he remembered Hoʻona telling how she sang the hymns
        louder than anyone with her voice somewhere up
in a tree he used to do imitations of her
        getting caught in the higher notes—This is for Reverend Rowell—
Koʻolau told her—What is it—she asked—It is for him—
        Koʻolau said—What is it Lali—he heard Mrs Rowell's
high foreign voice call from another room and then she
        appeared behind Lali the white sunken face and she said
—Are you not a student of Reverend Rowell's are you not
        from Kekaha you have grown so that I scarcely know you—
—Yes I am—Koʻolau answered—Yes your name is Koʻolau
        I remember you—and he said—This is for him
for Reverend Rowell——What is it—she asked—It is
        my sister's clothes to send to her——Your sister—she asked
—Niuli—Koʻolau said—She was a pupil of his too—
        —Was she the one they just sent away the poor child—
Mrs Rowell asked and put her hand over her mouth
        as Reverend Rowell appeared behind her—There you are—he said
—Bring it in—but Mrs Rowell turned and said to him
        in a voice like a whisper—Maybe by the other door—
—No No—the pastor said—It will be all right bring it in—
        and Koʻolau carried the box into the house
—Where do you want it—Mrs Rowell asked her husband
        and Koʻolau saw that she was afraid of the box
—Come with me—Reverend Rowell said—Yes of course it will be
        all right—Mrs Rowell said and Koʻolau followed
Reverend Rowell through the house to a room with a table
        papers spread on it books on shelves—Leave it there on the bench—
the pastor said—How beautifully you have carved her name—
        Koʻolau held out the key to him and said—Thank you—

7.

Kawaluna asked him that evening—What did you do
　　with the box—and he told her he told them all and she went on
asking until he told about the doctor's house
　　and then Judge Kauai and Reverend Rowell and writing
the letter and carving Niuli's name on the lid
　　and as he answered her he could hear his words fall with the sound
of a net dropping where there were no fish and Kawaluna
　　went on asking him what else was in the room what else
was on the bench what had he seen through the window
　　what were they talking about in the kitchen did the pastor
lead him out through the back door or return the same way
　　they had come in and then she stopped asking and looked at him
nodding and Ko'olau said—The pastor told me
　　that the doctor would be coming to church on Sunday—
—That is good—Kaleimanu said and Kukui was crying
　　to herself turned away from the firelight and Pi'ilani
was putting things away and Kaleimanu told
　　Ko'olau what he had done that day on the house
that they were building for him and for Pi'ilani
　　he said they could almost start putting the roof on you will see
in the morning and Ko'olau and Pi'ilani
　　went out to the back lanai where they were sleeping then
the child was already growing big in her and they
　　talked about that and what she was feeling inside there
and they talked about Niuli and Pi'ilani told him
　　that she kept thinking of when Niuli had seemed
to be so much older than they were and Ko'olau said
　　that there were times when he could remember Niuli
clearly and then he would look and not be able to see her
　　they fell asleep talking and there was a line of dark cliffs
and below the cliffs but above him in the light
　　that came through young branches there were some people standing
against the bright sky so that he saw only their shadow side
　　they were playing some game that he did not understand
passing something around among themselves that asked
　　the person with whom it stopped—Who are you—and a man's voice
said—The new arrivals go on playing that game—
　　and he saw that the one with whom it kept stopping was
the new arrival who was not a woman but a man
　　who turned in anger and pulled a young tree to the ground

139

8.

Through those days Pi'ilani and Kawaluna
     grew closer together they recognized some likeness
in each other a way of looking at daylight and darkness
     and when either of them laughed everyone paid attention
Kawaluna told Pi'ilani about things
     she never spoke of to anyone else and she taught her
something of what she knew of the healing powers of plants
     ways of touching the life in the body and of hearing it
and breathing strength into it she showed Pi'ilani
     bright designs to watch in the night sky lights that her father
had pointed out to her from the time before the tide of slaughter
     and Ko'olau and Kaleimanu put the roof on the new house
so that Ko'olau and Pi'ilani could move over there
     but when Ko'olau was away at Waiawa Pi'ilani
went over to spend the day with her mother or to be
     with Kukui and Kawaluna and when Ko'olau
went to Waimea he stopped to see Father Rowell
     who told him that he had given the box to the doctor
and the doctor had sent it on to Honolulu
     to the hospital and he had heard nothing since then
then one day as he stopped at the church to talk to the pastor
     there was a foreigner by the door watching him
a man taller than he was and thin with eyes like metal
     maybe about as old as Kua he remembered seeing
that man in Koloa fixing a door on the doctor's house
     and later at Makaweli with the foreigners
the pastor saw them looking at each other and he said
     —Louis do you know this young man he was a fine student
of mine when he was much smaller and now everyone says
     he is one of Valdemar Knudsen's most trusted men
his name is Ko'olau—and to Ko'olau he said
     —You must have heard of my son-in-law Louis Stolz
my daughter Mary's husband you know—and Stolz let his eyes rest
     on Ko'olau's bare feet and then raised them to his face
nodded and said—I am glad to meet you—speaking
     in English which he pronounced so that it sounded
to Ko'olau the way those foreigners spoke it
     who brought in new cattle sometimes from the boats in Koloa

9.

Once he had met the man Ko'olau kept hearing
    about him Ho'ona told him how helpful that
Mr Stolz had been to the foreigners in Koloa
    working as a carpenter with his brother when they first
came to the island a few years back they had made
    that balcony on the doctor's house with the shaped railings
and those upstairs windows toward the harbor on the Doles' house
    and he had become friends with the Pastor who took
pleasure in making furniture and had all those tools
    arranged in his workroom where he kept them as bright
as the spoons in the kitchen and the Pastor let Mr Stolz
    work with him there making arches for inside the church
that was how Mr Stolz met Mary when she came home
    from Makaweli on Sundays she was already
old enough for people to be wondering whether
    she would ever be married and that was the way
it happened that Mr Stolz became one of the family
    he even built the bed there for when they would be married
then Kua told Ko'olau that this man Stolz had
    some cattle of his own now that he kept out there between
Waimea and Makaweli and he called himself
    a rancher in Hofgaard's store and Ko'olau met
Judge Kauai on the street in Waimea and the Judge
    asked him whether he had been reading and he said yes
and the Judge said—I have more for you but never mind coming
    to my office this time for I have retired in favor
of my son who is now Judge Kauai the second and I am
    the Judge in name only so if you come by the house
out on Koloa Road in a while I can provide you
    with some more to think about Have you heard from your sister—
—No—Ko'olau said—We will talk about that too—the Judge told him

10.

A house still unfinished in a grove of mango trees
    half a dozen dogs barking as Koʻolau rode up the lane
the Judge was sitting at a table on the deep lanai
    in his hat with the broad straw brim and the band of pheasant
breast feathers around it that he seemed never to
    take off now that his hair had turned white and Koʻolau
saw how heavy he was becoming the chairs complained
    when he sank into them and the floor gave when he stood up
—You have been out here before the house was here I expect—
    the Judge said and Koʻolau said—There used to be cattle—
—It used to belong to Eliza Sinclair—the Judge said
    —We exchanged years ago you know I have been playing
peck and peck with land for years and now there is this Stolz
    got the land next door before I knew it was going
must have been Rowell passed him the word and he was quick enough
    do you know him——I met him—Koʻolau said—Keep an eye
on that one—the Judge said—Came here from California
    with his brother a few years older who took himself
away to Maui up country to Makawao where I
    come from so I hear about him I feel as though I had
bugs in my shirt with the two of them this one would like
    to carry the whole island in his pocket and the natives
should thank him for honoring them with his presence
    California is not where they started from they went there
with a cargo of hides I believe have you heard how
    he talks with that accent from South America they were born
in Argentina and grew up there and his parents
    came from Germany so he is a foreigner
among the foreigners and wants them to believe
    that he is the same as they are Well did the Doctor send
the box to your sister——Pastor Rowell told me he did—
    —And where is your sister now——We have not heard He sent it
to Honolulu where they take them but we have not heard
    anything from her or about her since they took her—
—You will learn something about the place from these papers—
    the Judge said—and I will see what else I can find out—

11.

—I cannot say whether I will be going over
  to the legislature in Honolulu again—the Judge said
—I have made my troubles here and there I have not agreed
  with all the agreements and there are those who have not
forgotten the time a while back when I stirred up
  that commotion over the manner in which the voting
was conducted and I threatened to have the ballot boxes
  called into court and opened and counted in public
you can imagine that some were displeased with that idea
  and in this matter of leprosy I have listened
and have read what I could find about it ever since they
  talked the old king into signing the law that was supposed
to get rid of the sickness by getting rid of the sick
  rounding them up and shipping them somewhere out of sight
they were afraid that having the occasional leper
  in full view would upset the delicate feelings
of foreign visitors and discourage them from bringing
  their money here but it was never foreigners
who suffered from the law they were not the ones who were taken
  by this sickness and deformed by it and lived with it
and died of it no from the start it was the people
  of the islands the blood of the islands that were being
got rid of it was our families that were being
  broken up once again and we had been disappearing
into the sand ever since the foreigners came here
  right here to Waimea hardly more than a hundred
years ago and now leprosy and this law and many
  now keep insisting that this is the only way
keeping the lepers apart from the righteous but it is not
  getting rid of the sickness they keep finding new cases
they say that by this means the lepers will get the best
  medical treatment but they are not curing them
Gibson himself says they are simply herding them together
  and feeding them but even the Queen now believes
that it has to be done and they sent her cousin
  to Kalawao for a while and still there are doctors
who argue against doing this and say there are better
  ways to deal with this and why should you know all this
I am not sure what can be done but if it did not matter
  for us to know they would not keep us from finding out

143

12.

—The schooner goes whether I am on it or not—
      the Judge said—and there are many ways of inquiring
have you spoken about this to Mr Knudsen——He knows
      that they took Niuli and afterward he told me
he was sorry to hear it but he knew it was the law
      and there was not much that he could do about it
and then he told me about Mrs Sinclair over
      on Niʻihau refusing to let the government
send over and take the lepers off the island—
      —Yes I have heard about that too—the Judge said to him
—and it may be true or was true once but she is not young
      and these days she is over here most of the time
up there at Makaweli and the government cares
      little about Niʻihau since the foreigners never
go there anyway unless the Sinclairs or their
      relatives invite them over there I expect Knudsen
is sympathetic and will go on trying to learn
      it was a doctor in Norway who found the germ
too small to be seen that makes leprosy and I know Knudsen
      reads medical papers from Norway—Koʻolau stood up
and thanked him—A fine horse that one you have—the Judge said
      —He is—Koʻolau said—but he really belongs
to Mr Knudsen though he is mine for now—and he rode
      back through Waimea and on out along the shore
toward Kekaha thinking as he went that he had just heard
      the voice of Niuli coming from inside the schooner
in the harbor at Koloa and he told himself
      that it was the stilts crying across the sand but it was not
the voice of stilts and yet it flew along beside him
      like the stilts with their long wings flashing into the light
and as he came to Kekaha he saw Kawaluna
      sitting looking out to the west toward the blue shadow
of Niʻihau and she heard him come up behind her
      and stop and when he spoke to her and dismounted
she did not look at him at first and then she said
      that she was sitting between Niuli and Piʻilani

13.

He told her of his asking and learning nothing
    about Niuli and then of the voice just as he was riding
toward home though he thought it had been only the stilts calling
    before sundown and Kawaluna nodded—It may be—
she said—You see the birds now flying all around us
    the shore birds and the terns out over the shallows and the owl
down from the valleys in the daylight Pi'ilani
    is near her time——Has it begun—Ko'olau asked
—Not yet—Kawaluna said——Maybe tomorrow
    maybe tonight sometime she does not know it yet
or maybe she knows it and has not said anything
    you know how she is there she is with Kukui do you
see the owl now—Ko'olau turned to where she was looking
    and saw the gray wings sailing along the edges
of the lagoon like a shadow through the dry notes
    of the insects shrilling the hour and the long quavers
of the toads the heron's bark the low hushing of the surf
    the owl swung through them and circled back without a sound
Ko'olau noticed that he had stopped breathing as he watched it
    as though the owl had held his breath and when he turned
to Kawaluna whose eyes were still following it
    he thought that she herself was the owl sitting there and when he
looked back he could not see it but as he looked for it
    Kawaluna was standing beside him—Time to go—
she said and they walked out from under the branches
    toward the houses and he thought how lightly she walked
his grandmother his mother's mother how she floated
    over the sand he heard his own footsteps and the horse
behind him and he looked at her as he had turned to her
    all his life to feel sure at the sight of her and she was
looking out ahead of them and said—Pi'ilani—
    and then he saw Pi'ilani in his parents' doorway
watching them come it was that night she went into labor
    not for long and the child was born before the ghost dawn
it was a boy and small and cried with a small voice

14.

In the morning shadows Piʻilani and Kawaluna
    filled the room with a slow undercurrent of comfort
Piʻilani remembered the way a canoe coming in
    rides at last the front of the wave toward the sand
the baby lay still and looked like a hatched bird lying
    asleep against her breast as Koʻolau stood over them
—Get out of the way—Kawaluna kept telling him
    and when she had gone out and walked down and into the sea
and stood there as she had done after each life that she had drawn
    into the daylight she came back with sea water running
from her feet and she took the cord from the navel
    to the place where she had hidden Piʻilani's
and Koʻolau's years before and she came back and bathed the child
    again and Piʻilani bathed herself and put on
a new dress as Kukui stood holding the baby then Piʻilani
    asked Kawaluna—Did you find a name for him in the night—
and Kawaluna shook her head and Piʻilani asked
    Kukui the same question and Kukui shook her head
Kaleimanu was in the doorway smiling at the child
    —I want him to be named for your father—Piʻilani said
to Koʻolau—I want his name to be Kaleimanu
    so that he answers to the same name as his grandfather
and if he grows up to be like him that would be a good thing—
    and they cared for the baby so that their friends laughed and said
that the boy would never learn to walk if his feet
    never touched the ground and each of them holding him
was overtaken by thoughts of Niuli of whom they
    heard nothing but for all Piʻilani's nursing her child
he stayed small as a fledgling and never put on weight
    his bones remained thin and nothing about him grew large
except his head and his bright eyes which soon followed them
    and lit up at the sight of any of them and he would
laugh and call out to them and he seemed to be a happy child

15.

In the year after Niuli was taken away
     whenever Koʻolau went to Waimea he would stop
at the Rowells' big house and ask whether there was any
     word about his sister until not only the pastor
but whoever answered the door knew why he was standing there
     and when she had been gone for a year he rode on
to Koloa to the doctor's house where they told him
     that the doctor was with patients and so he waited
until the woman with whom he had spoken came and asked
     what he had come for and then stared at him and went away
and came to tell him that the doctor knew nothing more
     and as he rode from there Koʻolau went to see the Judge
who told him that he had written to the hospital
     about Niuli and the answer from Honolulu
was that they had no record of anyone by that name
     but that he was pursuing the question and would do so
when next he went over to Honolulu in a month or so
     for it made no sense and he had no explanation
except that he had learned that patients when they were taken
     were told that they did not have to give their real names
if they were ashamed or were afraid of bringing
     shame on their families—But she would not do that—
Koʻolau said—She knew we were not ashamed of her
     she knows we are not ashamed of her she would not be ashamed
she was never ashamed she never did anything
     to be ashamed of——It is the foreigners who are ashamed
of us—the Judge said—and the sickness lets them show
     what they feel about us——Did they give her the box—
Koʻolau asked—Nobody knows—the Judge told him
     —I have been asking the authorities and now I am
turning to other sources both on Oahu and at
     Kalawao in the leper colony and I have been
finding out about both places and have saved more things
     for you to read but I still have no news of your sister—

16.

The Judge said—When nobody knows it does not prevent
    many of them from being sure and I listen
to the arguments in the legislature and at meetings
    in churches and among doctors and every one of them
is right and now the saints of the Board of Foreign Missions
    whom I have served as a trustee are as one supporting
this policy of seizing lepers and hiding them away
    as they have done now for fifteen years and upwards
trying to sweep them under the matting and meanwhile
    those who have gone to minister to those bewildered
souls in their separation and helplessness have been
    Catholics speaking French which scandalized the righteous
ministers from New England to whom God gave us first
    and who are content to know better at a safe distance
and who say such terrible things about the French priests
    that I decided I had to find out about it
and got to know the priest at the church in Koloa
    and the one over in Hanalei and they did not tell me
how the disease was God's judgment upon the natives
    for their sinful sensuality and the way they are always
touching each other there was none of that and they told me
    about the Catholic mission at Kalawao
and this priest Damien in particular who lives
    among the lepers not apart from them but eating
with them working with them through the days listening to them
    helping them bury each other and these people
have ways of their own for finding someone among
    the lepers there and they tell me stories of Kalawao
that have never been published and then there are still other
    kinds of inquiry that the foreigners do not know about

17.

In Kekaha they knew that Hoʻona and the woman
    he had been living with some of the time in Waimea
whose name they knew was Malukauai had a daughter
    and it was said that there was another daughter
but whether she was theirs or was Malukauai's child
    by another man or Hoʻona's by another woman
nobody was certain and they all talked about it
    in Piʻilani's family and in Koʻolau's
and Piʻilani's mother Kepola heard part of it
    from Hoʻona whose answers always left a door swinging
what was the daughter's name she asked him and he said
    that her name in Hawaiian was Kealia
but they never called her that and her name in English
    he never told her but he said the girl's mother
had taken her to Pastor Rowell's school without saying
    who the father was—But they all knew—Kepola said
and laughed and asked—How old is she now—And Hoʻona
    told her he could not remember—A little younger
than Piʻilani I believe—Kepola said—Yes younger—
    Hoʻona said—If I saw her one day in Waimea
I would not know her—Piʻilani said—Do they go
    to the church—Kepola asked—Sometimes—Hoʻona answered
—Do you sit in the same bench then—Kepola asked
    —I am the usher you remember—Hoʻona said
—so I stay by the door—Kepola said—I think we
    should go to the church more often—and she laughed again
Koʻolau thought of it as he rode home through Waimea
    and there on the street was Hoʻona walking with a young girl
then Louis Stolz rode past them toward the Rowell house as the bell
    in the church began ringing and Hoʻona looked up
at Stolz and saw Koʻolau and he stopped and when Koʻolau
    came up to him he said—Reverend Rowell is dead—
he was crying and then he added—This is Kealia—

18.

So that girl who looked up at him and then looked away
     was Piʻilani's half sister and he searched her face quickly
for anything he could recognize he stared for a moment
     and said her name and again she looked up at him
and mumbled something and turned away and he told her
     he was glad to know her and when she nodded he thought
he saw something familiar—When did the pastor die—
     he asked—Just a little while ago—Hoʻona said
—I was at the church and Lilia ran from the house
     to tell me—and Koʻolau looked at the tears on his face
and said nothing and for a moment none of them moved
     or spoke on the dirt street in Waimea late in the day
with the news spreading its shadow through the buildings around them
     and then Koʻolau said good-bye and rode on home
and when he told them in Kekaha about the pastor
     Kukui gasped and started to cry and his father
Kaleimanu said that they must go to the funeral
     and Piʻilani went to tell her mother Kepola
who said she would go with them and in the evening Koʻolau
     told them of meeting Kealia and they asked their questions
and he told Kepola he thought the girl was about twelve
     but it was hard to tell Piʻilani what she looked like
so as they rode together to the funeral
     they were wondering whether they would see her this time
now that Koʻolau could point her out and there she was
     with her mother outside the church as they arrived
and Koʻolau told them which ones they were and they all watched
     as the woman and the two girls went into the church
and they followed and saw where the three sat down and they
     took a bench where they could look at them and Koʻolau
saw Stolz beside Mary up in front with the family
     the Knudsens were up there and the Judge arrived with his wife
and sons and went up to his bench and there were all
     the foreigners from Koloa and from the foreign church
nearby and the bell rang and Valdemar Knudsen stood up
     and raised his hands like a preacher and announced a hymn
and then each of them was standing and singing the same words

19.

The singing itself took Ko'olau by surprise
    he had never liked the hymns back at the time when they
had to sing them in Pastor Rowell's school they were different
    from the songs and chants that he had grown up hearing
from Kawaluna and Keawe and Nakaula
    and the elders in Kekaha in the evenings
the hymns had felt to him like obeying a stranger
    and whenever the Pastor was not looking at him
he stood silent watching the others and watching Pi'ilani
    as she sang and Niuli as she sang and then
he would begin singing with them and as he stood there
    at the funeral the schoolroom that he had longed
to get away from woke up inside him burning through him
    and he looked at the Pastor's body in its box
white faced under the flowers this dead foreigner
    who had seen him born and whom he had looked up to
and had disliked most of the time until the day
    he had ridden up to the garden with the box
for Niuli and then back down by the river seeing
    the Pastor's back riding ahead of him and knowing
from watching the back of the Pastor's head under its black hat
    what the man was feeling about Niuli it was there
in the lines across the back of the neck then Ho'ona
    whom they had not seen slipped in at the end of the bench
beside Pi'ilani and Kepola and in the second
    verse of the hymn Ko'olau out of the corner
of his eye saw Ho'ona standing there and he saw
    tears on the man's face again and then he saw that Kepola
had her head bowed and there were tears running on her cheeks
    and he saw that Pi'ilani was singing and her face
was wet and shining and it startled him to see her in tears
    and between them their child Kaleimanu was gazing up at her
reaching up to her and at the sight of her tears he started
    to cry and Ko'olau picked him up and held him
to his shoulder and stood not singing looking at the lid
    of the coffin and he thought that he felt nothing now
for the man whose body was lying in it but only
    a strange ache that had come from the schoolroom and he began
to sing with the others and suddenly his throat grew tight

20.

At the end of the service when they had filed past
    the coffin and out the back door leaving the family
and the ushers and pall-bearers behind them in the church
    they went and took up places in the cemetery
facing the waiting grave and Piʻilani as she
    gazed at the piled earth and the long hole beside it
kept hearing the word for that dark pit that was Koʻolau's
    first name her hands were cold and the shadow of a kukui tree
moved like cold hands over the pile of fresh earth it was all
    coming to pass in whispers the trees stirring the words from
the bowed faces she saw the Judge's wife on the far side
    of the grave and the Judge and their sons and then her father's
arms loaded with flowers arrived at the mound and he
    set wreaths carefully on the grass to one side of it
and stepped away as the bearers came with the coffin
    slowly around the church from the front door she saw Valdemar
Knudsen with his wide beard and she supposed the tall
    old man beside him might be Reverend Dole from Koloa
and there was Doctor Smith who had taken Niuli
    and she saw a strange younger man with a long closed face
whom she had noticed in church standing beside Mary Rowell
    they were all foreigners and the preachers standing
beside the grave were foreigners and most of what they said
    had been in English so that she had let it float past her
the bearers let the coffin down onto the boards and stood back
    the men who held the ropes were Hawaiians and she saw
the way the man with the closed face was watching them
    as the man on the horse did when he was overseeing
the backs bent in the sugar fields then they lowered
    the coffin and the preachers all read from their black books
and she heard Valdemar Knudsen pray in a loud voice saying
    that this man's mind had been broader than most
and ahead of his time and later she tried to think
    what he had been talking about as she watched the family
come one by one to pick up earth and flowers and drop them
    into the grave the Pastor's wife the grown children and their
wives and husbands and last the one with that hard face

21.

That night Pi'ilani and Ko'olau lay awake
    recalling those who had been there at the funeral
and after a time they began talking about Niuli
    and where she might be and whether they believed she was
on this side of the grave or on the other side
    and Ko'olau said Now that the Pastor was gone
she seemed farther away and there was only the Judge
    left for him to ask about her and Pi'ilani
wondered who the man was next to Mary Rowell
    and Ko'olau said that was her husband and he told her
what Kua and the Judge had said to him about
    this Mr Stolz and his origins and ambitions
and she listened as Ko'olau said—He goes sometimes
    to Makaweli when Mary does and I see him there
but we never talk and now he runs some cattle
    of his own closer to town than Mr Knudsen's
and he calls himself a stockman—Then Kaleimanu
    woke up and they lulled him back to sleep with stories
but the next time Ko'olau stopped to see the Judge
    it was Louis Stolz the Judge wanted to tell him about
and how the man was getting his friends onto the Water Board
    and writing to the offices in Honolulu
for concessions and water rights that could give him
    advantages over his neighbors who had been there
since before he ever made his way out of Argentina
    the Judge said it seemed as though Louis Stolz had minded
his manners as long as the Pastor was alive
    but that once Reverend Rowell was out of the way
he began to show what he was like there were no
    Hawaiians at Stolz's place the men who handled
the cattle there were Mexicans but the Judge had heard
    of Stolz having his way with Hawaiian women
Married women—the Judge said—and I cannot be sure
    what truth there is in the stories but I keep hearing them—

22.

Then Ko'olau asked about Niuli and the Judge
        said that the priests in Koloa and Hanalei
had written to friends of theirs over at the mission
        at Kalaupapa and inquired about Niuli
but they had no record of her there by that name
        nor of any woman of that age admitted from Kauai
and they had found no trace of her at the hospital
        in Honolulu where she would have been taken
but they said that patients found many ways to hide
        and that they would keep trying to find her and the Judge said
that the priests had given him papers about Kalaupapa
        which he had saved for Ko'olau and they had confided
stories about the colony that were not public knowledge
        —We should learn what goes on in that place—the Judge said
—It has been happening in our own lifetimes and to
        our own people however the sickness first came here
first they got the old king to sign the law that would let them
        treat the lepers as criminals and they chose Kalaupapa
because it was isolated all the way out
        on a peninsula on Moloka'i cut off by sea cliffs
thousands of feet high and with the surf breaking around it
        it is there in the ancient legends and the histories
of the chiefs a promontory of spirits on an island
        of spirits with a lake of spirits in the middle of it
and when they chose that peninsula for their outcasts
        there were families who had been farming and fishing there
since the time of the legends and ships used to sail there
        straight from California just for the sweet potatoes
for they were the finest in the world and those families
        were never told of the plans for their rocky leaf
of land which was the world they had known all their lives
        they met the first twelve patients who were pushed into the surf
some of them with limbs crippled and shrivelled by the sickness
        and they helped them into their own houses and took care of them—

23.

—But that was long ago at the beginning—the Judge said
    —back when you were at the Pastor's school and at that time
none of us knew what went on there and the constables
    kept rounding up lepers and shipping them over
dropping them off at Waikolu along the coast
    to find their way to the grass roofs at Kalaupapa
some of them scarcely able to stand and they say that in less
    than a year two hundred of them had been thrown out like that
and the inhabitants could not feed them or shelter them
    but were crowded out of their own fields and houses
with lepers everywhere lying sitting hobbling begging
    until those who had lived there left the peninsula
where they had been born and they shipped out or climbed the cliffs
    into the rest of the world when it seemed that the world
was gone and the lepers moved into their empty houses
    and ate up whatever had been left there and they brewed
alcohol from the sweet potatoes and lay around
    naked so that the place became known on the island
as the crazy pen but the Board of Health kept sending
    more of them from Kalihi in Honolulu
putting up shelters and buildings sending a doctor
    and rations of meat and taro root so much a head
and not much of either and as for anything else
    they wore their rags while those lasted and were lucky
to have one scrap of blanket on that rainy coast
    and I hear the crippled were given nothing to eat
unless they did their share of the daily grave-digging
    and when it came to coffins those who had no money
were buried without them and this priest Damien says that
    he has seen a body dug up by the pigs and eaten
some died alone and unnoticed for days some forgot
    who they were and wandered into complete mindlessness
but now they tell me that with the mission it is better
    with more food and a hospital but just the same nobody
would go there willingly and now there are hundreds of them
    dragged away by the constables as your sister was—

24.

—And besides the priests—the Judge said—I have been talking
    with two brothers from Moloka'i who work on the schooner
Waiola and a friend of theirs on the steamer Pele
    they are all sons of the families who were crowded
out of Kalaupapa and now they go back to the place
    for a different reason there were always kahunas
all kinds of sorcerers at Kalaupapa and the lake
    in the middle of the peninsula has no bottom
but goes all the way down into the house of Pele
    and the sorcerers make their way at night to the water's edge
and talk with the darkness these men may be sorcerers
    they have kahunas in their families who return there
and among the patients at Kalaupapa there is one great
    sorcerer who was sent there years ago a woman named
Paniku Hua she has visions she talks of a dark cloud
    coming toward us reaching for the throne she has seen it
for years drawing closer I have sent messages to her
    and those men brought one back to me she says Less Than Ten
whatever that means Less Than Ten I asked them what
    she could reveal about your sister and she told them
nothing at first but after a time she said Shorebird
    and that was all and they tell me she is a healer
though her own sickness is one that she cannot cure
    they will be going back there soon and talking to her
asking the questions again and maybe she will have seen
    something more and there are sorcerers here who may
be able to tell us something we want to know
    but remember there was no word for this sickness
in our language before the foreigners came here——
    the Judge fell silent and Ko'olau saw him
staring down through the trees toward the sea and he thought
    it was time to go and he stood up but the Judge said
—I cannot say I cannot say and the older I get
    the less certain I am about how things come to be
and now there is Rowell taken we could never get along
    he was hard in the head and a foreigner in his heart
and I made trouble for him but I am sorry he is gone—

25.

Kaleimanu stayed small and they kept him home at Kekaha
    where Piʻilani taught him to read and write more or less
he wanted to know the exact name of everything
    and then why it was called that and what its story was
he coaxed the stories together believing that they
    would recognize each other and have things to tell each other
and as he walked he repeated the stories to himself
    and confided them to other children Piʻilani
would find him with the others listening to him
    for him all the stories were parts of one tale and he would
follow Kawaluna and Nakaula and all
    the elders of the village holding them in his wide eyes
begging for more stories and asking questions about
    the ones he knew and the people in them he was
little and funny and everyone liked him and he loved
    his girl cousin Ida whose mother Kinolou
was Piʻilani's sister the children were almost
    the same age they were together most of every day
they could recite some of the stories together
    or one would go on from where the other had stopped
when Koʻolau came home early he would lift Kaleimanu
    onto the horse in front of him and ride along the sand
and he told stories of the village and the legends
    so that it sounded as though there was no difference between them
Piʻilani's father Hoʻona spent less time at the church
    after Reverend Rowell died but he still brought back news
from Waimea telling how Mary Rowell now Mary
    Stolz seemed unhappy as everyone agreed and they said
Louis Stolz was high-handed and rude and they all knew
    which Hawaiian houses he visited by the back door

26.

Pi'ilani watched her father when he was with them
   behind his face she could not tell where his mind was
but he had settled into his own custom of passing
   like the tides back and forth between his two houses
and two families and at Kekaha everyone
   was used to it Pi'ilani heard him use one voice
to talk to Kepola and to others in the house
   and a different one to talk to men on the steps
dealing out bits of news from the mill and from Waimea
   one by one like a game played with Ko'olau's father
and Ko'olau and sometimes Nakaula and Kua
   who told what they had heard at Hofgaard's store and Makaweli
in those days they were talking about King Kalākaua
   how much money he was said to be losing and how angry
the foreigners were because of it and Ko'olau told them
   of the Judge saying for years that this king would ruin them
and that David Kalākaua was not the rightful king
   in the first place but it was one more bought election
and Queen Emma was the one who should have been on the throne
   he said that Kalākaua would run them into debt
until the foreigners had all the excuses they wanted
   he said Knudsen was guarded in his words but it was known
that he had no faith in Kalākaua and at Hofgaard's store
   they talked about Rice and Isenberg from Kauai
and the younger Mr Dole working against the king
   they called themselves The Hawaiian League with their own
militia The Hawaiian Rifles but they were
   all foreigners or the children of foreigners
and Pi'ilani listened to the talk eddying
   around the king with bits of rumor circling in it
his gambling his drinking but his faults as they talked
   seemed small beside the fact that he was their own king
and they would rather have him than be ruled by foreigners

27.

—A new day is upon us—the Judge said to Koʻolau
  —Louis Stolz has become a notary public
I suppose it is a kind of distinction for him
  and I am sure he intends to turn it to account—
they had met on the street in Waimea and Koʻolau
  noticed that the Judge was walking now with a cane
and had grown ponderous and sounded as though he were tired
  and the next time he saw him the Judge said—Now Mr Stolz
so I am told has had a suit brought against him
  for falsifying land records and I hear that Holi
is going to sue him for adultery with his wife
  or keeps threatening to do it—and as the Judge went along
Koʻolau was troubled to see that it was hard for him
  to walk and then one day that winter in Waimea
his father rode up to him and said there had been
  an argument at Hofgaard's store and the Judge had told
Louis Stolz that he had sworn falsely upon oath
  and Stolz had struck the older man and shouted at him
to keep his mouth shut and had knocked him down bleeding
  and when the Judge tried to stand he hit him again
and a woman had called out —Louis is trying to kill
  Judge Kauai—and they finally dragged Louis away
and now the Judge had brought a complaint and Koʻolau
  rode down to the Judge's house and saw the bandage
above his eye and heard the story in detail
  and the date of the hearing before the present Judge Hardy
and when the case had been tried he learned from Judge Kauai
  the program of that day in court witness by witness
foreigners and Hawaiians and how Judge Hardy had found
  Stolz guilty of assault as charged and had fined him
but Judge Kauai said—Dignity is not so easy to restore—

28.

The Knudsens had gone up to Halemanu for the summer
    Valdemar's beard entirely white by then and the children
growing tall he rode out less often into the forest
    with Koʻolau and Kua and the others when they
were all up there together and Koʻolau and Kua
    were out by themselves again and again that summer
tracking wild cattle which were harder to find each year
    as they traced the paths over the mountain skirting
the Alakai swamp and climbed to the sharp ridges and down into
    the steep green clefts where water was running on the rock walls
through curtains of fern within arm's reach as the horses
    slid down the muddy trails written over with the split prints
of cattle washed dim rewritten gone and the tracks switched back
    and clung to steep ravine sides coming out at the edges
of canyons with white wings circling a vast distance below them
    drifting across blue shadows and the far red rock face grooved
stained split with age where the white threads of waterfalls
    hung swaying in the silent sunlight then one day above
Kalalau they came to where a young man was watching them
    from under the trees but he came out when they called him
and told them that he was Iwa and that he had come up
    out of Kalalau down there where he was living
and they told him who they were and asked about the valley
    the families they knew there and Iwa asked them
how long it had been since they had been down there and they
    did not answer at first but looked at each other and then Kua
said—I have heard of the new people who have gone to live
    in these valleys—and Iwa looked down at his feet and said
—My father's brother Nihoa came home and they had taken away
    his wife for being a leper and had left the two babies
just screaming and they took away my friend Kuhi
    off the cane wagon he never came home we heard how they
went and got him and now some of us live down there
    where we hope it would be harder for them to find us—
—Did you come up looking for something to eat—Kua asked him
    nodding toward the gun in the shadow of a tree
and Iwa said smiling—Maybe a goat or something—

29.

As they were riding back down to Halemanu
    Kua said—Knudsen has known about them for a long time
longer than I thought he may have known they were there almost
    from the beginning hearing from friends out by Hanalei
or people at Haena and Wainiha they all knew
    and the canoes that go around Māna and bring
word back to the ranch at Waiawa whenever Knudsen
    asks me about them I can see how much he knows
he wants them to be let alone there he told me and he said
    he saw it all happen in Norway when he was a boy
he does not want the rats from the Board of Health prowling
    out at the ranch or coming up here he was talking
about the three of us going down into the valley
    to find out what he could do for them maybe later
in the summer when it dries out some more we could
    go down the way we used to when he was looking
for birds on the cliffs I think he is as strong as ever
    only more quiet—and Koʻolau watched Knudsen
those next days with Kua's words in mind and he watched him
    on the day when Knudsen left his family there
with Makaʻi and the others and he and Kua
    and Koʻolau rode down to Makaweli and on the way
Knudsen said he was anxious to hear what was happening
    over in Honolulu he told them he had been hearing
rumors of coming change there and as they were riding
    beside the house it was silent without the family
hens out in the back field the voices of doves in the trees
    Meʻeawe came around the corner and stopped in surprise
and stood stiff as though he had been caught at something
    he stood still until they were close to him—What has happened—
Knudsen asked him—What is it—Knudsen repeated
    —It is the King—Meʻeawe said—It is about the King—
Kila brought the mail for you it is in the house there—
    and Knudsen thanked them all and went in by himself

30.

—Now they have him tied down hand and foot—the Judge said
    —it is what they have been wanting to do from the start
he will not be able to waste money now or command
    any troops at all the foreigners will do the voting
they will let him sit there on the throne in his uniform
    and will tell him how lucky he is not to be in jail
because of this money or that money while they let
    the Americans take Pearl Harbor for their warships
in exchange for making the sugar planters rich
    and we will see what it all means to the likes of us
we will still be their problem their embarrassment
    on the one hand the King and on the other the lepers
and the same voices that profess to be horrified
    at any resistance to authority are the ones
that are shouting to be rid of the King and the last
    remnants of rule by Hawaiians in Hawai'i
they believe we are here for the profit of foreigners
    I hear my neighbor Stolz was there at the legislature—
and Ko'olau saw the sweat trembling on the Judge's cheeks
    heard the shortness of breath felt the waves of anger like heat
from the baking pit—What will they take from us next—
    the Judge said—The last of the dirt under the houses
or whatever we still think is ours you can be sure
    they will clean out the lepers now once and for all
they have a thousand lepers over in the settlement
    but that number will multiply and no more of these
lepers kept hidden by the rest of the family
    those will be dug out one by one and there may be others
up there in the windward valleys before long—and Ko'olau
    saw his hand fall in despair onto the table
and it seemed to him that he rode home through a shadow
    Ho'ona was there in Kekaha and Kepola
and her parents came over and that evening they all sat
    talking and trying to understand what had happened

31.

Piʻilani woke in the dark and lay listening
      Koʻolau was sleeping Kaleimanu was sleeping
she got up and went out the door touching nothing
      knowing the feel of each board underfoot she slipped the latch
without a sound and stepped onto the lanai smelling
      the air above the sea before morning and there beside
the post at the top of the steps was a dark form
      and she stopped breathing it did not move and she saw
it was Kawaluna sitting there and an arm stirred
      a hand came out onto the step beside her and turned
upward in welcome and Piʻilani sat down next to her
      and they stayed there without a word looking toward the sea
Kawaluna put her arm around Piʻilani
      and after a while Piʻilani leaned her head
on Kawaluna's shoulder and they sat hearing the whisper
      of the small waves finishing along the sand as the first light
of the ghost dawn began to seep into the darkness
      and Piʻilani saw a wave beginning to
lift and move in toward them on the flat sea it rose
      higher with the face of it dark and beyond it
in the dim light was Kekaha out there and the whole coast
      that had been her world since she had been born the wave kept rising
until she could not see over it and it had cut off
      everything she knew it kept growing as it came closer
until she thought it was going to break over them
      there it stopped and stayed where it was and blacked out half
the sky darker than a night without stars and she stared at it
      but there was nothing to see she opened her eyes and the light
before daybreak was spread on the calm sea all the way
      to the horizon there was not a wave nor a cloud
she felt Kawaluna's arm around her and it was the next
      of the days in which they were learning how little
they knew about how their lives were being directed
      from somewhere out of sight and by decisions they never heard made
then from the capital came word of a rebellion

32.

Ho‘ona came back from the mill in the morning
    to tell them what he had heard and Ko‘olau and the two
Kaleimanus his father and his son were down
    at the canoes with the fish that they were bringing in
the news had come from Koloa when the Pele
    docked at daybreak but it was a tattered story
and what seemed to have happened was that somebody
    in Honolulu by the name of Wilcox who was part
Hawaiian had marched to the palace wearing a red shirt
    he had his own army behind him some of them Hawaiians
or part Hawaiians all wearing red shirts and armed
    they had their own constitution for the King to sign
instead of the one that the foreigners had forced
    upon him and this one would take back the power
from the foreigners and return it to the Hawaiians
    and would let them decide whether Kalakaua or his sister
Liliuokalani would sit on the throne but the King
    was not at home and the government troops in support
of the foreigners had killed no one knew how many
    of the red shirts and driven them out of the palace grounds
then it was all over and the foreigners were still
    in control of the government and the King had done nothing
and could do nothing and through that day and the days
    that followed as they talked about it there were foreigners
in Hofgaard's store who laughed at this Wilcox or growled that he
    deserved to be hung and there were Hawaiians at
the mills and the ranches who said less and who sensed that
    one more wisp of hope had just blown away from them
before they knew it existed and there were other Hawaiians
    who said it was shameful to show so little respect
for those in authority and it brought shame on all of them
    and the Judge told Ko‘olau that he supposed Wilcox
had his head in some cloud and never knew what he was doing
    but he said he wished he had been in the legislature
to hear the big Hawaiian Bipikane roaring like a bull
    shouting that he would gore them all until they charged him
with contempt and threw him out—he was a clown—the Judge said
    —but there are times when that is the best you can hope for—

33.

When Koʻolau told his family in Kekaha
    about the encounter with Iwa on the cliff top
and about the lepers hiding in Kalalau Valley
    and when they had asked him question after question
and had fallen silent it was Kawaluna
    who began to ask her own questions as though her voice
were coming from somewhere else so they could hardly hear her
    she asked when he had first gone into that valley
what path he had entered by and where he had gone the first time
    which stream he had followed who had been with him and what
he had seen then who had spoken to him and what they had said
    what sounds he had heard in the valley that time that were
still clear to him so that if he shut his eyes now
    and heard them he would know them and he answered her
as well as he could Piʻilani had crouched to listen
    they were all listening and Kawaluna asked how often
he had gone there how well he knew the valley and when
    he had been there last and he told her everything
as well as he could remember and then he asked her
    whether she had ever been there but instead of answering
she sat looking straight at him and said nothing at all
    then in the morning at Waiawa Knudsen and Kua
were talking and Knudsen waved and called him over
    and asked them both about Iwa and what they knew
about the people hiding in Kalalau and told them
    that they had written asking him to request the Board of Health
to allow them to remain where they were and they wanted
    him to be their doctor and he had written to the Board
and they had said that in view of the isolation
    and inaccessible situation of that place
they would consent but they warned that this exemption
    was temporary and that their intention was still
to remove those fugitives on some future occasion
    when weather and other circumstances favored it

34.

—It did not mean much—Valdemar Knudsen said to them
      —the Board of Health is not making any real promises
and as for my being able to provide those souls
      with medical attention that suggestion may be
there in the hope of quieting the official
      contention that the lepers must be rounded up
to be given proper treatment for their condition
      and of course with only two doctors on the island
neither of whom approves of allowing victims
      of leprosy to remain at large and neither of whom
could include the fastnesses of Kalalau within
      his practice there could be no pretense of medical care
for those who have chosen that place as a refuge
      but on the other hand all of the treatment we have now
in the hospitals is inadequate at best
      there is nothing that could be called a cure and the means
of delay sometimes seem more cruel than the sickness
      except for whatever hope they permit but these people
who have chosen to manage without any of that
      should know that my medical qualifications are too
limited to deserve the name and that I could not promise
      regular visits into the clefts of Kalalau
how many years has it been since the last trip we made there
      but I will spend as much time as I can at Halemanu
where they can reach me and I will send them medicines
      and perhaps for some emergencies I might be able
to go into the valley but no one must count on that
      I understand that most of the time there is one of them
somewhere along the edge of the cliff above Koke‘e
      would you be so good as to tell him what I have said—

35.

Ho'ona arrived in Kekaha one day with news
    he had brought from Waimea while Ko'olau was away
at the ranch and they all saw that Ho'ona was burning
    to tell them something but he was having trouble
saying it right out and he knew he would have to repeat it
    when Ko'olau came home Kepola was beginning
to find it funny before she even heard it
    and he saw the way she and Kawaluna and Pi'ilani
were looking at each other and he said—You remember
    what they have been saying about Holi's wife——You tell us—
Kepola said—But you know it—Ho'ona said—
    Everybody has known it now for a long time—
—What do you know—Kepola asked—And how do we know we know
    if you will not tell us what it is—and Ho'ona who was
the only one in the family who wore shoes every day
    and who had not yet taken them off when he got home
shuffled his feet and then unlaced his shoes and set them
    up on the lanai beam out of reach of the dogs
and stood looking at his feet—I never met Holi's wife—
    Kepola said—Does she have a name of her own—
—Holi has brought suit—Ho'ona said—against Mr Stolz—
    —I remember Mr Stolz—Pi'ilani said
—He was standing beside Reverend Rowell's grave
    and I can still see the small top of his head with his hat off
and that thin woman next to him in church——Holi has charged him—
    Ho'ona said—with what is termed Mischievous Sleeping—
—Mischievous Sleeping—Kepola said—Now what is that—
    —You know what it is—Ho'ona said—I am not sure
I do—Kepola said—You will have to explain—
    —It means adultery—Ho'ona said—With Holi's wife—
—The unnamed one and is that what we know—Kepola asked him—
    Ho'ona said—And it will be tried in the court
and Judge Kauai's son will be one of the witnesses—
    —Mischievous Sleeping—Kepola said—What a shameful thing—

36.

When Koʻolau came home they lost no time telling him
    that Hoʻona knew something and they got everyone
together to hear it and made him say it all over again
    —With a jury too—Koʻolau said—Who is to be
on the jury——They have not been named yet—Hoʻona said
    —But they say six foreigners and six natives—It will be
nothing but shame—Koʻolau said—And maybe they will not
    even find Mr Stolz guilty he is a foreigner
and she is only one Hawaiian woman and married
    to one Hawaiian man and Mr Stolz has made important
friends there is Dr Smith who sent Niuli away
    and then never could say what happened to her and there is
Reverend Dole who surely would not let it be said
    that a friend of his had been doing things of that kind
with some native woman——But everyone knows—Kepola said—
    —And there are witnesses there is young Mr Kauai—
—Wait and see—Koʻolau said and he added—I think
    Judge Kauai will have something to say about it
Holi kept announcing that he was going to do this—
    But it was the summer then and Koʻolau was away
much of the time up at Halemanu or between
    the ranch and Makaweli and once Piʻilani
and their son Kaleimanu whom Koʻolau still carried
    half the time and held on the horse in front of him
went along up to Halemanu and stayed there with him
    for days and Koʻolau and Kua went several times
to meet Iwa at the top of the cliff beyond Kokeʻe
    carrying medicines and they went in with him
and went in by themselves all during that summer
    down the razorback ridges the steep crumbling ledges
along the cliff walls above the bottomless chasms
    through clouds and then up into side clefts in the buttresses
to the caves and grass houses and the lepers and their
    families who were living there with them and they took in
tools for them and clothes and bedding and chalmoogra oil
    for the sickness and it was late in the summer
before Koʻolau rode back to the harbor at Koloa
    and turned aside in Waimea to see the Judge again

37.

—No of course it was nothing like justice—the Judge said
      they were sitting on the lanai looking out through the trees
toward Koloa Road and the Judge's wife Kaenaku
      had come and joined them—And of course I never went
to court—the Judge said—On that day it would not have been
      proper for me to be there for the purpose of watching
my neighbor on trial for furtive activities
      that everyone in the courtroom knew he had committed
and to hear the questions and hear him lie under oath
      to them all as I have heard him do in the past
and all of them listening and knowing that he was lying
      you know one of our sons was the lawyer for the plaintiff
though Holi has no money and another of our sons
      was a witness for the plaintiff but they got former Judge
Hardy a successor of mine and Mr Hofgaard
      who had heard me tell that man to his face that he
had borne false witness and who had seen him try to kill me
      and each of them in turn stood up to profess their esteem
for their fellow foreigner's character and to deplore
      the distress such a case must cause to a decent man
and his wife and that was more or less how the court
      viewed it and encouraged the jury to see it
and nothing different was to be expected I think
      with the present complexion of the government and with
the foreigners in power I wonder how much longer
      they will let us go on pretending to be ruled
by a king from our own people—and Ko'olau was thinking
      how his face had changed in the course of the summer he searched
the shadows under the broad brim and they seemed to be melting
      Kaenaku said to him—You told us you had been
into Kalalau and had seen the people who have gone there
      because of the sickness I would like to know about them—
and Ko'olau looked at her and saw that she meant it
      and he tried to answer her question about them

169

38.

The Judge had been sitting there in that same position
    when Ko'olau walked up the steps that day and he did not move
when Ko'olau got up to leave as Kaenaku's
    questions about Kalalau seemed to be ended
and she was silent and stared off into the leaves
    then she said—My father knew that coast and he left me
the land over there near Wainiha and Hanalei
    I remember him talking of Haena and Kalalau
and Nualolo he called them the owl's valleys
    but I do not know what he had seen there what they did there
or how he went there a whole life ago and the one
    story he told me of that coast was about a ship
the most beautiful ship that anyone ever saw
    it drifted ashore there and ran aground and an old chief
Kiaimakani got the people to make ropes of *hau* bark
    and tie them to the mast and crouch down in silence
while he chanted to Lono and they held their breaths staring
    and he blew the conch shell and then they pulled and the mast
broke and the ship rolled away onto the rocks and sank
    and they stood with the ropes they had made slipping over their feet
out into the waves and that is what my father told me
    I am not sure why but perhaps because it always made me
be quiet—and she laughed—But I know you do not go
    along the coast to that valley you go down over the cliff
it is hard to imagine that—and she looked away toward the road
    and the Judge said—It is getting harder for me to walk now
I suppose it is age and my weight there comes a time
    when everyone starts complaining about some part
of the poor body and it is my feet that are failing me
    I mention it only because I can scarcely pretend
it is not so and I see you have a fine pair of feet
    I think they will take you anywhere you have to go
how foolish to come to notice such things out of envy—

39.

The Judge had always liked riding in a carriage
    and they had a small family of carriages
out in the stable one of them dating from the days
    of Kaumuali'i and the sandalwood trees
and all of them too delicate for most of the roads
    most of the time but he and Kaenaku had taken
one or another of them into Waimea
    to church on Sundays or into Hanapepe
or Koloa for celebrations or weddings or funerals
    their carriages were well known along that coast and their
horses and their clothes and the Judge surely had never
    driven barefoot in any of them but he could
no longer get his feet into the tops of his boots
    and at last he stood up without them and waded down the steps
with the cane and heaved himself into the waiting carriage
    beside Kaenaku they were dressed as though they were
going to a birthday party and they rode to Koloa
    and tied up outside Dr Smith's and made their way
to the railing at the foot of the steps and up the steps
    where the door was opened to them by a young Hawaiian girl
who looked at them with surprise that turned into something
    like fright and showed them into the parlor and left them
sitting in the high-backed chairs and the Judge began
    laughing to himself recalling the arguments
in the church more than thirty years earlier and how he had
    cited church law to the foreigners and how the pastor
had nailed the doors shut and all that melodeon business
    and the Doctor always long-faced as the spine of a book
he thought of their muttered civilities all these years
    when they met in some doorway and then the Doctor came in
and greeted them with unsmiling correctness keeping
    his eyes away from the Judge's feet and the Judge said—We have
come for a medical examination so perhaps
    I should come into your office when you are at liberty—
and the Doctor looked at him as though he were an object
    and said—Of course although it may not be necessary—

40.

—It appears to be some kind of dropsy—the Judge said
    as the Doctor showed him into a room heavy with
the smell of disinfectant upon former disinfectant
    with sheets at the windows—Please sit there—the Doctor said
pointing toward the end of a long table I can give you
    an examination in the usual way
listen to your heart sound your lungs and so on if you so desire—
    —It is my feet—the Judge said—But I believe you know—
the Doctor went on—I believe you have known for some time
    what this ailment is and it is common to cling to some
other explanation as long as possible—
    He paused and the Judge said nothing and the Doctor said
—Do I have to tell you——No—the Judge said—You have told me—
    —But you knew—the Doctor said—The Chinese sickness—
the Judge said and the Doctor as though he had not heard
    said—It is still called leprosy but that name may change
since a doctor in Norway a man named Hansen
    has determined the cause of it in a minute form of life
too small to be seen——Has he found the cure—the Judge asked
    —Not yet—the Doctor said—but we can delay the course of it
chalmoogra oil corrective surgery you need them both
    and I am afraid you will have to be sent for treatment
to Kalaupapa I will give you some time of course
    to make preparations——Not everyone goes—the Judge said
—The law requires it—the Doctor said—You are a man
    of law some have to be taken by force——There is
a resistance growing—the Judge said—Armed resistance—
    —That is true—the Doctor said—Police officers have been
threatened and have resigned I think Knudsen has made it
    worse by encouraging that band that has gone into hiding
over in the windward valleys——They have permission
    from the Board of Health I understand—the Judge said—I have
read it—the Doctor said—and it is regrettable
    but temporary—The Judge hauled himself to his feet
—Did you ever learn what happened to that girl from Kekaha
    named Niuli who was sent to Kalihi ten years ago—
—I have no recollection—the Doctor said—I believe
    Pastor Rowell asked you about her——Did he—the Doctor said

41.

As they went out the door the Doctor said—Your wife will be
     able to go with you——But I heard the law was changing
about that—the Judge said—She will go as a patient—
     the Doctor told him—The marks of the sickness are obvious
on her face I will let you tell her in your own time
     if she does not already know—and he escorted them
out to the lanai and when they were in the carriage
     they rode off in silence until they had left Koloa
then he put his hand on her arm and looked at her face and nodded
     and they drove on home where their sons were waiting for them
they all sat around the big table on the lanai
     and the Judge told them what the Doctor had confirmed
and told them which boxes to bring from his office and he
     and Kaenaku signed over to their sons all of
the lands in Kikiaola and in Haena
     and in Hanapepe and Koloa and they drove to town
to register the changes in the courthouse and then
     they began the last days in the house there packing
boxes and bundles going through papers and the messages
     went out to Kekaha and up to Waiawa
and then the morning came when they got up in the dark
     and the lamps were lighted on the tables and the pack horses
were loaded by lantern and Koʻolau rode in
     long before daybreak and three of them helped the Judge
into the saddle and set his feet in the slings
     they had made instead of stirrups and they turned
at the end of the drive and looked back at the house with the lamps
     burning and the figures crying and waving and they
rode out and up the mountain—The house will be ready
     they tell me—Koʻolau said to the Judge and Kaenaku
as they paused after the sun rose and ate and drank
     without dismounting and then they rode on toward Kokeʻe
stopping no more than they had to and arrived late in the day
     where a camp was ready for them and the Judge's family
those who would stay and those who would go in sat up talking
     and slept and at daybreak the men who had come up
out of Kalalau to make the camp helped them to the cliff's edge
     where they said their good-byes and four men from Kalalau
picked up the Judge and started down into the valley

THE VALLEY

1.

The valley is the mountain split open to windward
    to the northwest to the sea to the horizon
where the ancient peaks sailed away sinking before there was
    anyone before the archaic words were first uttered
and from the crags at the head of the valley to the winding
    stream beds and the drapery of forest tumbling into
the braided ravines it is so far down that only
    sections of that carved land can be seen glimpses caught
between drifts of clouds as they travel in to the cliffs
    along the pinnacles and the waved fins of buttresses
and through gaps in the stone facades cloud shadows pass
    across blue slopes all the way below and in the partings
of the clouds waterfalls spring white from distant scars
    high in the rock walls beyond the chasm and the silent plumes
descend slowly through the air of another time until they
    melt into mist but the veins gather somewhere below them
and down toward the rocks along the shoreline stone terraces
    had been stepped some of them raised in the remote past
fanning out from banks of the main stream like bones of a fish
    toward the cliffs and a scattering of thatched houses
was settled among banana trees near the taro ponds
    the roofs of families that had lived there for longer than
the stories told and now their boats waited on the shingle
    their donkeys and goats were tethered near the houses
and up in the head of the valley on the ledges
    in the steep gorges were the caves and shelters of those
who had come in recent years because of the sickness
    and the police raids breaking without warning into
the houses of the poor to hunt for those with the sickness
    up there the fugitives had improved what they called The Big House
when they heard that Judge Kauai was coming to live among them
    it was not as big as Ko'olau's house in Kekaha
but it had two rooms and a good roof and a door
    and a sheltered outhouse tucked back against the cliff
and a stream ran a few steps below the front door

2.

When the word spread from Koloa and from Hofgaard's store
    that Judge Kauai and his wife Kaenaku and others
of their family had gone over into Kalalau
    rather than let themselves be sent to the hospital
at Kalihi in Honolulu and the settlement
    at Kalaupapa everyone had something to say
about the sickness and the manner of dealing with it
    and the constabulary and the tales of those who had
driven them off with guns and the growing bands of
    fugitives in the upper valleys of the islands
the tearing apart of families the persistance
    of the disease the torments of the treatment and the failure
to find a cure the way that leprosy seldom
    attacked the foreigners the fact that it was costing
so much even to try to confine it for treatment
    everyone had something heated to contribute
over and over some exhibit of fear and shame
    Damien had died of leprosy at Kalaupapa
and the photographs of him on his deathbed had been published
    in the American papers as far away as New York
and those of the missionary persuasion were so
    unhappy about the choir of praise carolling after
this Catholic that in Honolulu the Reverend
    Charles McEwen Hyde wrote to a fellow preacher deploring
the extravagant laudations as though this man
    had been a saintly philanthropist when the simple truth
was that he was coarse dirty headstrong and bigoted
    had no hand in the reforms and improvements and was not
a pure man in his relations with women and his
    death resulted from his vice and carelessness and Hyde's friend
arranged for this corrective statement to be published
    in San Francisco and a copy was sent from there
to Robert Louis Stevenson who had stayed at the settlement
    not long after Damien's death and as he taught the patients
croquet he had learned how they remembered this man

3.

In Hawaii on his way to Samoa and the hill
    at Vailima Stevenson had observed for himself
a precarious moment and had made the acquaintance
    of this minister with the echoing name of Hyde
he remembered clearly the comfortable neat pastor
    in his pleasant parlor on Beretania Street
and courtesies for which he could have been grateful
    except this letter of the later Hyde absolved him
as he put it from any bonds of the kind and instead
    he was impelled in the cause of public decency
to right the name of Damien and deal fitly
    with a letter so extraordinary I conceive you he wrote
to the Reverend Doctor Hyde as a man quite below
    the reticences of civility one of those
missionaries who in the course of their evangelical
    calling had grown rich until the cab driver commented
upon the size the taste and comfort of the minister's home
    he thought readers should be aware that the letter maligning
Damien had been penned in a house that could raise
    the envy of passers-by and your sect he wrote
which had enjoyed in Hawai'i an exceptional
    advantage when calamity befell its innocent
parishioners and leprosy took root in the islands
    had been sent an opportunity by God which they
had failed sitting and growing bulky in their charming mansions
    while a plain uncouth peasant stepped into the battle
brought succour to the afflicted consoled the dying
    was afflicted in his turn and died upon the field
of honor and the battle could not then be retrieved
    as the Reverend Hyde's unhappy irritation
suggested but it was lost forever and such rags
    of common honor as remained to him he had made haste
to cast away and Stevenson wrote on concerning
    Damien and cleanliness and life at the settlement
and adversions in the clerical parlor to misconduct
    with women and is it growing at all clear to you
he asked what a picture you have drawn of your own heart
    the man who tried to do what Damien did is my father

4.

His open letter was published on Kauai in
     the newspaper 'Elele The Messenger and its message
ran like the burning of a cane field the heat and smoke
     soon rolling far away from where it had started
there were the missionary offspring for whom the document
     was an outrage rendered particularly shocking
by the author's descent from elders of their own persuasion
     there were the functionaries of the Board of Health
already nervously revising inadequate
     budgets and justifications and they took public
objection to the use of the leprosy question
     as a political lever while at the same time urging
stricter enforcement of the segregation of lepers
     which was adding to the growing civil unrest
and accounts of Kalaupapa re-echoed like choruses
     two small orphan girls from Father Damien's orphanage
at the settlement had been ordered by the Board of Health
     to be sent to Honolulu on the schooner and they
had been met on the causeway after nightfall by native
     police officers who dropped the trunk containing
one girl's belongings into the water and a fight
     broke out between the officers and two patients
who had escorted the girls that far and two officers
     were stabbed and died a third barely survived the patients
were given ten years and then on the island of Hawai'i
     when the police went to arrest a certain Kealoha
assumed to have leprosy he refused to go with them
     and when the police shot him in the leg he returned fire
with a Winchester killing the sheriff and wounding
     one officer who ran away with the others
Kealoha himself died in jail not long afterwards
     the tales summoned others and recommendations
for dealing with the situation multiplied
     in the newspapers in the legislature in statements
issued by the Board of Health and in Hofgaard's store

5.

It depended to some degree on who might be listening
    in the store but there was recurrent low-rumbling
assurance of no-nonsense in the new directors
    of the Board of Health and persistent speculation
as to whether the disease was not in fact a form
    of syphilis and so a visitation of the wrath
of a too-patient God upon the natives a sentence
    which they had brought upon themselves with the abominations
of their behavior their dirty sensual ways
    their touching and their sharing of food as they licked it
from their fingers and all their doings from their infancy
    many of the regulars at the store could remember
the papers raging after Little Big Horn most of them
    had stood there discussing the hunt for Geronimo
they had shaken their heads over what they understood
    of the Ghost Dance and had agreed that Sitting Bull
deserved what he got and they had hoped that Wounded Knee
    had driven home the lesson at last they supported
their men from Kauai Rice and Isenberg over
    in the legislature in Honolulu and they approved
of the new constitution rendering the King helpless
    and depriving most natives of the vote and they sympathized
with American expansion in the Pacific
    spoke of annexation as the way of progress
but meanwhile there was this unpleasant situation
    that would not go away and a crumbling government
a constabulary unequal to its duties
    one day in Kekaha Pi'ilani heard the dogs
sounding serious in front of the house and she stepped out
    and saw the tall man whose long face she remembered
from beside the open grave of Pastor Rowell he was
    sitting his horse looking down at the dogs in front of him
and she could see what he thought of them but when he looked up
    he smiled without raising his hat and he called out
—Is this the house of Ko'olau—and she nodded
    —I wanted to have a talk with him—Louis Stolz told her
—I will tell him when he comes home what is your name—
    —Tell him Louis Stolz thank you—he said—I may find him
myself—and he rode off with the dogs barking after him

6.

As she turned in the doorway she saw Kawaluna
     watching her from the steps of Koʻolau's parents' house
she felt a chill along her arms and she went to talk
     with Kawaluna but kept watching that man's back
and the older woman said nothing but stood looking after him
     by the time Koʻolau came home it was almost sundown
and she told him about the visit and he said—Yes he came
     to the ranch looking for me and father and I were there
with the new horses I met this man years ago
     in his fine boots and all he could look at was my bare feet
I think I know what he wants but he told me he had heard
     that I was good at making saddles he told me
there were those in whose opinion I was the best but I said
     Kua was the best and he should go talk to Kua
he said he had heard about Kua and he might just do that
     but that he wanted to talk to me first he had heard a good deal
about me he said and that was true I heard Pastor Rowell
     speak to him about me and I know things Mr Knudsen
has said but this Stolz never paid attention before
     all that time and now he wants to get me to make
a saddle for him he says of my best work I told him
     that was the only kind of work I did he said this
saddle was a matter of importance to him
     to mark his new duties as Deputy Sheriff
looking at me as though he had caught one big fish
     and this saddle he said was to be made like one
that some officer in the American cavalry had
     I said I could only make saddles of the kind
we use here and then he said I can show you a drawing
     I said no this is the kind I make the kind I am riding
he said with that strange way he bites the words I understand
     that it will cost more if it is made to a design
that is unfamiliar here but that will present no problem
     and I sat there making no promises watching
Mr Knudsen's horses the young ones and waiting for him to go
     and he said you can look at the drawing and think about it—

7.

Up beyond Halemanu riding the mountain with Kua
        that summer there were turns on the trail where Koʻolau
could see all the times he had passed there every step that he
        had ridden among those trees along those rocks through that light
they floated in front of him and then in a moment
        they had moved on and it was a day like any other
they were getting meat for the people at Halemanu
        for Mrs Knudsen and the children and the guests who would
be coming up from Makaweli with Valdemar Knudsen
        and they rode up along the cliff edge at Kokeʻe
looking for someone from Kalalau with news of the Judge
        they had been talking about Stolz and that visit of his
to Waiawa to find Koʻolau and of what he had said
        about a saddle and his being Deputy Sheriff now
and what that was really about and Kua said
        nothing on the subject for most of the day and they
met not Iwa this time but Puhipaka under the trees
        above the rocks where the Piliwale sisters
were turned to stone and Koʻolau gave him newspapers
        for the Judge and his family and Puhipaka
said they were all right it was a good house and the people
        took care of them and went to see them and sat talking
they had enough to eat and the Judge had those books he read
        but his feet were getting worse there were others down there
like that—With me—Puhipaka said—it is my face
        but you can see that—and when they had left him Kua said
—I think Mr Stolz wants a saddle that he can say
        you made for him a saddle like nobody else's
because I think he wants to make use of you in some way
        in this new position of his and it has to do
with how close you are to the Judge and to the others
        in Kalalau—and Koʻolau nodded—That is
what I thought too—he said and Kua said—One of the guests
        who is coming up with Mr Knudsen is Dr
Campbell who says that the people in Kalalau
        should be let alone and he is a government doctor
but others never thought that way and Stolz is one of those—

8.

—It is better if they go out in the evening—
    Kawaluna said to Pi'ilani as they stood watching
the two Kaleimanus the child and his grandfather
    taking their canoe down the sand to go fishing
—For that child the sea is good but the midday sun is not—
    Kawaluna said—I know—Pi'ilani said
—I see how his eyes look in the sunlight—Kawaluna said
    —and the brightness hurts them——And he loves to go fishing
with his grandfather—Pi'ilani said—but I know
    it is true about the brightness though when it is night
I lie awake until they are back——Next week the moon
    will be right on the third night and we will all take the net out
and nobody will sleep—Kawaluna said and they laughed
    seeing the canoe reflected on the calm sea as the light
widened between them and they sat on the steps while the stilts
    waded along the water's edge lifting in flight
a little way with the white flashing as the wings rose
    then gliding back down onto their feet to run and stand
vanishing into their shadows and then appearing again
    It was after the night when they all took the net out
with Kawaluna herself directing the fishing
    a night when the net came in heavy with fish and they
ate fish on the beach before the sun was up and then began
    to clean and salt some and dry some and in the afternoon
they slept and the next day Ko'olau went back to Waiawa
    and the young horses and again Mr Stolz turned up
and sat watching him work with them and when Ko'olau
    had stopped for a moment he went over to talk to him
and told him he had brought the drawing for the saddle
    —There is only one kind I can make—Ko'olau told him
—and that is my kind—and Mr Stolz said—I have also heard
    that you are the best pig hunter on this part of the island
I would like a chance to go hunting pig with you—
    —I have not hunted pig for a while now—Ko'olau said
Mr Stolz said—I expect you have not forgotten
    anything could we go the day after tomorrow—
—It would have to be later—Ko'olau said—some time later—
    but before Mr Stolz left he had agreed on a day

184

9.

The dry still days of later summer and the beginning
     of autumn had already gone and the rains were coming in
again along the upper valleys—He thinks I will
     help him talk big about what a pig hunter he is—
Koʻolau said at home at the end of the day
     on the steps of the house looking out past Mānā
to Niʻihau—But maybe we will not see one pig
     in a whole day—he said and he told Piʻilani
what Kua had said and what they both thought Mr Stolz
     had in mind—He wants to get up in the world—Koʻolau said
—and it may be the Judge he is after so he can say
     I am the one who arrested the Judge I brought him in
I cleaned out that place and maybe he thinks I will help him—
     —What makes you think that—Piʻilani asked and he sniffed
—That rope is rotten—he said—I know it—Piʻilani agreed
     —But I wanted to hear what you said—and Koʻolau took
Kaleimanu onto his lap and sat looking out
     to the far island darkening with the sun beyond it
and the red seeping into the light and after a while
     he looked at Piʻilani sewing beside him and he said
—Do you see anything different about my face look at
     both sides—and she looked up at him and looked closely and said
—No there is nothing different about it maybe some little
     red there from the sun you should not spend so much time in the sun
and you should protect yourself better and wear your hat—
     But he said to her—We did not work in the sun today
we have not been much in the sun these last days run your hand
     over my face there do you feel anything—and she said
—No it is smooth do you think you rubbed it too hard
     when you were washing—and he said—I saw it in the mirror
these red places they go away and they come back—
     —Wear your hat—she said—You should have been wearing it
all summer long and now the summer is gone but you
     should be careful wear it when you go out tomorrow—
—We should all be wearing hats—Koʻolau said and they laughed

10.

In the early morning before he left when they were alone
    in the house she felt how silent he was and she said
—You will be up in the forest today and the sun
    will not be so hot and the winter is almost here
but try to be careful—and he said—What if it is not
    the sun—and she put her hand on his arm and said
—We will watch it and we will hope and you know you are strong—
    He put his arm around her and drew her against him
and said—I did not want to talk any more about it
    last night with our Kaleimanu there but I have seen
red patches like that on him too on his legs and his chest
    then I did not see them and then I saw them again—
—Yes—Pi'ilani said—I have seen them and I know
    that Kawaluna has seen them too but she talked about
his eyes and the sun hurting his eyes and keeping him
    out of the sun and maybe it is only the sun
how dry and hot it has been these last months I cannot
    remember such a hot summer—Ko'olau stood looking away
—What stays with me—he said—is that I think I remember
    red places like that on Niuli on her arms
and on her neck that patch that Kukui pointed to
    as an old birth mark that had come back do you remember—
—They never told us about those—Pi'ilani said
    —They never told us anything they simply took her—
—They never told us anything—Ko'olau said
    —but we know more now although not about Niuli—
and they stood together in their house without a word
    with their arms around each other and then she reached up
to the rack by the door and took his hat and put it on him
    with the cord under his chin and handed him the gun
from behind the door and he laughed and swung a belt
    with a few cartridges over his shoulder and picked up
a saddle bag and then turned and embraced her again
    and stepped out the door—A fine day for it—she said

11.

She stood watching as he saddled his horse and she saw
    Mr Stolz come riding between the houses and he
called out—Good morning—to Koʻolau and looked around and saw her
    and this time he raised his hat—Good morning—he said again
—I thought I would save us some time and ride out here early
    to meet you—and Koʻolau said—I am ready—and mounted
Mr Stolz waved to her and she nodded and they rode off
    she knew it would be late when Koʻolau got back that night
and the lamps had long been out in the houses she could see
    when he rode in on the tired horse and she thought how he
never seemed tired himself but this time he looked tired
    as he took off the saddle and led the horse to the paddock
and came and put his arms around her and stood still
    then he went and washed and sat down at the table
where the lamp was burning—Today no pig—he said
    with a laugh—Lucky the pigs safe tonight—he sat looking at her
with his hat still on and she brought fish and poi over
    to the table and bananas and he caught her hand
as she was passing—Where did you go—she asked him
    —I took him up Kaʻawaloa all morning
not many pigs there you know but I heard one and told him
    One pig there and he spent some time trying to find it
then we came back down and up Niu a way toward
    Puʻu Opae I showed him tracks and we followed them
but we never saw anything—Koʻolau stopped talking
    and she asked—And was that all—and he said—As far as pigs go
But after a while he started to ask me about
    the Judge and others in Kalalau little rain questions
little by little you know and I had nothing to tell him
    then he comes out and tells me it is a bad situation—
—Is it—I asked him he said—Yes and it cannot go on
    it is unclean—he told me—and against the law—and I said
that I understood that the Board of Health had given
    permission for those people to stay where they were—
Where did you hear that—he said—I work for Mr Knudsen
    I told him—And I work for the Board of Health now—
he told me—as a special agent—and so I said nothing
    and at the end he said that I appeared to be sunburned
but that he thought I should show it to a doctor

12.

—If he comes out here again—Koʻolau said to her
      —try to keep him from seeing Kaleimanu—and she said
—He is over at my aunt's most of the time these days
      playing with Ida they spend the whole day together—
—But you saw the way that man comes shadowing around
      looking at everything——Yes I saw that—she told him
—And that low voice of his if he talks to me I will make sure
      that people hear us and what we are talking about—
But for some time nobody came out that way except
      those who lived there Hoʻona came from the mill
and said he had heard that Mr Stolz had been out
      hunting pig with Koʻolau and Piʻilani said nothing
then one day when Koʻolau was at home a man they knew
      named Pokipala whom Kua had known for years
and who was working for the government one of those
      they called rats who slipped around behind the houses
looking to see whether someone was living back there
      trying to hide came riding along with his head up
out in the open and up to Koʻolau and showed him
      a paper he had that was an order to go with him
to the doctor to be examined because someone
      who had seen him suspected that he had leprosy
—The sickness—Koʻolau said—that separates people—
      and he said—You stay there—and went to his horse and Piʻilani
caught his arm at the corner of the house—Whatever
      they tell you—she said quickly—I want to stay together
if you have to go away I want us all to go—
      then his father Kaleimanu came and asked where he was going
and when he told him his father said—I will come with you—
      and as they rode off Koʻolau asked Pokipala
—Who was it who said they thought I might have that sickness—
      —I am not supposed to tell you—Pokipala answered
and Koʻolau said—I know who it was he says he works
      for the Board of Health——And he does—Pokipala said
—It was Mr Stolz—Koʻolau said—is he afraid that
      people will know——He is not afraid—Pokipala said
Then Koʻolau said—You do not have to ride along with us
      we know the way——It is my duty—Pokipala said
and they rode on to Dr Campbell's office in Waimea

13.

At night on the schooner coming back from Honolulu
    Valdemar Knudsen sat out on the deck for a while
in a sheltered corner against a bulkhead with a blanket
    and a piece of sailcloth over him and watched the masts
waving across the dark clouds and the stars behind them
    and as the wind crossed his face it seemed that he had never
ceased to be the child bundled up in his wooden carriage
    with the blanket tucked under his chin and he could feel
somewhere near him out of sight warm figures who loved him
    then he remembered that they had been dead for years
in Norway far back in the frozen ground which he did not
    think ever to see again and there was his beard lying white
on the shadowy sailcloth and he felt alone and felt age
    rushing across dark water and he growled a few bars
of a hymn low to himself and then a phrase of Norwegian
    from a hymn he had sung as a child recalled to him
a moment from the book he had been reading on this trip
    on which he had come alone this time it was a new
edition of Ibsen and he had been reading *Ghosts*
    again and pondering these incurable afflictions
and the judgments that echoed from the mouths of the spared
    Reverend Dole preaching to the natives about the Lord's
vengeance upon their sins and his son Sanford Ballard's wife
    Anna never touching a doorknob in her own house
without covering it with a handkerchief for fear
    that a native might have touched it before her and he thought
what I feel is not age yet for I am as strong as ever
    but in him was a new distance an alien floating sadness
and he went over to Honolulu much less often these days
    than in the years when he had sat in the legislature
and when he and his own Anna had gone there together
    and each time had felt young again but he had taken this trip
to try to arrange some improvement however
    tenuous some more practical and kinder way
of providing for those found to have leprosy
    because at present he saw nothing but useless cruelty
but he was coming back reaching for hope in the empty dark

14.

He had managed to obtain one tentative permit
    to take care of those on Kauai whom the doctors there
were convinced had leprosy and already he was providing
    care for them at Kekaha while those who had gone
across into Kalalau to whom he had been sending
    such medicines as existed had signed petitions
asking for his treatment to be made official and their
    refuge sanctioned by the government but the Board
kept sending him letters urging the segregation
    of lepers and insisting upon their removal
from contact with their families then a notice arrived
    stating that unless doctors pronounced those in his care
cured in a matter of months they would have to be sent
    to Honolulu and Moloka'i and now Sheriff Wilcox
on Kauai was resorting to increasingly rougher
    tactics surprising native houses searching and seizing
everyone even suspected of harboring
    the disease and the cases of violence the shootings
and rumors of shootings multiplied and that summer
    the Board had informed Knudsen that he would be allowed
to keep his patients at Kekaha only for three more months
    and in Honolulu he had learned that his friend George Trousseau
whom he considered much the finest of the doctors there
    best informed and most clear and gifted was on the point
of resigning from the board of examiners because
    his own findings and the conclusions of the latest
Indian Leprosy Commission had left him convinced
    that the policy of enforced segregation
had always been useless and impossible and that there were
    more effective and humane ways of dealing with this disease

15.

But then there was that colleague of Trousseau's Moritz
    one of the predominant medical authorities
at the leprosy settlement of Kalaupapa
    who made it obvious that he alone understood
this disease in its sources and shifts both pathological
    and racial and who would discourse exhaustively
on the unclean eating habits of the Hawaiians
    and in his view the segregating of those with leprosy
was an unquestionable necessity and his voice climbed
    as he described the improvements that had been effected
at Kalaupapa the facilities the expenditures
    the misconceptions while at the Board of Health
under its new director Knudsen heard heavy rumblings
    about a policy of no nonsense and of smoking this
thing out at last and he might as well know that Sheriff Wilcox
    was disgusted at what he called the incompetence
and cowardice of most of his native constables
    who he said frequently let people know in advance
when they were coming and were easily frightened off
    and that the Sheriff's grumblings had been echoed respectfully
in letters and then a visit from Louis Stolz
    who now had the confidence of the Board where a friend could
quote his letters of application for the post of deputy
    not for the sake of the office as there is neither
money nor glory in it for me but I would like
    underlined to see the laws a little better
enforced in this district than they are at present
    and believe I can say without boasting that I can do
better than the present incumbent and they had given him
    special authority for dealing with the lepers
on Kauai those now cared for at Kekaha those still at large
    and the fugitives at Kalalau whom the Board
fully intended to clear out by force if need be
    as soon as a vessel was available and the weather
allowed a landing for the waves there along that coast
    would make it dangerous to anchor and go ashore
during the winter months and in the meantime the plan
    was to remain a secret for obvious reasons

16.

The night wind was rising and the sea was growing rough
    he went below feeling stiff and damp and his sleep was shallow
he kept running over it all sensing the fabric
    of what he had known and been sure of dissolving
under him and sliding out like a tide to the sound
    of the creaking of the vessel that was taking him home
then it was the morning and they were coming to anchor
    off Koloa and then the whaleboat reached the ramp once more
and he saw it all as though it were under water
    and as he stepped onto the wharf he heard his name called
a voice like an unwanted touch and he looked around
    and saw it was Stolz himself with that smile and his arm raised
he was pushing through the others toward the ramp and there he stood
    the extended hand the pleased face the opportune greeting
there was something they were to deliver to him here
    this morning he said but what a pleasant surprise
and so on into questions which Knudsen found himself
    diverting and he managed to divulge nothing at all
about the trip except the weather on the way back
    and then Stolz told him of the special authority
granted him by the Board of Health which Knudsen said
    he had known about—and in that connection—Stolz said
—Dr Campbell informs me that your employee from out past
    Kekaha there you know that Koʻolau has been examined
and found to have leprosy and I am afraid I will
    have to send him to the settlement—Knudsen looked at him
and watched the moustache and Stolz said—I have been thinking
    of urging you to use the influence you have
with Judge Kauai and those lepers now evading
    the law over in Kalalau and perhaps between us
we could resolve this disgraceful situation
    in a civilized manner——This is scarcely the place
nor the moment to talk about it—Knudsen told him
    and he turned to his son Eric and the Hawaiians
from Makaweli who had come down to meet him
    —I may call on you then—Stolz said and Knudsen nodded

17.

Anne had come down from Halemanu and the children
    were away at school and she and Knudsen lay talking
in the big bed at Makaweli and when he had told her
    what there was to tell they were both silent for a while
then she said she wondered what would become of Koʻolau's
    family they had that little boy and she asked whether
they would go away to the settlement with Koʻolau
    and Knudsen said he did not think so but she said
—But you remember there were some who were allowed to have
    their wives or husbands go with them if they wanted to
as helpers—and Knudsen said—The Board has not been
    consistent about that and recently they are set
against it in general and of course they will not
    admit children there unless they have the disease—
Anne said—I keep seeing them when they were younger and how
    beautiful Piʻilani was do you remember
when was that day when she was wearing the head lei and standing
    in her white dress outside the church in the sunlight
I seem to have forgotten all but the happiness
    and how she looked with that stillness she has—and Knudsen
said—Yes—and kept trying not to let his mind go on
    turning back to Stolz he did not want to mention the man
and he said nothing until at last she said it for him
    with a kind of laugh—You never did like him did you
from the beginning that Louis Stolz—and he said—I did not—
    and took her hand and said—I never could abide him
not when he came here to see Mary Rowell when she was
    taking care of the children and not when he married her
not when he went on toying with Hawaiian women
    threatening them if they ever told I could not bear his wiles
and his overweening and he makes me ashamed of myself
    because I think I disliked him before I even knew him—

18.

A man came to Makaweli one morning with a note
       for Knudsen from Dr Campbell and the next morning
the doctor himself came and asked to see Knudsen alone
       He said—I wanted to tell you that I have been informed
by the President of the Board of Health that he is
       proposing to come over here shortly perhaps next week
to go out to Kekaha with Dr Smith and I believe
       Dr Emerson and me to examine the leprosy patients
now in your care would you prefer to be present
       at the time of the visit——I would not—Knudsen told him
—and I would not want those helpless people to suppose
       that I was one of your party and I shall make it
clear to them that your visit has nothing to do with me—
       —In that case my calling upon you this morning
may be an embarrassment—Dr Campbell said—I thank you
       for your courteous intent—Knudsen said—And I respect your own
difficulties—Campbell looked at the floor for a moment
       and then at Knudsen—You are a man of science—he said
—And I have admired you for years and hope that you will
       understand me when I tell you that not all members
of the medical profession entertain the same views
       of the present methods of dealing with leprosy cases
and the policy of segregation and removal
       for treatment away from their families——Yes I know that—
Knudsen told him—And I believe you delayed having
       Pake and Keola sent over from Kekaha
to Honolulu after their diagnosis
       some months ago I sympathize with your position—
Campbell said—I should warn you further that the Board
       plans to elicit the help of one of your wife's
family Mr Gay to persuade the fugitive lepers
       in Kalalau to put themselves in the hands of
the authorities—Knudsen said—I would be rather
       surprised if he did that and still more if they agreed to it—
—It was young Mr Rowell on the Board who suggested it—
       Campbell said—And he proposed taking part in it himself—
—Did he now—Knudsen said—It would be worth watching
       one of the Rowells charm Judge Kauai out of his tree—
and they both laughed at that and bowed and said Good Morning

19.

Knudsen was at the ranch at Waiawa with Kua
      watching the foals running when Louis Stolz rode up
and fingered the brim of his hat and when they had traded
      civilities Knudsen asked Stolz what his errand was
he allowed Stolz to see that his arrival had stalled
      a conversation and he followed the way the man's eyes
slipped over the ranch and over Kua and the men
      working there that morning and Stolz said—I hoped I would find
you here—and there was a pause with the sound of hooves
      drumming through it and then Knudsen said to Kua
—We can go on with this later—and Kua nodded
      and rode off and Knudsen considered moving into the shade
but decided to stay where they were and he sat waiting
      until Stolz said—The President of the Board of Health
has been to the place in Kekaha where you house the lepers
      he took three doctors with him to examine them there—
Knudsen said—I know of the visit—Stolz said—They inform me
      that two of those you have living there are confirmed lepers—
—That conclusion was reached months ago—Knudsen said
      —They have been pronounced incurable—Stolz told him
—And they are to be sent to the settlement——So that they
      can die there—Knudsen answered—I have heard that too—
Stolz said—It is my duty to see that the law
      is carried out——Ah—Knudsen said—your duty—and Stolz went on
—And we have spoken of that other who lives in Kekaha
      your cowhand Koʻolau and I have learned from the Board
that Mr Rowell wants Mr Gay to support him
      in bringing the lepers in Kalalau to their senses
but I think you and I would be more likely to manage that—
      —You mean—Knudsen said—because Judge Kauai was your neighbor—
—Because they trust you—Stolz said—and they trust this Koʻolau
      who could bear a message from you and I could offer him
concessions of some kind perhaps——Do you think so—Knudsen said—
      —What concessions could you offer considering your duty—
—I can talk with him—Stolz said—We hunt pig together—
      Knudsen said—I can see how it might serve your purpose
but I must talk this over with my relative Mr Gay—

20.

On a Sunday in the autumn when the big mill at Kekaha
    was all but silent with the wind echoing in the slatting walls
Ho‘ona was over there part of the day checking
    shipments and storage and talking story with whoever
came along with nothing to do but Pi‘ilani’s
    and Ko‘olau’s families were spending those days
together around the house on the way to Māna
    preparing too much food and talking talking as though
there was not a trouble that they knew of in the world
    Ko‘olau and the elder Kaleimanu his father
and his son Kaleimanu were cleaning and salting fish
    that they had brought in that morning and Ho‘ona walked in
and sat down in the shade looking sick and Pi‘ilani
    asked him what was the matter—That one Pokipala—
—Where is he—Ko‘olau asked and stood up—He is not here—
    Ho‘ona told him—He came to the leper house
I saw his horse there and heard crying and then I saw him
    come out and ride away going toward Waimea
he said he is coming back in two weeks with the wagon
    to take Pake and Keola off to the settlement—
Kukui began to cry and the rest were silent
    —Only those two—Ko‘olau asked—That is what he said to them—
Ho‘ona said and Ko‘olau asked—What about Nalu
    who was taking care of Pake he told me that if she went
he wanted to go with her are they going to take him too—
    —He will not be allowed to go—Ho‘ona said
—And Keola’s sister who he lived with——They will not
    let her go either—Ho‘ona said—And you know
Keola has almost no fingers left to feed himself
    cannot reach his mouth right and then it was Malea
who started to laugh when they were all crying and she said
    We going to make one big dinner once and for all
with our friends and we all get drunk for our own funeral—

21.

—Do you think he will come back here then that Pokipala—

Kukui asked and none of them answered—The doctors
only went to the leper house—Ho'ona said at last

—And so did Pokipala——That was this time—Ko'olau said
—What can they take when they go—Pi'ilani asked Ho'ona

—One box with their things and you know they do not have much
there in that house——More than they let Niuli

take with her—Ko'olau said and the child Kaleimanu
started asking his questions about Niuli again

and about the settlement and then he too gave up
and they ate in silence and when they had said good-night

and gone to bed and the house was still Ko'olau
slipped out and walked down between the canoes to sit

on the sand looking out toward the dark rim of Ni'ihau
and in a while Pi'ilani came and sat there beside him

without a word and they lay back as they had done
years before and for a long time they said nothing

hearing the small waves breaking along the shoreline
Then Ko'olau said—That Keola has lived there a year

more than a year and that Pake was there for that long
they thought they could live like that doing nothing wrong

and their friends could see them they thought they would die there
all that time they thought so and then he just came for them

and he will come again you remember the doctor told me
they would send me away—Pi'ilani said—Yes—in the dark

—And I want us to stay together—she said—But I
do not believe he will let me go with you——If Kaleimanu

did not have the same kind of red places on his skin
I would want you to stay here and be with him—Ko'olau said

—But they will find him too and I do not know where they send
children where did they send Niuli—and Pi'ilani said

again—I want us to stay together—and they sat there
in silence and then Ko'olau said—I will not let them

take me to the settlement and I told Pokipala
that day the doctor examined me that I would go only

if we could all go together after what you said to me
but I do not trust them and I know the time has come

to go away and to go over into Kalalau
and live with our friends there—Then we will go together—

Pi'ilani said—We will be there together—

22.

Hoʻona and Kukui hung ti leaves around the doors
    as the church did at Christmas and Kawaluna watched them
as she helped with the food and Hoʻona said that the neighbors
    were going to the leper house for the good-bye dinner
—We could send them food—Kukui said and they packed up
    baskets of things to eat and to take to the leper house
and Hoʻona and Piʻilani and Koʻolau's father
    carried them and Hoʻona took an old cloth runner
the women at the Waimea church had sewn years before
    which Reverend Rowell had given him one day saying
it was too faded to put up again and he wondered
    whether Hoʻona might like it the pale words read Peace
On Earth Good Will To Men Hoʻona took it
    to the leper house and they hung it up though few of them
could read it and by that time they were afloat in cane liquor
    and ʻawa It was the next day when the eating and drinking
and the visits were over that Kawaluna was sitting
    on the front step as the sun went down and only family
still there and Koʻolau went to Kawaluna
    and sat at her feet and leaned his head on her knee
and she laid her hand on his hair and then he said to her
    —I will not let them take me to the settlement—
and when he looked up at her she nodded without answering
    —I am going over into Kalalau—he told her
—Yes—she said—Koʻolau—and then she said his name again
    —Koʻolau—so that they heard it mean the windward cliffs
and the time of trouble that name that she had known was his
    before he was born the others were all listening to them
as he said—Piʻilani is coming with me and we will
    take Kaleimanu with us——Yes—Kawaluna said
and Piʻilani's mother Kepola said—I could come
    if you want me with you——Yes—Piʻilani said
and Kepola's sister Kinolou was there with them
    and Kinolou's little girl Ida who had grown up with
Kaleimanu and Ida said—I want to go with
    Kaleimanu——Oh no—Kinolou said but Kepola told her
—I can take care of her if she comes—and as they began
    to cry Koʻolau stood up and said to Kawaluna
—When you decide what night would be good for us to go
    I will tell Kua and we will get the horses for it—

198

23.

That first time that she had climbed down the steep crumbling
    narrow path along the top of the ridge that flared out
into the clouds over the valley when she looked back on it
    afterwards the way came and went in the braid of
later times when she had travelled down that trail something
    of each emerging just as the trail would appear
where the clouds parted and then they would cover it again
    There would be nothing below her and small echoes drifting up
through deaf cloud and always it was hard to balance and always
    she was carrying something although that first time
when the horses were unloaded they had hidden
    some of the bundles and the rolled blankets back under
the bushes for someone to come up and get them later
    She remembered the rain the first time it caught them
with the wind whipping it cold against them and pushing them
    toward the cliff but then she thought how the rain had found her
somewhere on that trail every time going up or down
    but that first time it came as the clouds were turning
into shadow and the daylight was going she could still feel
    the first touch of night in the valley but by then they were
down from the screen walls of the cliff and the trail twined
    between broken rocks and across scree down to the first
small clutching trees and she knew that the sound she had come to
    under the wind was a stream running below her
then as they went in among the branches it was darker
    and ahead of her she could see Koʻolau's shirt
which she had not seen up in the white cloud and she knew
    that he had taken off the cloak he had been wearing
and had wrapped it around Kaleimanu over his shoulder
    at last she heard him call out a strange sound that was a signal
and a moment later she heard the answer to it
    coming from below and they picked their way down through the dark
until she saw a lantern flickering up through the woods
    like a burning insect and Koʻolau called out his own name
and a voice shouted—Ho—with pleasure and the lantern swung
    and rose toward them and it was Iwa carrying it
who laughed to see them and reached to take everything
    he had arms for and he led the way through the trees
to Naoheiki's house in the lap of the mountain

24.

—We were hoping you would come over to us—Iwa said
        —That Pokipala talks and the ripple goes all the way
you never told me about the doctor in Koloa
        and Kua never told me but we heard all the same—
Koʻolau said to him—I have been thinking about it
        but when we made our decision there was no time
to find you and tell you and besides it was better to have
        no more ripples going around   They sat down by a small fire
between rocks behind the house and Iwa said—If we
        had known what day you were coming we would all have been here
the ones who could get here and we would have the pig
        all baked and the dinner ready——We have plenty—
a voice said from the side of the house and Kauila
        came around the corner laughing and walked to Koʻolau
and embraced him—You remember me—Kauila asked
        —I think now I am wearing another face and I am
still younger than you are Naoheiki is up here asleep
        and the Judge and his family over there they will all
be glad you people came but maybe you should go see them
        tomorrow because they would all be asleep now
and here we have plenty to eat only it is cold—
        Koʻolau said—I think mostly now we are tired—
Kauila said—And thirsty I am sure and must be hungry—
        —My my—a woman's voice said and it was Kalaina
limping into the firelight—I know they are thirsty—
        and she held out a big water gourd to Kepola
—I am Kalaina—she said and then she was gone
        and as they drank she came back with baskets of fruit
—Wait there—she said and turned to get more—Thank you—
        Kepola said—But the children are too tired to eat
they are both asleep——You eat a little—Kalaina said
        —and then we can all sleep and start new tomorrow—
and she kept bringing more food cold fish cold taro
        she went for more water and then she took Kepola
by the hand and Iwa picked up Ida and led the way
        into the house and Koʻolau stood up with Kaleimanu
still asleep on his shoulder and Kalaina led them all
        one by one through the low unlit doorway

25.

Kalaina drew them through the dark to a soft pile
    where they could lie down and Pi'ilani saw the doorway
behind her lighter than the darkness around her
    there were paler shadows out there above the fire
Kaleimanu made distant sounds in his sleep as they put him
    between them and she lay gazing up at the black
above her in the smell that kept soaking into her
    smell of damp and dirt smell of decaying wood and moss
smell of rags age mouths with no teeth old food incontinence
    rancid and bottomless so that she felt hot in there
though she had been cold out by the fire and as her back
    sank into the pile she was half asleep but when she looked up
she was awake again and thought she could never sleep
    and kept seeing her feet moving down through the fog again
ahead of her and then she woke hearing the owl very near
    and she thought it was Kawaluna but the smell told her
where she was and she lay listening to the child's breath
    and when she opened her eyes again she saw the doorway
filled with the first gray of the ghost dawn in the silence
    before the birds were awake and she tried to imagine the place
now that it was day and she could make out the matted grass
    and the poles of the ceiling and she saw that she was lying
on a heap of rags and moss with a crowd of baskets
    and gourds watching her from beyond her feet and then they were
all outside with Kalaina limping ahead to show them
    the stream for washing and for filling water gourds
and telling them to eat and she looked up to where the cliffs
    disappeared in the cloud and Kauila was telling them
that the Judge said he needed a while to be presentable
    and Kauila laughed as he said it and told them to eat
and she saw that Ko'olau who had carried the gun with him
    down the cliffs along with the roll over his shoulder
and Kaleimanu on top of the roll now took the gun
    with him wherever he went and set it next to himself
when he ate and when she raised her eyes from the children
    and looked at his face she saw that he was watching her
and then she heard the unbroken sound of the stream flowing

26.

—Not too clean in there—Naoheiki announced to the world
　　as he hove around the corner still half asleep
—If I had known you were coming we would have got it up
　　like a wedding for you with flowers and all that kind
makes me ashamed now—and he embraced them one by one
　　as he talked—But we can still do that today—he said
—This is my mountain house and I let my friends stay there
　　in the lean-to when they are up here and sometimes
they let it slip for a while the front of the house is around here
　　where we were sleeping when you came and this whole place now
above the stream with the rocks around it they call
　　the Big House where the Judge and his family are staying
and now there are other houses around some you can see
　　from here some wood houses some grass ones since you leper friends
started coming with your families and there are more
　　down through the woods that you cannot see from here they are even
growing some taro up here now I am happy you have come—
　　he said it to Koʻolau and embraced him again
calling him brother and then he said it to all of them
　　then Kauila reappeared to say—The Judge says come now—
and they filed over with Naoheiki as the host
　　leading the way and found the Judge sitting up in a chair
as big as a throne made out of planks with blankets
　　folded around him for cushions he had his broad hat on
and a dark coat buttoned like a man in a picture
　　and as they came in from the sunlight he looked like that
like a faded page or a shadow his feet were wrapped up
　　and propped on a box but he raised his arms—Come in Come in—
he called—How glad I am to see you and I see you all know
　　Naoheiki but you cannot know what a friend
he has been to us like a son to us and I think you know
　　Kaenaku and my family we are all here all well
more or less—and he laughed and looked around at his wife
　　and his older sister Mere and as they embraced
he went on asking questions about their coming over
　　and their health and what news they brought and Koʻolau
when his eyes had settled into the room was shaken
　　to see the Judge's face wrung and crumpled with the skin
by his mouth like the rind of a dry orange and he looked
　　at the Judge's wife Kaenaku and could scarcely see
through the knotted features before him the woman he had admired

27.

Kepola was looking at Kaenaku out of
    the corner of her eyes not wanting to appear to be
staring and she was thinking back to Kaenaku
    coming out of church wearing ginger leis her elegance
her hats her fragrance the way she sat in the carriage
    her manner of speaking and inclining her head she looked
at Kaenaku's mouth like a chicken's foot and she wondered
    how much older Kaenaku might be than she was
and Kaenaku caught her eye and they both looked away
    thinking that they would be neighbors and the Judge praised
the children and then told Koʻolau that they had been
    preparing another petition but Koʻolau
told him of the Board of Health doctors and Sheriff Wilcox
    going to Valdemar Knudsen's house for the lepers
in Kekaha and about them sending Pake
    and Keola off to the settlement after that
Piʻilani and Kepola took the children outside
    with Naoheiki going ahead to make them all at home
and Koʻolau talked with the Judge about Knudsen saying
    to Kua that this was a bad time when the best doctors
at the Board of Health were on the point of resigning
    and the harsh voices were having their way and proposing
sending a vessel to Kalalau to take off the lepers
    Knudsen had said they kept discussing the matter
what boat to charter and when and kept putting it off
    but he was afraid that some day they would do it
and the Judge said—It sounds as though there is not much hope
    of their favoring a new petition and perhaps less now
than there was with the others but I am for sending it
    even so to have it on the books and make it plain
that our intentions were serious and honorable
    though they may choose to make light of them and ignore them
but they will have trouble making light of me if they come
    I suggest a sedan chair—he said laughing—If they can find one—
Koʻolau said—I will not go with them and I know
    Pokipala told everyone I had the sickness but he
never knew that our child Kaleimanu is sick the same way
    and I will not let them take us with them—and the Judge looked
past Koʻolau's head and saw the gun leaning by the door

28.

Pi'ilani would look back on those first days in the valley
     first days first weeks she could not tell how long it lasted
that time that season that age in itself and it would seem
     to be a sound ringing all alone that she had not
heard before and could not call to and even when
     she could no longer hear any echo of it there was
its silence and she went back in silence to something
     she thought had been there even in the new strangeness
of whatever she had touched and even in the cold
     and the missing Kekaha and the bed and voices back there
and in those moments of nothing but cloud and wet and not
     knowing with the knowing waiting under them even
there she knew it had been and she had breathed it and looked
     through its air for however long it lasted and she
could turn to it in her mind afterward and see it as a clear
     suspended time when she had once had everything Naoheiki
showed the children a pool up along the stream where small fish
     swam straight up the rocks inside the waterfall and he took
Kepola and Pi'ilani to his house and told them
     that he would be staying at his place down near the shore
so they were welcome to the whole of his house up here
     and he started to clean it out saying he had to make it
right for them and he told them that he would take them all
     down to the lower part of the valley where people
had always been living and they would have a big feast there
     so they would get to know the ones who lived there now
he went on talking as he swept and carried and they worked
     together and he told them who they would meet down there
stories of the families who was who and who they
     were descended from until Pi'ilani and Kepola
could no longer tell who he was talking about and they
     were all laughing drawing out threads of stories while
the Judge was trying to tell Ko'olau what he had learned
     of those living down in the valley now—You knew it—he said
—long before I came or any of the lepers up here
     and I know it only from up here where they had
the house ready for us and were glad to put me down at last
     I have not managed to get down there yet and I know
only the ones who came up here to see us bringing us
     things we need but I have never known such kindness—

29.

—It has been that way since before I came—the Judge said
    —Word arrived that they would have a house ready for us
and that we would be welcome and by that time there had been
    lepers living in hiding up here for years some of them
and with their families so those people knew what to expect
    they had seen something of the sickness by that time
the helplessness and the dying and they knew how lepers
    are regarded by the foreigners and the government
and what the law is and although I decided to come
    even then I believed only a part of the welcome
they extended and I thought it came only from
    the lepers here in the upper part of the valley
the ones for whom Knudsen has been getting the medicine
    for you to bring and even when I had let them know
that I was scarcely able to walk any more
    and would never be able to climb down the trail and they
said they would carry me I set out only partly
    believing and thinking that if I fell it would be
better than rotting away as a favor to those
    who pray for a world without us and then they picked me up
and started down and it seems that I must have been
    in a fever perhaps or something like it with the fear
cold in me shaking me and the sickness so that I
    felt nothing in my body at all which I had been
prudent enough to empty before we started
    but part of the way down I did not know who I was
I looked into the clouds and slipped out into them
    I looked up through tears but I was not weeping I was
not there and then they were heaving me over the rocks
    at the foot of the cliff and it was beyond believing
but I learned that they had carried down others before me
    though maybe no one so heavy and still they treat it
as no big thing and some go daily to houses
    to move those who cannot stand up but what has surprised me
almost as much is the way those who were here before us
    in the lower valley have behaved toward us and how
good they have been to us we have heard in the stories
    that people once treated each other this way but I thought
that was long ago and probably was made up—

30.

—They keep telling me that we are their family—the Judge said
     —the word makes me feel more like a foreigner the more
I would like it to be true and after what I have known
     and what my family and Kaenaku's have known it seems stranger
that they should all welcome us in that way without question
     I know that some have seen leprosy in their own relatives
and some have seen people taken away with it
     but most of them know simply that this is an affliction
that has befallen us and those of our own blood
     recurring like an inheritance how many of those
with my name have died of it these last years I cannot tell
     and in this valley everyone knows of the household
by the wet cave outside Hanalei where they grow taro
     who were cursed and one child in each generation
has been claimed by leprosy nobody understands that
     but here they treat us as their own kin think of Naoheiki
who got his house ready for us and has given his own to you
     and Kaumeheiwa down by the shore is another like him
some of our people up here who have the strength for it
     go down and work in the taro beside the friends there
and Puheliku has restored a small taro pond
     that had been abandoned down there a long time ago
and they all went and planted the first taro with him
     and then ate and drank and danced that was after I came here
some go out fishing together and they bring fish up here
     they bring it to me and what good am I to them
they sit and listen to me as an elder and what they ask
     I answer as well as I can but the best of it is
their own stories—Koʻolau said—Our boy Kaleimanu
     has always loved stories——This is a place for them—
the Judge said—Will you bring the boy over to see me—
     —That will make him happy—Koʻolau said and he took the rifle
to leave at Naoheiki's house and he told Piʻilani
     that he was going down to the valley to see about fish
and he followed the stream path all the way to the shore
     and there he saw a tall imposing man and a beautiful
boy standing by the water and he knew the man who was
     named Pā from a family that had always lived in the valley
where everyone knew that this gentle figure was a shark spirit
     —Koʻolau—he said and embraced him—You have come to stay—

31.

She remembered that it was only a few days after
　　the great feast of welcome that Naoheiki had planned
and brought together for them at his house down near the sea
　　to which everyone in the valley who could walk
or was not too sick or too old or taking care
　　of someone who needed them came bringing what they could
they came with fish and fruit with taro shellfish seaweed
　　fern shoots chickens a goat from the cliffs and Ko'olau had gone
with Kala up a ravine toward Nualolo and they
　　had brought back a pig there must have been more than a hundred
who came and they chanted part of the ceremony
　　for the new year in a procession along the water's edge
and there were other chants there were love songs and dances
　　and the children played by the water until dark
and Pi'ilani kept remembering the feast
　　at the lepers' house in Kekaha only a month
behind her and that woman's drunken voice shouting
　　—Come and eat and drink we are celebrating our
funeral and now this was Kalalau and after that day
　　he went out fishing with Kala and the Pā's and sometimes
took Kaleimanu with him and Kepola and Kaenaku
　　liked spending time together talking and it was into
that time toward the end of one day filled with the luminous
　　green of the year's beginning that Iwa arrived
at the Judge's and stood in the doorway catching his breath
　　—They have taken the Queen—he said and the Judge said—What—
Iwa gave him the bundle of papers that he could not read
　　saying—You have to tell us what is in there they have taken
the Queen maybe she is dead because they said there is no more Queen—
　　and the Judge opened the bundle and groaned as Ko'olau
and others who had seen Iwa running to the house
　　pushed through the door and stood listening and the Judge
groaned again as he read—They have taken the kingdom—
　　he said—They have finally taken it from us
that stiff-necked gang those partners in foul play they have
　　got the American Navy to help them and they
have locked up the Queen in the palace and taken over
　　and who do you suppose is the ringleader in all this
but our own Sanford Dole from Koloa that ruthless prig—

32.

—My son is a good boy—the Judge said—He has sent all these
     Commercial Advertiser The Friend and in Hawaiian
Ka Leo o ka Lauhui I cannot trust one of them
     and a letter here saying he will send the rest and it is
as bad as it sounds—he read on with all of them asking
     question after question and they stood in tears listening
some unable to comprehend it and some understanding
     only too well—And who will be playing the footstool
for Sanford the Great—the Judge asked——But Lorrin A Thurston
     born to know better I remember him telling at length
of how his admiration for Sanford went back
     to the days of their youth when they went out walking together
with their guns and one day as they were passing
     through a native village a native dog barked at them
so Thurston shot it and they walked on but when that
     village was behind them Sanford said he was thinking
that trouble just might result from that which was one thing
     I doubted about the story so according to Thurston
in the next native village they came to Sanford
     shot the first native dog he saw and turned to Thurston
with that righteous look he has made his own and said Now
     I cannot be required to testify against you
and Thurston said I thought here is a man of foresight
     the kind of man we need which is what he was
for the mission boys the annexationists
     whatever they will call themselves next it is
in their pockets now—and Pi‘ilani saw that there were tears
     on the Judge’s face and on all the faces in the room
and for a moment then they all stood there without a word
     and then one and then another slipped out through the door
and some talked later asking the same things over again
     some said nothing and worked in the taro looking down
at their faces in the water and knew nothing to say
     she worked among them and listened and in the days
that followed more papers came and more of the story
     and the Judge read to them about the Provisional
Government and its proclamations and about the Queen
     but nobody knew what to expect and it seemed
to Pi‘ilani that nothing had changed except in their voices

33.

In the new year at the new roll-top desk in his office
    Louis Stolz was reading of new things in the papers
among them a new Krupps Howitzer the latest
    thing of its kind manufactured in Germany
newly arrived the performance it promised its caliber
    weight of projectile range number of rounds possible
in a given time accuracy all of it on paper
    the gun scarcely uncrated the crew not yet named
Pokipala was standing in the doorway—I have told you
    to knock—Stolz said turning—I knocked—Pokipala said
—Then you wait—Stolz said—I waited—Pokipala said
    —I came to say I think Koʻolau has gone——Gone where —Stolz asked
—I was over Kekaha way to the leper house and I
    went out Mānā side and the Koʻolau house looked to be closed
his mother was next door watching me and Where is Koʻolau
    I asked her Not here she said You know where he works
Is his wife home I asked She is out his mother said
    Koʻolau's father came out and walked to Koʻolau's front step
and sat down on it facing me and I came back asking
    whoever I saw where Koʻolau was and they told me
they did not know—So the next day Stolz rode over
    to Kekaha and asked about Koʻolau and they all
said they did not know where he was and Koʻolau's father
    went again and sat on the steps next door—And where
is his wife Piʻilani—Stolz asked and Kaleimanu
    answered—Has she some sickness why do you ask about her—
—I am looking for Koʻolau—Stolz said—And you have been told
    that he is not here——And his wife is not here either—Stolz said
—We do not tie her up—Kaleimanu answered—And nobody—
    Stolz went on while the dogs kept barking at him
—nobody knows where she is and is the little boy
    with her—Kaleimanu stared at him—Are these dogs
all yours or are they his——They get along together—
    —When he is away you feed all of them do you
how long has he been gone——Piʻilani is with her mother—
    Kaleimanu said looking across to Niʻihau
and the year was some days older before Stolz could be sure
    where Koʻolau had gone and when and who was with him

34.

So whatever thought he might have had of using Koʻolau
    to talk the Judge and the rest of the fugitive lepers
into leaving the valley in some semblance of order
    and putting themselves in the custody of the Board
represented by Louis H Stolz who would be given
    credit for the operation he would have to
go about it in some other way now and no doubt
    he would have to go into the valley himself at some point
and try to arrange to speak to all of them there
    but he had no authorization for going in there
and his supervisor Sheriff Wilcox who never stopped
    trumpeting about wanting to clean out that valley
kept telling him to wait until the weather was right
    and they had the right boat and enough men to do it
for there would be deaths on both sides so Stolz wrote to the head
    of the Board Dear sir a leper belonging to
this district after having been examined by Dr Campbell
    and notified that he would have to go to Molokaʻi
asked for and received permission to stay a week
    in order to settle up his affairs this request
as has been our practice here was granted upon his
    promise to be ready and willing to go
upon the return of the steamer Pele he has broken
    his promise and gone over to Kalalau where
so many other lepers are as this is the first
    person who has escaped from this district while I have been
deputy sheriff I am anxious to bring him back
    and have requested Doctor Campbell to get out
a warrant for him which he will do Unless I receive
    positive orders to the contrary it is my
intention to proceed shortly to Kalalau
    and endeavor to arrest the person in question
who is a man named Koʻolau I think it is quite
    probable that unless I happen upon him
unawares resistance will be shown as almost
    every man in Kalalau is armed and much as I
should regret it and endeavor to avoid it
    somebody it may be myself or a constable
may be hurt or killed and as the Board has tacitly

tolerated the lepers in Kalalau the man being
therefore justified to a certain extent in going there
      I would be pleased to receive any orders or advice

35.

But other questions of authority were occupying
    the capital and before Stolz received an answer
news came of the takeover and the dismantling
    of the kingdom by the annexationists and he nodded
as he read of the new Provisional Government
    name after name that he knew and thought well of so that
he was elated and rushed around to Hofgaard's store
    where they were shouting and drinking toasts but he wondered
how all this might affect his own position and duties
    Wilcox was there and assured him that nothing of that kind
would change—It is just that our friends have taken over
    which is something they should have done a long time ago
and ended the circus—he held out a bottle of Hofgaard's
    best iron-bottom cane liquor and they cheered but Stolz
still received no answer to his request and the winter
    slipped away and the President of the Board of Health was changed
and in the spring Stolz wrote to the new president starting
    over again Dear sir allow me to respectfully
call your attention to the fact that if it be
    the policy of the Board of Health to remove
during the present year the lepers now residing
    in Kalalau it would seem necessary that steps
in the matter be taken shortly as the months during which
    a steamer can effect a landing at Kalalau
are at hand if a system of segregation is to be
    carried out undoubtedly these people should be removed
it cannot be otherwise than that healthy persons will
    and are at the present time becoming infected
with leprosy and this time the Board replied telling him
    that An attempt to remove the lepers from Kalalau
simply means reducing the place by force of arms
    and they requested Stolz to send them a full report
of the number age and sex of all lepers at Kalalau
    also if possible a like list of other people
residing in the valley and it would also perhaps
    be interesting to the government they told him
to know the quantity and kind of firearms in their possession

36.

Stolz sent an answer by the next steamer respectfully
        begging to differ with the view that removal
of lepers from Kalalau would probably lead to men killed
        on both sides and suggesting that effectual work
could be done before force of arms was resorted to
        but he called their attention to the fact that at present
he was merely agent for the district of Waimea
        with no authority in Kalalau and he was not
hankering he assured them for any work in connection
        with lepers but the work ought to be done and somebody
twice underlined must do it Should the Board desire me
        to act further in this matter I suggest that
a commission be sent me as Agent for the Islands
        of Kauai and Niʻihau then a few days later he wrote
urging that before further steps were taken
        in regard to the lepers in Kalalau should the Board
decide to remove them first a stringent quarantine
        be placed on the valley allowing no communication
either for lepers or non-lepers between Kalalau
        and other places boats are engaged in taking taro
to Niʻihau and other places and presumably
        taking visitors should this source of income and communication
be cut off and the well people told plainly that this quarantine
        would not be lifted until the sick people were removed
I am sure that it would have a salutary influence
        on the non-lepers and cause them to assist
in the removal To carry into effect such
        a quarantine three stations would in my mind be necessary
one on the Hanalei trail of two white men and four natives
        one on the Waimea trail of like get up and strength
and one on the beach at Kalalau as soon as the Board
        decides on the removal of the lepers a good man
should be sent into Kalalau to urge and persuade them
        to give in peaceably my only object in giving
my poor views to the Board is that time is flying
        he wasted none himself but went to Mānā and hired
a canoe to take him around under the cliffs to the valley

37.

It was cold up at the head of the valley among the rocks
     at the foot of the cliffs with the winter rains beating down
and the streams crashing around the small mountain houses
     tucked up in the cloud much of the day and while they were
still numb with the news of the Queen and the kingdom
     some of the people who lived in the valley and some
of the lepers who worked with them built a few more houses
     lower down where it was warmer and they gave the first
and biggest of them to the Judge and his family
     and brought him down gathering to welcome them all
and then other families and lepers living alone
     moved down nearer the taro and the beach and Koʻolau
and Piʻilani and their household moved down under
     a small new grass roof and were out most days in the taro
or along the shore and it was turning to spring with the days
     passing like clouds until they began to imagine
that they had been forgotten but Piʻilani kept watching
     the red spots swelling on Kaleimanu's body
always new ones appearing and one eye looking strange now
     not shutting right and tears coming from it when the other
was not crying and sores on his feet getting worse
     though he said they did not hurt even when the rocks cut them
she saw the same swellings coming on Koʻolau's body
     and she washed the sores and swellings with the powder
that was kept at the Judge's house and they swallowed
     the bad-tasting oil and then one day when she was
alone in the house and the valley seemed peaceful she looked
     over to where the two main streams come together and there she saw
that man Louis Stolz who had come to Kekaha
     to hunt pig with Koʻolau and who had seen the red spots
on his face and with him was the one called Penikila
     the steel pen and she thought they had come down the cliff trail
from Kilohana and she saw Penikila point
     to the house where she was watching them and they came along
and Stolz put his head in the door and looked around
     for a long time before he saw she was there and then he
spoke to her like the feel of a fish asking her
     how she was and how she liked it over here and did she
miss her friends in Kekaha asking her who her friends were

in Kekaha who her friends were here and telling her
what he thought was news of Kekaha and she kept saying
yes yes as he stood there looking at everything

38.

—And where is Koʻolau—he asked finally and she said
   —He is working down below there——When will he be back—
—Sometimes he comes at noon sometimes at the end of the day
   you can come in and wait for him—she said with Stolz
already standing inside the door—No—he said
   —Please tell him that I would like to speak with him down there
near the beach when he comes home today and how are those
   red spots on his face that I noticed at Kekaha—
—About the same—she said—They come and go and most of the time
   they are hardly there——Please tell him that I will be
down at Kaumeheiwa's house by the beach tonight
   I want to see him at any time—She said—I could
make you two something to eat here while you wait—but he thanked her
   in that sliding way he was talking that day and then he told
Penikila to stand up and she watched them go
   down the trail by the stream and she slipped around toward the cliff
and down the banks of the terraces to the one
   where she knew Koʻolau had gone to work and she saw
that he was not there but she watched Stolz and Penikila
   come to the far end of the terrace and talk to those standing
below them in the water and she turned at a sound
   and saw Koʻolau and Kaleimanu under a tree
smiling at her and Koʻolau said—We saw them coming
   and we said to our friends Nobody has seen us for some time
and Makuale said I never saw you all morning
   only this face of mine in the water—and Koʻolau saw
that she was crying and Kaleimanu buried his head
   in her skirt and cried and they stood watching the others
across the water and then she saw Stolz go on down
   toward the Judge's new house and the others climb out
and go off and the surface of the water was empty
   except for the small shoots of taro the delicate arching
stems the green heart faces of the leaves waving together
   in their youth and the three of them stood under the tree
with tears on their faces and Piʻilani said—He has come
   to take you—and Koʻolau answered—Whatever happens
he will not take me and now we can go down to the meeting
   and hear him tell us that he will take all the lepers
to Molokaʻi and will not let you come with us—

216

39.

—It is some time—the Judge said to Stolz—since you lit up
    my doorway come in come in word of your arrival
went before you——How are you—Stolz asked—It depends—
    the Judge said—As you may have noticed in your own life
some days only lack of music keeps me from dancing
    some days I do not stand up and this is one of those
you must excuse me and you must lower your head
    not to strike it on the beam there a gesture worth
bearing in mind—The Judge was enthroned in his plank chair
    with his broad hat on and a bright fabric far from its
original purpose drawn around him like a shawl
    his bandaged feet were propped up on a long box and his hands
trembled gripping the arm of the chair but the rest of him
    sat motionless as he deflected Stolz's phrases
and then said—Can we tempt you with something to eat—
    —Oh no—Stolz said—I am going—and there the Judge stopped him
—Of course—he said—I never imagined that you had come
    for old times' sake—Stolz said—I have come for your own good
I have been making a survey of Kalalau—
    We know that—the Judge said—why else have Penekila
and Sam Ku been turning up asking their long-nose questions—
    Stolz said—And now I have come to tell you that the time has come
for the lepers in this valley to go to the settlement
    on Moloka'i and I want to know whether you will
agree to go willingly—The Judge said—Do you think I became
    sick willingly——You will get medical treatment there—
Stolz told him—How many have they cured by now—the Judge asked
    —And those others who are sick in your family can go
with you—Stolz said and the Judge looked around at Kaenaku
    and at Mere—When are you planning this move—he asked Stolz
—In a week or two—Stolz said—When we have what we need
    by way of men and equipment which is why I am asking
these questions—and the Judge laughed—Willingly—he said
    —willingly and forever Well as you have not come
for us yet I see no reason to say no today—
    —You are being sensible—Stolz said—I am continuing
to act as though I had a choice for as long as I can—
    the Judge answered—Watch out for your head as you leave—

217

40.

Hon W D Smith Pres Bd of Health Honolulu
     Sir in accordance with your request herewith a complete list
of the residents of the valley of Kalalau there are
     twenty three households four of which consist of only
one old man each In nine households no leprosy
     is visable sic to a casual observer
in three households all the inmates are afflicted with leprosy
     while in eleven underlined households the inmates
are part lepers and part non-lepers the population
     numbers one hundred and two with seventy four apparently
non-lepers and twenty eight lepers eighteen of them male
     eighteen adults ten minors only six rifles
could be heard of and only three of these are available
     one of them belongs to a non-leper the lepers do not wish
to be taken away as they believe the new Japanese
     doctor at Kilauea may be able to cure some of them
J Kauai and Paoa are the two lepers most likely
     to give trouble it is my belief that if these two
and perhaps one or two others were removed most underlined
     of the others would go voluntarily I also believe
that these leaders could be taken with a small force
     two or three men like Sam Ku with what material
we have here would do Two weeks later after Stolz's own visit
     he wrote again to Hon W D Smith now
Attorney General Dear Sir in accordance with your
     instructions I went to Kalalau and interviewed
most of the lepers six of the reported cases
     I would not undertake to move some of them I am sure
being non-lepers As for their going peacefully
     my trip was only a partial success the majority
among whom is J Kauai desire to go and will
     make no trouble but about four or five of the young
strong fellows say they will not go while as many more
     were non-committal the amount and kind of intimacy
existing between lepers and non-lepers at Kalalau
     is simply abominable I believe there will be fifty cases
of leprosy in consequence of lepers having been
     allowed to remain in Kalalau Then three weeks later
he wrote again that eighteen of the lepers had decamped
     for parts unknown including J Kauai They had vanished
into the tangle of ravines up at the foot of the cliffs

THE CLIFFS

1.

The cliffs rose before him straight into the summer sky
     it was a week after the solstice and along the headlands
the trades were blowing Stolz stood at the mouth of the valley
     looking up into it and in the sun it all seemed to be white
the glittering on the leaves and across the blank taro ponds
     the water running over the rocks and the frayed clouds
slipping behind white crags with the tropic birds wheeling
     around them and thousands of feet above him the cliff faces
appeared to be white against the white sky that was falling
     upward behind them nobody in this place would give him
a straight answer to anything he asked he opened the white
     page again with the sun on it and wrote I will
hurry up things as fast as possible and report
     the progress as it occurs folded it over and addressed
the envelope to send at the first opportunity
     he had sent word early in the morning for everyone
in the valley to come down to Kaumeheiwa's house
     and as he waited he kept seeing Ko'olau's face
at the last meeting when Stolz had told him that no one
     except those with leprosy would be taken to Moloka'i
and Ko'olau saying in a low voice that when they married
     they had promised they would never be separated
and that no man would separate them now Penekila
     and Peter Nowlein had unloaded the canoe
while Stolz questioned Kaumeheiwa about Judge Kauai
     and the others who were hiding in the upper valley
and while he waited he had Penekila and Peter
     set up the tent on the hill above Kaumeheiwa's house
where he could see up the valley and he told them
     to carry the chest of guns up the hill behind the house
and hide it in the rocks there and by the end of the morning
     when they had gathered for the meeting there were only three
lepers from the lower houses though there was one other
     who could not walk and all of them including Kapahe'e
the famous swimmer had decided to go to Moloka'i

2.

They gathered a few at a time and sat in the shade
    at the foot of the bank waiting until Stolz decided
that he had waited long enough and that no one else
    would be coming it was already past noon and a hush
seemed to fill the lower valley with the sound of the waves
    brushing the shingle those who told of the meeting later
said it was not like the first one at which he had spoken
    as though he wanted to be kind to them this time
all but three of those gathered in front of him were
    residents of the valley and most of them had lived there
all their lives and he threatened them like a preacher
    promising Hell He said that anyone helping
the lepers who were in hiding was breaking the law
    and that if they did not help him their lands would be taken
and they would have to leave the valley and go to jail
    —And as for this Koʻolau—he said to them—You see
how he has run away from me into the mountain
    you will see how his head becomes bigger but the rest of him
grows smaller and smaller and I will capture him
    I will take him alive if I can but I will take him
living or dead he has brought this trouble among you
    all the ones who are hiding have brought this trouble among you
and they are making you sick with their own sickness as long
    as they are here in your valley—and he waited
to see whether anyone else was coming and they watched him
    and turned away and he told Penekila and Peter
to pick up their guns and the three of them started
    along the main stream toward the head of the valley
by then Puhiliku had reached the mountain houses
    and the caves in the cliffs and told everyone there
about the meeting Stolz had called at Kaumeheiwa's house
    and Koʻolau said—We should go down there and hear
what he has to say this time—and he picked up his gun
    whose name he said was Death Winks Far Away and Piʻilani
went with him down the trail by the cliff and as they went
    they kept stopping to listen for someone coming

3.

—Because I think Louis Stolz may try to wait for me
   out of sight—Koʻolau said—And take me from ambush—
and when they were down by the taro ponds they saw
   the tent on top of the hill and they stood watching it
for a while to see whether anyone was there
   then they went on down the stream to a place called Kahaliʻi
where they found a raincoat with the name Louis Stolz
   stitched into the collar and a package of soda crackers
inside it rolled in a blanket and Koʻolau said
   —He seems to have dropped these we had better not leave them here—
and they went on down to the trail behind the houses
   and Koʻolau held up his hand and in a moment
Penekila came along the trail and Koʻolau stepped out
   and greeted him and asked him where he was going
and Penekila said he was looking to see
   who was in the houses and Koʻolau asked him where
Louis Stolz was and Penekila said he did not know
   but he thought Stolz had gone off to Hanalei on the trail
—That surprises me—Koʻolau said—Because we were told
   that he wanted to speak to us down here by the houses
and so we came down to see him—and he began to ask
   Penekila about his family because he had known him
for years in Waimea and he said it did seem strange to him
   that Stolz would ask them to come to the beach to meet him
and go off to Hanalei—But the meeting is over—
   Penekila said as Peter Nowlein came up the trail
and Koʻolau asked Peter where Louis Stolz was
   and Peter told him that Stolz had gone up the valley
hoping to surprise Koʻolau somewhere on the trail
   and capture him up there—You see Penekila—
Koʻolau said—I thought you were my friend but it is Peter
   who has told me the truth—and he and Piʻilani
went down through the houses to Kaumeheiwa's house
   where they found friends waiting and others came from the houses
and the ones who had been hiding were carrying their guns

4.

Koʻolau said to them—I have heard what this Stolz told you
     about how he is going to capture me and I have come
to meet him here We have all been friends up until now
     but if any of you is afraid you should not stay with me
because nobody knows what will happen and I understand
     he means to take me alive or dead—then he turned
to Penekila who had followed him down and he said
     —Penekila you are no friend of mine you lied to me
you told me Stolz had gone to Hanalei when you knew
     that he is up there now somewhere lying in wait for me—
Penekila said—I saw him take his raincoat
     so I thought he was going to Hanalei—but Koʻolau
was studying a few strange faces along the beach
     new constables whom Stolz had brought with him and posted
to guard the lepers he planned to take away with him
     and Koʻolau and Piʻilani and their friends who had come
down from the cliffs with their guns spent the night above the houses
     out of the sound of the surf with two of them always awake
listening to the darkness and they stayed there all the next day
     keeping watch in turn and talking with their friends who brought
fish and taro and the rumor that Stolz had captured
     Paoa and that he was coming that night for Koʻolau
and Koʻolau said—We will be here Everyone knows where I am—
     Iwa and Kala had been there with them and they went down
to the trail below and it got dark but the moon rose
     and Koʻolau and Piʻilani watched from behind a rock
listening to the leaves until Koʻolau breathed to her
     I hear two of them coming—and then they saw Kala
and Iwa running down the slope and they heard Stolz
     shouting after them—Halt Halt I warned you Halt—and then
the click of a gun and at that Koʻolau took aim
     and fired and they heard Stolz groan and in the moonlight
they could see that the man with Stolz was Paoa who turned
     and began to beat Stolz with his handcuffs and they heard
the chain each time he struck and Koʻolau shouted to him
     to stop and he stood up but Paoa called out to him
—He is going to shoot—and Piʻilani saw Stolz
     on one knee and the gleam of his rifle and Koʻolau fired
a second time and they saw Stolz fall over and roll
     onto the rocks and they went down and found him dead

5.

Paoa said to Koʻolau—That was my rifle
　　　　that he was going to shoot you with when you stood up there
in the moonlight so we could see you as though it was daytime—
　　　　And Koʻolau said—I thought you were killing him
with that piece of chain——My handcuffs—Paoa said
　　　　—He put them on me he was hiding up there in the rocks
and I came out and he put that pistol in my back—
　　　　Paoa reached across the body and with both hands
drew the Colt from its holster and stood up looking at it
　　　　—And when he had these on me Sit there he said and he went
all through my house turning everything over and took my rifle
　　　　and said Now we are going to find Koʻolau and we came down
to where we saw Kala and Iwa and he said
　　　　There he is and when they ran he was going to shoot
but you shot first—They turned the body over and saw
　　　　the blood glittering as though there was a sound in it
which they were not hearing and Koʻolau patted the pockets
　　　　until he heard the clink of keys and he fished them out
and found the one for the handcuffs and then put the keys
　　　　into his own pocket and found a box of cartridges
for the Colt and by that time Kala and Iwa
　　　　had crept up the path and Koʻolau said to them—Come
He is dead He was going to shoot you when you ran
　　　　He thought one of you was me Now pick up the body
and bring him down to the lanai in front of the house
　　　　and they came to one of the lepers Kapaheʻe
the swimmer waiting by a rock and Koʻolau
　　　　told him what had happened and said—You can go ahead
and say we are coming with the body—and then they saw
　　　　Wahinealoha who said Penekila had sent him
after they heard the shots and they all carried the body
　　　　down to the house lanai and Kapaheʻe said
—We were frightened when we heard the shots and we knew
　　　　that the trouble had come——There will be more—Koʻolau said
Kapaheʻe said—When Kaukeheiwa heard what had happened
　　　　he ran to that old rotten canoe of his and said
he had to go and tell them and that he was paddling
　　　　to Mānā if that canoe gets there—And they put the body down

225

6.

Even in that light Pi'ilani could see how frightened
    many of the gray faces were as they gathered
at the top of the steps like seaweed moving in the waves
    and stared up at the body she saw that some of them
were afraid of Ko'olau and some were simply afraid
    of whatever was before them the constables were afraid
the eyes were afraid and the whispers and Ko'olau
    told them how it had happened and said they should not be
afraid of him they were still his friends and he reminded them
    of Stolz insisting that he was going to take Ko'olau
alive or dead—And he did not come here with orders
    from the Queen—Ko'olau said—But from those others
who took the Queen away from us they stole her from us
    what they call now the Provisional Government
he came from them—And now more trouble will come from them—
    a voice said with a silence around it and it was
the tall man named Pā and Ko'olau said—We will leave
    the body here and if they do not come for it we will
come bury it ourselves—There were seven lepers with guns
    down there with him and he motioned them to come with him
and whispered to Iwa—Come—and in a low voice said
    —Show us where the guns are—but Iwa said—Penekila
is watching——Then tell me—Ko'olau said—Up in the rocks
    only a few steps in back of the tent going
toward the cliff—and Ko'olau was looking away from Iwa
    as though he was not listening and he said—Good night—
to them all there and went down the steps with Pi'ilani
    and the friends with guns went with them as they started
up the trail and climbed to the tent in the moonlight
    and stood looking inside it and Ko'olau told two of them
to search among the rocks until they found the chest and he took out
    the keys and opened the lock and they lifted the rifles
out into the ghost dawn and then the boxes of cartridges
    and they handed them around whispering until the chest
was empty except for one metal box which Ko'olau
    held up and opened and he could see that it was packed
with bottles and bandages and he turned to Pi'ilani
    and gave it to her and then they closed the empty chest
like a coffin and went on up the dim trail carrying the guns
    through the valley which seemed to have become a different place

7.

Kaumeheiwa the gentle Kaumeheiwa the smiling
　　Kaumeheiwa who had always been happy when
anyone asked to stay at his house above the beach
　　near the Pā family and Naoheiki's big house and the others
who had always lived in that valley Kaumeheiwa
　　who had welcomed the lepers and then Stolz and the constables
felt the cold breaking over him heavier than the waves
　　and he was used to the night sea in the old kukui canoe
that leaked so that he had to keep hitching the paddle
　　under his leg while he scooped with the baling gourd
and he seldom felt the cold but however hard he paddled
　　this night his teeth chattered and as he rounded the white
headlands of Nualolo he kept saying to himself
　　Trouble trouble as the paddle bit and went by
Like the Pā's and Kapahe'e and many of the others
　　in the valley he had been able to swim before he
could stand and the deep water was like his own sleep
　　that he could float into but the cold kept climbing through him
in the moonlight as he paddled outside the white surf on the cliffs
　　past Mākua'ike and Miloli'i Keawanue
where the valleys ran out from under deep shadows
　　Mākaha Kauhoa Mākole Ka'aweiki
Polihale of the springs and the temple walls and the underworld
　　Kapa'ula and then the long sands before Mānā
and he ran the canoe ashore below a dark house he knew well
　　making the dogs bark and rush down the beach as he climbed
calling and his friend came to the door hardly awake
　　and Kaumeheiwa breathing hard told him he needed
a horse right away and told why as they saddled her
　　behind the house and he galloped off to the mill and shouted
at Mr Faye's door with the dogs barking around him
　　and then one light appeared and the door opened and they telephoned
to Sheriff Wilcox for a long time before anyone answered
　　waiting to the sound of Kaumeheiwa's breathing
with the dogs barking on and on around them and then
　　Kaumeheiwa telling the story and Mr Faye
repeating it into the receiver and the buzzing of flies
　　coming back out of the earpiece and he said what his name was
and mounted and rode back to the house and they took off the saddle
　　and he pushed the canoe back out into the same night
and paddled home to Kalalau as the stars were fading

227

8.

All the way it had seemed to him that if he could tell
    what had happened it would be gone then gone away
and not be there afterward wherever he was
    and not be still coming wherever he looked but when he
pulled the dead weight of the water-logged canoe from the surf
    onto the shingle below his house and heard the muffled groan
of the wood dragged over the stones he knew it was there unchanged
    all of it whatever it was and he saw the first light
welling up in the valley and the tent limp on the hilltop
    and along the beach in that light friends of his by the whaleboats
he saw neighbor after neighbor from the valley and they were
    bringing things of their own to take away with them
he saw that they were putting them into the whaleboats
    getting ready to leave and Penekila and Nowlein
were up at his own house watching them from the step
    he did not at first see the body lying behind them
by that time Wilcox had sent the news from Waimea
    to Deverill his deputy in Hanalei
and Deverill had taken the steamer Waialeale
    with Captain Smythe and was making for Kalalau
to get Stolz's body and Koʻolau and Piʻilani
    and their friends watching later from the head of the valley
standing on ledges above the mountain houses could see
    the steamer arriving and anchoring inside the headlands
and the boat making for shore and they watched as it
    went out again and returned three times before it was finished
and more smoke rose from the funnel and the steamer turned
    and moved out and away and Paoa went down
to see what had happened and late in the day they gathered
    at the Judge's house and from there they could see that the tent
was gone and Paoa said that the four lepers
    who had already decided to go and one other one
had been taken on the steamer he said Kapaheʻe
    had gone and Kamali and Hakau and Pauwahine
and Mele and besides there were nine from the valley
    who were not sick but were afraid now women living alone
Kapoli and Puahi and Kahalehei
    some who had relatives they could go to in Kilauea
or Kapaʻa and that Kaumeheiwa had gone

228

Deverill and Smythe said they wanted him to tell
his story again and they asked him about everything
and promised that he would be famous and had him sit with them
by the head of the body and as the boat steamed out
the father and the boy named Pā were watching from the headland

9.

—Well now they have two heroes—the Judge said—and you can be sure
    they will make the most of them dress them up for a little while
and wave flags over them blow their horns and Kaumeheiwa
    will tell them again about how he carried the news
of this catastrophe through mountainous seas at night
    to the proper authorities and for a while he will be
the good Hawaiian and Kapaheʻe who I know is
    as old as I am and has been improving upon
stories about himself all that time will bring them out
    in up-to-date versions The Society of Stranglers
he belonged to in his youth and the man he passed one day then
    up in the forest above Kalalau following him
but walking backward so they both stopped to fight and when
    a twig fell on the man's shoulder and he looked aside
Kapaheʻe caught him in the Stranglers' Hold and killed him
    and the one where he sailed from Kalalau in the whaleboat
with a load of taro and two old people who were hoping
    to visit Niʻihau and a fierce storm hit them halfway
the waves pounding the old whaleboat until it broke apart
    and they were all hanging onto the wreckage and swimming
and he tried to keep the old couple afloat and then swam on
    for help and heard them singing a hymn the way he tells it
and he swam all night and woke up on the reef at Lehua
    and then got up and swam on to Kiʻi that one has
gained with fond repetition and then there was the time
    when Valdemar Knudsen decided to swim ashore
from the whaleboat past Nohili and the surf had him
    helpless and as you might have guessed Kapaheʻe
arrived just in time to rescue him and then swam back out
    to the whaleboat to wave and so on I expect that he
seldom revived those stories here in the valley
    where they knew him and he had the Pā family
as neighbors who are said to swim with the sharks and have sharks
    for guardian spirits but he will recall the stories now
wherever he is taken and the reporters will make notes
    and nobody will have heard those tales in Honolulu
or on Molokaʻi and so for a matter of weeks
    he will be the good leper unlike the rest of us
when voices are rising about this news from Kalalau—

10.

Koʻolau said—I think now they will be back soon
    for the rest of us this Louis was going to take us
all by himself big man but after the way it turned out
    they will not let it pass and they will send others for us
but I have said from the beginning that I will not leave here
    alive I said that to the haole and what I did then
is what I still think I had to do and I will be buried
    in this valley as my name says and some of you
have said that you would fight to stay rather than be
    taken away from here but I think you should all consider
once more what you will do if they come with a large force
    maybe soldiers to take us or kill us and if you want to go
you should try to decide now before they are there in front of us
    Piʻilani has told me her mind but I will not
say it for her—And then Piʻilani said—I came here
    with my husband and our son so that we could stay together
this is the only place where we can stay together
    and I will not leave them no matter what happens to me—
Then the Judge said I could scarcely leave on my own feet
    but Mere has already gone and I doubt that I
could fight off many of them I hope they will not find me—
    and Kaenaku said—Now I keep thinking about
things my father told me when I was a child and they all
    used to say how beautiful I was how beautiful I would be
he came to this island when it was mourning and bleeding
    with grief and under everything I remember
going to see old Deborah Kapule and her answers
    to my questions and her huge sadness and my father
seemed to me far away from the people on this island
    so I did not know and then I would find myself crying
and now it seems to me that I have turned into the grief
    I did not touch then and my father never showed and into griefs
that I know nothing about for things that I never knew
    I will hide here and stay with my husband if I can
I am not afraid of their guns but I cannot keep them
    from taking me away—And then the seven who had taken
rifles from the chest with Koʻolau one by one said they would
    stay and fight to the last but Koʻolau said to them
—Wait and see what comes and if they arrive in force
    heavily armed there will be no reason for staying
unless you would rather die here than go with them—

11.

In Hofgaard's store the news of the shooting of Stolz
    brought out the bugles a rehearsal of rising notes
in the brass choir of unquestionable righteousness
    the refrain returned to having been soft with them
the lepers and the natives and this is what comes of it
    and suggestions grew violent before several of the more
seasoned champions of order composed a letter
    to W O Smith Pres Board of Health and Att General
in red ink Sir We the undersigned request and demand
    that every effort possible be promptly and diligently made
to bring to justice and punish the murderer
    or murderers of the late L H Stolz and to clean out
the valley of Kalalau of its leprous population
    or we will take the matter into our own hands and promptly
revenge the death of our friend murdered in cold blood
    T H Gibson Professor English niceties
be damned Th Brandt E E Conant C B Hofgaard
    H P Faye who was happy to recapitulate
for new arrivals the appearance of Kaumeheiwa
    at his door in the dead of night gasping out the news
and they all expressed satisfaction in the strong wording
    and the red ink and made copies for themselves before
going in a band to present it to the captain
    of the steamer to Honolulu announcing to him
that this outrage was a challenge to the new Provisional
    Government in which all their hopes were invested
and by that time something of the same view of the matter
    was awake in the capital assembling a military
expedition under Special Order 67
    dated on the second day after Stolz's death
boarding the steamer Iwalani with twenty four
    privates under Sergeant-Major Pratt Lieutenant
G W R King and Captain W Larsen
    and as they were stowing their gear around noon a carriage
drove onto the wharf and a uniformed courier
    from the president's office introduced to Captain Larsen
with ill-concealed embarrassment Prince Kunuiakea
    representative of the deposed royal family
who had offered his services for addressing
    the insurgents and persuading them to leave peacefully

232

12.

There were reporters from the papers standing around
    the gangplank and the emissary in his gold braids
and his piping explained in a low voice to Larsen
    that the man had presented himself at the governor's
office in a public manner and because of
    the recent overthrow and the American hesitations
about recognizing the Provisional Government
    it had seemed politic to accept the proposal
with a certain flourish of welcome however
    belated and awkward and the official hope
was that the man's presence on the expedition
    could be utilized as a kind of symbolic
accompaniment however unnecessary
    —I think you understand Captain—he said and Larsen
saluted and the salute was returned and the courier
    drew from the gloved hand of his attendant a roll
of something like parchment which he unfurled and began to read
    announcing the full name of the heavy man in the carriage
and the principals in his genealogy beginning
    with his forbear Kamehameha I the courier
picking his way with evident caution through the names
    getting them right in his dead voice and then turning
to the carriage and introducing Captain Larsen
    who stepped forward as the Prince's two attendants
and then the Prince himself stood and stepped down to the wharf
    Larsen saluted with a sidelong glance at the courier
the Prince bowed slightly and Larsen told the Sergeant-Major
    to show the Prince to his cabin in the officers'
quarters and he watched as the Prince's attendants
    carried his trunk aboard and then the Prince followed
Larsen watched the top hat the black coat with its tails
    the trousers and shoes that he supposed were the garments
of an ambassador and he saluted the courier
    and went on board and the steamer Iwalani sailed at three
that afternoon with its contingent of reporters
    the men working up jokes about the Prince and his entourage
the officers raising their eyebrows to the reporters
    and Larsen and the officers came on deck before daylight
at five thirty off Hanalei to find the Prince
    and his pages clad more simply in white gowns facing the coast
where the day was about to break above the mountain

13.

From the landing at Hanalei Larsen telephoned
     to Wilcox and then on the wharf read a proclamation
of martial law in the presence of those who could
     be summoned to the place then they boarded and sailed on
and one of the Prince's attendants said to Captain Larsen
     that the Prince requested a word with him—It is about
the landing—the Prince said—and the conduct of it
     I propose to go ahead and meet with the lepers first
with as little threat as possible and I prefer
     to approach them simply and without pointless formality
I will be dressed just as I am but on the other hand
     it is important that they should be aware of who I am
and have some idea of who I represent
     in the traditions and story that are theirs and mine
I shall require to go ashore with a guard of honor
     such as befits and will indicate my position
I think four men might be enough one at each of the four
     corners around me and my own two attendants in white
going in front without arms—Larsen said—I will allow you
     a boat when we get there for yourself your companions
but if you intend to speak with the lepers you will have to
     introduce yourself to them I have no intention
of sending men ashore in the way you describe and there is
     nothing in my orders that suggests it—Larsen
was aware that the reporters had been listening
     and he continued—You have heard my offer Prince
will you go in the first boat or will you not we have heard
     that the lepers are resolved to resist any force
sent to capture them—and the Prince said—I thought I had
     made it clear that what I requested was not a show of force
but a guard of honor indicating my heredity—
     —Fall in—the Sergeant-Major shouted to the men on deck
and the flag was run up for sunrise—There will be
     no guard of any sort from my command—Captain Larsen said
—Will you go or not——I will not—the Prince said and turned
     to the rail and the passing coast and Larsen muttered
to the nearest reporter—Did you see how the Prince turned
     a little white when I told him he would have no protection—

14.

—Fall out—the sergeant major shouted and the men sat around
      smoking and polishing their rifles and whispering behind
the Prince's back and Larsen said to Lieutenant King
      —Once he learned that we would not cover him he decided
not to play the part after all and I had been thinking
      before we were assigned the privilege of transporting
royalty of sending one of the native constables
      ashore first to find out from the ones who are there
how things stand now but I have decided simply to land—
      At nine-fifty off Haena Point they saw a group
of several families on the beach around whaleboats
      whom they learned by sending a boat had come from Kalalau
rather than be caught in a battle between lepers
      and soldiers and when they were asked whether they thought
the lepers would resist a landing no one would answer
      they steamed on to an anchorage off the beach at Kalalau
there the men were lined up on deck and Larsen addressed them
      concerning the objects and duties of the expedition
and the possible risks saying that some were convinced
      that the lepers were resolved to resist any force
that was sent for them and then with a glance at the reporters
      he asked for volunteers for the first boat and each
of the officers later reported proudly
      that All of the men volunteered underlined and they loaded
the first boat with as many as it was meant to carry
      there were sixteen and they landed without opposition
forming at once into a column of twos and marching
      quickly across the beach and climbing to take possession
of a tableland overlooking the lower end
      of the valley where they halted until the others
came up to them and then they marched on up the ridge
      to a point where one of the native police informed them
that they were some three hundred yards above the place
      where Mr Stolz had been killed and there they pitched their tents
and hoisted their flag over what the reporters
      were told was Camp Hitchcock and the sergeant major
noticed as one man handed it to another
      a tattered yellow copy of a book he had noticed
on deck that morning something about Geronimo

15.

Early that morning Kaleimanu and Ida
      were playing along the stream above the mountain house
and Pi'ilani was talking with her mother Kepola
      saying that perhaps Kepola should take Ida
and go back to Kekaha now before more trouble arrived
      but Kepola said that she wanted to stay with them
and Ida wanted to stay and Kepola said
      she kept thinking of Kaenaku and wondering whether
she would see her again and they heard the children's voices
      high with excitement and went upstream and found them
bending over a clear pool before a cleft in the rocks
      Ida was saying maybe it was only the fish
swimming upstream—Look at the fish—she said but Kaleimanu
      said—It is the water too—and she said—Maybe it is
just turning around—and he said—Yes it is turning
      but it is going back up look there—and he pointed
—It is going up—he said—The soldiers are coming—
      and Ida started to cry—It is going up—he shouted
and then he looked at Ida and said—You must not cry—
      and he put his arms around her—They can never come up here—
he told her—It does that so that we will know about them—
      and he saw Kepola and Pi'ilani and told them
in his high voice and they all went down and found Ko'olau
      sitting in the doorway with his rifle on his knees
and Kaleimanu ran and told him about the water
      and Ko'olau asked the children about it and then said
as though it were part of the childrens' game—There is a steamer
      down in the bay I have watched it come in and anchor
and a boat has left it for shore it may be the soldiers—
      And Ida was crying again and Kaleimanu
kept telling her that they would not come up past the waterfall
      but they all went out and sat among the rocks at the end
of the ledge where they could see down the valley and at last
      they saw Paoa hurrying up the trail by the stream
when he got to the ledge he said before he had caught his breath
      —They are here soldiers a lot of them—then he gasped and said
—I hid behind Kaumeheiwa's and heard their officer
      read from his paper shouting and he is going to kill us
is what he said unless we let him take us away—

16.

After a moment sitting there hearing him
     breathing heavily Koʻolau asked Paoa
—What will you do then—and at first Paoa said nothing
     staring down into the valley and out to the steamer
and the whaleboat going out to it almost too small to see
     —I will stay with you—Paoa said—and fight if they come—
—You are frightened—Koʻolau said—Yes I am frightened—
     Paoa answered—The captain said they will hunt for us
and if we do not give up before nine tomorrow morning
     they will shoot us on sight but I will stay and he will
not catch us up here only now I have to go down
     one more time to bring my wife—and Koʻolau said to him
—That is how Stolz caught you when you went back to your good house
     and he took you away from your wife it is not long
since the time when we lived down there one by one we moved down
     closer to the beach and the rest and it was good then
all the children together it was there that we lived
     just down there and it is gone since the day he came
now you should go down and let them take you and your wife
     you do not want to stay up here and she would not like
having the soldiers come—Paoa looked down the valley
     then he stood up—I will try to come back—he said
—A few are ready to go with them and I hope
     the Judge escapes this time the same way as the last time—
then they watched Paoa picking his way down the trail
     and at the mountain house they began to pack up the things
they would want to take with them if they needed to move
     to some other shelter in the cliffs and the things they meant
to hide and come back for and Piʻilani watched her mother
     who she thought had always seemed to find every trouble
from her own ailments and her husband's multiple life
     to the coming of the sickness and the setting out
from Kekaha and all that came after at once familiar
     and amusing and she saw it again as her mother
folded and packed and went out with the children to find
     hiding places in the low cellars under the cliffs
as though they were playing a game she had grown up knowing

17.

Captain Larsen had lined up his own men on the beach
    and sounded a bugle to call what inhabitants
might be within hearing and had read the proclamation
    of martial law following it with his statement
that his men would shoot on sight lepers who had not surrendered
    within forty-eight hours he was maintaining the conduct
of the campaigns in the western states which he had studied
    then he sent out parties to begin searching the houses
those near the beach first and by mid-afternoon three lepers
    had emerged saying they were ready to go away with him
one was badly disfigured one a woman with deformed hands
    one an older man who had been living by himself
they were herded into the neatest house near the beach
    which was said to belong to that same Kaumeheiwa
who had carried the news of the murder of Stolz to Mānā
    though accounts varied as to where Mr Stolz met his death
some said there near the house and some said it was farther up
    on the way to the cliffs but that house was requisitioned
and the lepers left there under guard until such time
    as they should be removed supplies meanwhile being ferried
from the steamer by whaleboat and stored there and the night
    passed quietly then after reveille the searching
of the houses continued Neil Boyle and Louis Toussaint
    coming to the closed door of the house where they had been told
former Judge Kauai had been living though Mr Stolz
    on his last visit had found no one there and the neighbors
told him the Judge had not been seen there for some days
    and may have gone up to the cliffs somewhere Boyle and Toussaint
struck the closed door with their rifle butts and then
    opened it and found the house empty but went on looking
pulling down tearing open poking with bayonets
    Boyle jabbed at a pile of blankets and tent halves and heard
a muffled sound and dragged out a woman who told him
    her name was Kaenaku and admitted to being
the Judge's wife but said she had not seen him and turned
    her back on them as they went on searching the house
until a bayonet under the bed touched something yielding
    and Boyle and Toussaint put their heads to the floor and found
themselves looking at a dark roll of sail swaddling
    a wad of dirt-colored bandages that they discovered
were protecting the feet of the retired Judge Kauai

18.

—If you burst in upon us so rudely—the Judge said to them
    when he had managed to crawl out and sit up with his back
propped against the bed—You will have to allow some time
    for us to make ourselves presentable and if I
am to go anywhere I can tell you that I shall require
    considerable assistance since I can no longer walk
—We want no more of your tricks—Boyle said to him—And this house
    will be watched until I receive further instructions
for dealing with you—He stood looking down at the Judge
    —We know about you—he said—We call you the Archleper
It is your fault that all the rest of these lepers are here
    and all this has happened and Mr Stolz was murdered—
—Still wearing the King's old uniforms I see—the Judge said
    smiling up through his mat of hair—Hand-me-downs they too
were young once upon a time—and Boyle and Toussaint
    left the door open when they went and Kaenaku closed it
The search continued and the number of lepers huddled
    in Kaumeheiwa's house grew and another three were brought
out of a beach cave and meanwhile the tents at Camp Hitchcock
    were struck and moved a mile farther up the valley
to a place on the ridge overlooking the stream
    They named the new site Camp Dole and put up their flagpole
while a search party found the grass house of that same Paoa
    who had been arrested and with Mr Stolz when he was killed
inside they found a rifle and cartridges several issues
    of the newspaper Holomua in Hawaiian
with Ko'olau's name on them two baskets packed ready to go
    and outside in the undergrowth they found Paoa
and his wife and arrested them and took them to the beach
    where one Wahinealoha had also been arrested
though later he turned out not to be a leper at all
    and he and the tall man named Pā both said they knew
where the stronghold was that the lepers had in the cliffs
    Pā said he would not go up but Wahinealoha
and Paoa were sent to talk with the outlaws and before
    sundown they were back saying that eleven lepers
were coming down behind them which Wahinealoha said
    was all of them except Ko'olau—Is that true—
Larsen asked Paoa who answered that he did not know

19.

—And what will Koʻolau do now—Larsen asked Paoa
        —He will never come down—Paoa said—But what of those
who are with him does he not care about his family—
        —His wife says she will not leave him—Paoa answered
—and their child is a leper and does not want to leave them—
        —What are you smiling at—Larsen asked him—Something
the boy said about you—Paoa answered—No he will not
        leave them——And what if we corner them——Koʻolau
will fight to the last—Paoa answered and Larsen said
        —You are telling me that he will allow them to be
killed I expect a man like that might kill them himself
        if it came to that——Those are your words—Paoa said
—I believe he would—Larsen said looking at the Lieutenant
        and the reporters—But I am happy that the rest of them
are being sensible though I am a little surprised
        we had been told that they were a strong force heavily
armed—and as he said it the first of the lepers
        from the cliffs appeared on the trail sick and weak and crippled
Paoa said—Some of them want to speak with the Prince
        before giving up—and the Captain laughed—Oh the Prince—
he said—I am not even sure where he is this is martial law
        we do not have time to waste on nonsense——And some of them
wanted to speak first with Sheriff Wilcox—Paoa said
        —It is too late for that—Larsen answered—I am in command here
put them all inside—and a soldier guided them
        to the doorway and turned back for the rest
—And our hunt—Larsen said—has scarcely begun——Tomorrow—
        Lieutenant King said—we can begin to shoot on sight—
—And out of sight—Larsen said pointing to the beached whaleboat
        from which the new Krupp howitzer was being unloaded
They watched and the reporters watched as it was turned
        and rolled up the beach to sit facing up the valley
—Give the ones in the house there something to eat—Larsen said
        —and tell them that they will leave on the steamer tomorrow
along with the other residents of Kalalau—
        and he started up toward Camp Dole leaving the reporters
taking notes around the gun crew before they went off
        to their own camp on the beach complete with jester Marmont
government detective and dandy who returned from his own
        explorations with long yarns about naked hobgoblins
which that evening offended his more earnest companions

20.

In the ghost dawn Piʻilani heard the owl and she reached
     and touched Koʻolau's arm—I heard it too—he whispered
—I think it is Kala—but he put his hand down
     on Kaleimanu's lips and as he rolled from beneath
the blanket he was holding the rifle and he sat up watching
     Then they heard a whisper—It is a friend Koʻolau
it is Kala—and Kala slipped from the bushes
     —I came down last night—he said—I have been out there
I did not want to surprise you in the dark—and Koʻolau
     put the gun down and stood up and embraced him—They have
caught Kilohana—Kala told him—I had to tell you
     They have four men hiding up there on the top of the cliff
where the trail from Waimea starts down and Kilohana
     was ahead of me and they caught him they never saw me
I heard them talking he was good he answered them
     he never told them anything and now they think
they have everybody except you they have a mirror
     up there on top and one down at their camp and they flash
messages back and forth and tomorrow morning
     they say when the signal comes they will start to shoot on sight
They do not know where you are yet but they have brought
     a big gun and they will come trying to find you
They say that this morning they will take away everybody
     from down in the valley so that nobody will be left
except you by then—Piʻilani and Kaleimanu
     and Kepola and Ida were sitting listening to him
—I would stay here with you Koʻolau and fight against them
     because we are friends and my own chiefs are all gone
but I was thinking about Piʻilani's mother
     and the little girl if they want to go now I can take them
we can take the pig trail up that side that these people
     do not know exists we could start in a little while
and go up that stream and get behind that rock wall
     and they will not see us—Koʻolau looked at Piʻilani
and nodded and Piʻilani looked at her mother
     and said—You have to take her now—and they stood up
and embraced crying silently and made a small bundle
     saying nothing and the children stood facing each other
and put their arms around each other and then Kala
     embraced Piʻilani and Koʻolau and said
—I will get them home—and Kepola and Ida followed him

21.

In the morning the soldiers of the Provisional Government
    got the lepers down to the beach and gave the remaining
residents of the valley one hour before sending them
    to the steamer named for the mountain where they had lived
and as the whaleboats were taking them out a man on a horse
    with an entourage of rough-looking dogs rode down
from the ridge and the sergeant major challenged him
    informing him that the valley was under martial law
the man told him that his name was Kinney Wili Kinney
    and said he had land over Haena side up into
Wainiha and cattle there and he said no he had seen
    no lepers anywhere and the sergeant asked him
how he had passed the sentries—What sentries—Kinney asked
    then the sergeant major told him that they were hunting for one
Ko‘olau the murderer of Deputy Sheriff
    Louis Stolz—Oh I know Ko‘olau—Kinney said
—but I have not seen him for a long time now—and the sergeant
    asked whether he had known Louis Stolz—I have met him—
Kinney said—But not here though I heard about his visits here—
    —What did you hear—the sergeant asked and Kinney answered
—I understand that the last time here he was angry
    and he told the lepers that those who did not go with him
he would hunt down and shoot them——Who did you hear that from—
    the sergeant asked—From some of the women when I was
over here looking for cattle——We are clearing out
    the valley now—the sergeant told him—and I am
ordering you to leave it at once—and Kinney
    called his dogs and rode off without another word
glancing once at the steamer before he disappeared
    The last whaleboats reached it and the Waialeale
got under way and rounded the point toward Haena
    and Kalalau seemed empty in the morning sunlight
under the white tropic birds wheeling far up toward the cliffs
    They drew the howitzer up from the beach and fired it
toward the distant rock face five rounds the sound crashing
    and rolling like a storm around the stone buttresses
and the crags and pinnacles thousands of feet up the echoes
    falling over each other before they sank and then nothing
and one search party went up the west side of the valley

taking Paoa and they found nothing and they burned each house
after looking inside it and another party
    under Lieutenant King went up the east side of the valley
and found nothing and burned each house as they left it

22.

The largest group in the hunt fifteen of them under
    sergeant major Pratt began by burning the beach houses
and then started up the stream burning and late in the morning
    where two streams flowed together they found fresh tracks
in the mud showing that a number of people had passed there
    shortly before but they grew uncertain as they traced
the marks along the stream because they seemed to continue
    in several directions finally they decided
to follow tracks leading up toward the cliff and they crawled
    through a dense tangle Pratt said it seemed like a pig trail
they picked up a broken gourd with some taro in it
    and came up from the thicket onto a level patch
that they saw was a campsite with sleeping places
    for at least eight and it appeared to have been used
until some time that morning they found fresh pieces
    of orange peel and a bundle of food including fish
wrapped in ti leaves bags of taro and of salt and a coat
    with two cartridges in it and Miller said either they
had left in a hurry or they planned to come back
    it was Pratt's belief that they had just abandoned
the site when they heard the soldiers and the tracks led on up
    crossing the stream between rocks and went on climbing
several hundred feet to the base of the straight rock face
    where they could see what might be a way up and Pratt ordered
one or two to volunteer to see whether that was
    the trail and Anderson and Evanston said they would go
and they started up with McAulton and Johnson
    and McCabe and Herschberg and Reynolds and the others
behind them they had been climbing then for hours
    Anderson was from Norway a village in the mountains
and Herschberg was from Sweden from a stony farm
    McCabe was almost fifty and said he had been
at Gettysburg thirty years before and in the long campaign
    that ended at Appomattox and that he had seen action
in the west and he would mention things from those times
    in the army before he shipped to the islands
and married a Hawaiian woman and settled down
    —And if you settled down—they would ask him—What are you doing
back in the army again after everything
    and no advancement for all that—they said that was hard
to understand and he would tell them it was a living

23.

Of the seven who had come up from the valley
    with Koʻolau and Piʻilani bringing the rifles
two had gone with Paoa when he was sent up to talk
    and the other five had moved into the clearing
in the thicket below the cliff where Koʻolau
    and his family had been staying since the soldiers landed
They sat watching down through the trees and when the steamer
    got under way and left the five had made up their minds
that there were too many of them to hide in such a small place
    and they had decided to move across the valley
to a cave they all knew and if they were driven from there
    they would take the back trail to Wainiha and they were packing
to leave when a spur of cliff over to the east
    and some way above them seemed to burst all at once
and broken pieces of rock clattered down and then they heard
    the hollow boom of the howitzer and the echoes
began rolling up around them into the cliffs overhead
    five times it happened while they crouched waiting and when
the stillness crept back again Koʻolau said—Go now
    they are sure to be coming up—and the five picked up
what they had ready and made their way into the thicket
    Then Piʻilani looked down through the trees toward the sea
and saw the smoke rising and said as though she could
    not believe it—I think one of the houses is burning—
They stood watching then and saw another smoke start to bloom
    and then another and Koʻolau said—Now they are coming
It is time for us to go up and we may not be able
    to take everything—but they picked up what they could carry
the three of them and went up beside the stream to the cliff
    and Koʻolau showed them how to go up the rock face
then he came back for their belongings and they settled
    on a ledge under a deep overhang with big rocks
out in front and between these they could see the valley
    and the columns of smoke rising into a spreading cloud
and the dark fold of the stream and then the glint and flash
    of metal the flicker of soldiers on the trail
there was the sound of water back under the overhang
    a cool breath from the cliff as they waited until the first
soldiers emerged from the trees below and started toward the cliff

and they could hear the voices and Ko‘olau stood braced between
rocks with his rifle raised and then a soldier's head appeared
in front of the ledge and he shouted—I have found
the trail—and Ko‘olau shot twice and the man was gone

24.

No one was looking up at that moment their eyes
    were on the rock face in front of them when they heard Anderson
shout—I have found the trail—and the two shots rang out
    the echoes ricocheted through the sounds of bodies
thudding down and rocks rolling and the scree sliding around them
    no one saw where Anderson fell from the ledge overhead
Evanston climbing below him was knocked from his handhold
    and slid down onto Aulton who in turn fell onto
sergeant major Pratt and Miller fell onto all of them
    Johnson who had been poised on a loose rock fell onto the scree
to one side dropping his gun and he rolled down they guessed
    six hundred feet and they were all sure he must be dead
and they picked themselves up cautiously covered with blood
    barely able to stand and Pratt said—We will retreat now—
and they crawled along to where they could see Johnson
    caught by some bushes and when they reached him they found
him still alive but scarcely conscious a long head wound
    shoulder seemed broken and knee badly pulped and Miller
started trying to bandage him while Pratt said—We will
    return fire before we go—and he ordered the others
to aim just above the ledge and they propped themselves up
    against trees and bushes and fired until they were low
on ammunition and then they limped and crawled
    over the scree looking for Anderson's body
but they could not find him and Johnson was bleeding and they
    had to take turns helping to carry and drag him
down through the thicket to rest in the empty camp site
    the afternoon clouds filling the valley had become
an acrid fog and the smoke of the day's burning
    kept them coughing as they slipped down through mud with light
beginning to fade out of the day and it was dark
    long before they saw lights in the tents and groped toward them
and there Pratt made his report beginning with the statement
    that they had located Koʻolau's stronghold and then
that Anderson was presumed dead and the body not found
    then they all began going over their wounds by the light
of the kerosene lanterns turning three of the tents
    into a field hospital for the night and Johnson seemed
to be in bad shape and would have to be shipped off
    when the next steamer got there and Captain Larsen
announced that they would go at first light to find the body

25.

At first they heard nothing except the echoes and echoes
        of the rifle and then the sounds of falling and slides
and shouts from below them and then only the cries
        of white birds sailing circling the cliffs and then voices again
smaller and farther down in waves like rain blowing
        then bullets began banging into the rock over their heads
bounding away screaming and pieces of stone spattered around them
        as the rattle of the shooting climbed over the ledge
and Koʻolau drew Kaleimanu and Piʻilani
        back under the steep overhang and said—Stay in here—
and he crawled along the ledge to where he could watch
        the shore until they stopped shooting at the cliff
and he saw them carry and drag one man from the scree
        along into the trees but it was not the one he had shot
who would not have fallen over there and he waited
        until they had gone and then crawled back to Piʻilani
and said—I have to see—and he slipped over the edge and down
        below the cliff to where Anderson would have fallen
found the man rolled far down and checked for signs of life
        took off cartridge belt shirt necktie to look at the wounds
still bleeding and he plugged them with ferns from the woods
        started to haul him to where they would be sure
to see him and left him in plain sight with the hat
        under the head and he noticed a bayonet by itself
off on the scree and no sign of a rifle and went back
        up the cliff where Piʻilani had unwrapped fish and taro
and held some out to him—There is water back there—she said
        —a little and some in the gourds—and they ate and Koʻolau
took one of the rifles and gave it to her and said
        —You remember when we would go shooting there behind Mānā
this rifle is better than the one you shot in those days
        if you need it—And she said—Why did you go down there—
Koʻolau answered—I wanted to be sure he was dead
        I saw them carry away somebody I thought
was not the man I shot and I went down to see—
        —You knew he was dead—Piʻilani said—They never
went near him—Koʻolau said—I needed to see—
        —Would you have gone if you had thought he was not dead—
she asked—And left us up here—He answered nothing
        Kaleimanu whispered to him—Is it the story now—

248

—What story Koʻolau asked him——Where the soldiers
    come up the cliff one at a time and he throws them down—
Koʻolau said—It is like that story in some ways
    as you are like Kaleimanu your grandfather
but not all the same—And he felt the child shivering

26.

Larsen and King and Pratt sat up late in the tents
    at Camp Dole writing their reports in the night heavy
with damp smoke and the aftertaste of smoke Larsen
    fought it off with cigars and each of them at some point
looked up at the shadows in the tent wall and heard
    the owl hunting down along the valley over
the charred remains they all slept badly Johnson was moaning
    they were awake before the bugle and the morning gun
and Larsen and Reynolds led a party up to the fork
    in the stream and on up to the cliff where Anderson
had been shot and they looked for his body and found it
    finally shirtless the hat under the head the wounds
plugged with ferns the cartridge belt off to the side and they
    carried him down to the woods and Larsen examined
the ledge through his glasses and ordered an attempt
    to climb the cliff to one side to a place where they
would be able to fire onto the ledge and the men
    started up through the woods to a crevice in the rock face
Larsen was watching and there was not a sign from the ledge
    McCabe was climbing up the rock face and when he appeared
to be almost high enough two shots rang out and he fell
    and then another shot but this one came from the edge
of the woods where Herschberg's rifle had caught in a vine
    and Herschberg had been killed by his own gun
they took the bodies down into the campsite that Pratt had found
    every man in the expedition who was not wounded
was there by then several of whom claimed to have seen action
    against the Indians on the plains and they stood smoking
agreeing that this beat anything they had ever seen
    they knew where he was now but they saw that he could not be
approached except by one man at a time and would be sure
    to pick him off before he himself could be seen
it would be suicide to try to get him that way
    so they took the bodies down to Camp Dole and buried
all three together Mr Hoogs reading the service
    and fired three rounds over them and kept a detail
on watch up under the cliff and that evening a message
    came from Sheriff Wilcox saying that he had five lepers
who they knew had been somewhere in the upper valley
    they had been out near William Kinney's above Haena
and it seemed they had given up for a good meal

27.

From the ledge they could hear the voices before daylight
    and at dawn the shooting began again a few bullets
at a time and they heard the voices coming closer
    they could look down through the rocks to the edge of the woods
and again a man was climbing up toward them Pi'ilani
    could see him moving up with two others behind him
and then Ko'olau's rifle fired and she saw the man
    fall back and it fired again and another man fell
and the rest went back into the trees and the shooting
    kept on and then stopped and they stayed there looking down
through the rocks trying to move around into the shade
    as the sun rose higher and Pi'ilani brought a gourd
she had left in the cave to fill and gave it to Kaleimanu
    and in the middle of the day as they sat waiting
Ko'olau said—There may be more of them coming
    and what will you do if they kill me—And Pi'ilani
picked up her rifle and said—I would rather die
    than be taken by them—And then she said—But what would they
do with him if he was alone It would be best
    to die all together—Ko'olau said—If it seems
that there is no other way I will try to kill us all
    quickly and we will not see the rest—And they pulled the child
to them and sat with their arms around each other
    Pi'ilani said—Yes that would be best—And she felt less
frightened after that and the sound of the bullets
    troubled her less striking the rock above them all that day
a few at a time then stopping then coming again
    she watched Ko'olau studying the cliffs and the valley
and she sat in the shade rocking Kaleimanu
    and looked up to see tears on Ko'olau's face and he
said to her—Let us take off these dirty clothes and put on
    the clean ones in case we are killed They know where we are now
and there are three places up on the cliff and one place
    on the trail from which they could shoot into the ledge here
and they will find those and find a way to train
    the big gun up into the ledge here so I think we must
go down to the cliff after dark taking only what we have to
    we will have to get past the sentries and wade down the stream
and up the stream on the other side to a place I know
    I think it will be some time before they can find us there

28.

They ate the rest of the food and Koʻolau took two rifles
    and Piʻilani one and they took all the cartridges
and a few things in two blanket rolls tied to their shoulders
    Piʻilani knew that the sores on Kaleimanu's feet
were getting worse every day and it was not easy
    for him to hold things because his fingers had grown stiff
and were twisting up tight but Koʻolau told him
    to follow close behind him and they started down
a foot at a time feeling the rock in the dark
    slowly as snails over lichen and came at last to the foot
of the cliff face and the treacherous scree and Koʻolau
    picked up Kaleimanu and put him on his shoulder
while they skirted the trail and went down into the steep dark
    under the trees to where they could hear the stream running
and when they came to the water he put Kaleimanu down
    and told them not to step in the mud but on the rocks
then they knelt and drank and felt their way down the stream
    until they began to hear the soldiers talking
above them in the campsite where they had stayed before
    they went up to the ledge and they slipped past the soldiers
down through the water between the rocks where the current
    pulled them they hung on and slid down rock by rock
and came to where a stream flowed in from the other side
    and they inched their way up that stream to a leafy hollow
with walls of stone on three sides and Koʻolau drew them out
    under the small trees there onto a beach of shingle
and then moss and they lay there in the dark holding
    Kaleimanu who was shivering again and she asked him
whether his feet were hurting and he told her no
    They lay there and slept some until it began to be light
and Koʻolau said—The name of this place is Koheo
    and it always seemed to be a good place but now we must go on—
and they slipped back into the stream and up the valley side
    and Koʻolau left Piʻilani and Kaleimanu
part way up and went off to see whether his friend
    Kelau who had a house at a place called Kaluamoi
was still there and he crept to where he could see the house
    and saw PG soldiers sitting in front of it
laughing and playing cards and other people around there

he thought it must be one of the guard posts now and he left
and they climbed farther up to a place called Limamuku
with a cave above a waterfall and banana trees

29.

Pratt wanted to use the howitzer Larsen opposed it
    saying it took too many men from the scouting parties
King wanted to send a contingent up to a corner
    on the Waimea trail and fire down into the ledge
and Larsen opposed it saying that at that distance
    they would accomplish nothing and he sent a note
down from the mountain to Pratt asking for six men
    for the Wainiha trail adding that there was no danger
over there which King read by mistake and as both men
    had been finding Larsen's temperament hard to endure
his lofty moods and caprices the note as they construed it
    led to heated words at Camp Dole later in the day
and a rivalry dividing the expedition
    with Special Police on one side and Provisional
Government troops on the other became more deeply entrenched
    and after relieving the guards up at the clearing
which they now called the lepers' campsite or the police camp
    King returned to Camp Dole to find that Larsen had left
in a whaleboat with instructions to do as he pleased
    with his plan for firing down into the ledge but that he
would take no responsibility for it and Pratt rolled
    the howitzer farther up the ridge to a flat spot
where they could aim it above the ledge and after signals
    to the men at the camp they fired several rounds but as they
could barely see the ledge above the trees they withdrew the gun
    and resumed the occasional rifle volleys around it
during the day and that evening Larsen came back
    from Kekaha by whaleboat bringing with him two natives
a woman he said was Koʻolau's sister and a man
    who was her husband and he said they would go next morning
up to the ledge to talk to Koʻolau they were frightened
    and were kept under guard that night and before they left
in the morning he told them that any treachery
    would cost them their lives and then he started them up the trail
with soldiers behind them bayonets fixed and Larsen
    had never pronounced her name and was not aware that the woman
was not Koʻolau's sister but a cousin who was called that
    and they had scarcely set out before she began pleading
—Koʻolau Koʻolau do not shoot it is only Palila
    sister Palila sister Palila—At the police camp

254

a skirmish line was formed to move up behind them
    and Palila and her husband climbed to the empty ledge
where they found old blue overalls a pair of boys' trousers
    a cotton shirt some dried eel and empty cartridges

30.

Through one tree above the waterfall they could see
    framed in leaves Waimakemake the ledge that they
had come from and when they heard the rifles begin
    again in the early morning they looked across
and saw here and there a splash of stone where a bullet
    struck the cliff and then later in the morning they heard
the crack and roar of the big gun again and the echoes
    reeling around the cliffs they could see the puffs of smoke
rising from down in the valley at a place Pi'ilani
    thought must be the ridge at Pune'e and they saw rocks
shatter above the ledge at Waimakemake
    and fall onto where they had been lying and she thought
they would destroy it all but then the shooting stopped
    and they could hear voices from far down in the valley
but then it was quiet for the rest of that day
    and the next morning a long way off they thought they heard
a woman's voice calling very faintly and they moved back
    from the waterfall to try to hear it and at last
Pi'ilani said—Yes I think it is Palila—
    and Ko'olau said—Yes they have gone and brought her and made her
come up how frightened she must be they must be with her
    just behind her the soldiers and that is why we heard
those signal shots from the top of the cliff this morning
    and they sat hearing the frail sound and whispering
about where she must be now as she called—Sister Palila—
    —Poor thing—Pi'ilani said—They went to Kekaha—
Ko'olau said—Frightening everybody with their
    guns and their uniforms and those faces Provisional
Government or whatever they told everybody they were
    and made her come with them—Pi'ilani said—They are going
up onto the ridge—and they kept trying to hear her
    and then far over on the ledge they could just see her
and someone with her a man and then soldiers and then they were
    all gone and bits of voices floated up from the valley
but for the rest of the day they heard no more shooting
    except signal shots from the cliff top and they found food now
fern shoots and shell fish and small fish out in the stream
    and bananas and after another day of hearing
nothing from below Ko'olau climbed to where he could see

the whole valley and there was the steamer in the bay
but the next day the bay was empty and from farther on
he saw that the tents were gone and there were no boats on the shore

31.

He sat for a long time looking down into the valley
      watching the shore the sides of the far headland the glint
of the taro ponds and the ridges as far as he could follow them
      he looked across at the ledge at Waimakemake
and the cliff above it but he saw no one no sign
      of anyone there and as the light began to go
he went back to the green hollow above the waterfall
      and they ate and drank and began to ask each other
whether the soldiers could have left Kalalau hardly daring
      to say it at first but they asked whether it could be
possible and if the soldiers were gone whether they would be
      coming back and whether they had left guards on the trails
or at the cliff top and after a while Koʻolau said
      —They made Palila go up onto our ledge over there
and they saw we were not there and the shooting stopped after that
      maybe they think that we have climbed out of the valley
there is that trail up from Waimakemake that they
      might have heard about because Mr Gay had it cleared
a few years back and there is the way Kala went up which they
      would never find under the deep ferns they would not
think we could have come down at night past the sentries
      and if they believe we have left the valley they would have
no reason to stay but they might have left guards hidden somewhere
      or send in spies or offer rewards to get people
to come into Kalalau looking for us and even if they have gone
      they could be planning to draw us into the open
so we must watch carefully all the time and see whether
      anyone at all is still in the valley and if they are
we must not let them know we are here because someone
      may be watching them or someone may visit them
and look for us and so for days they slipped out carefully
      from Limamuku and the banana trees by the water
and down the stream and they left Kaleimanu to watch
      the cliff top and the upper ridges when they climbed down
along the rocks of the stream to get food and when Koʻolau
      made his way silently farther and farther
from the waterfall to look up the side valleys and down
      to the trail and climb to crevices where he could see
the ridge where the soldiers had camped already the mark of them

was disappearing under the green and that night
back under the shelter where it could not be seen
    they built a small fire of dry sticks and cooked a meal

32.

Then for a quarter of the moon they lived that way
    going out from Limamuku in the morning
together sometimes and sometimes Koʻolau alone
    scouting the valley farther and farther from their hiding place
sometimes Piʻilani and Kaleimanu would wade
    down over the slippery rocks catching shellfish
and the little fish that climb upward through the current
    sometimes Kaleimanu would stay in one place listening
he seemed better now that their life was quiet again
    but the seizures of cold and the shivering kept returning
he would go to sleep and wake with his teeth chattering
    and then he would sleep again and she would lie awake
One morning when he was asleep she went with Koʻolau
    to the old campsite on the other stream below the ledge
they found pieces of clothing boxes that already
    seemed to have been there for lifetimes and out on the rocks
there were empty cartridges everywhere and under bushes
    another rifle some more rags and nothing else
they did not climb to the ledge for fear it was still being watched
    but they stayed for a long time looking down through the trees
to the valley below and the shore and up to the cliff top
    they stood where the soldiers had been talking that night
when they had slipped past below them in the sound of the water
    and after all those days they were still whispering
She said—The medicine that we brought up from the Judge's house
    was all gone by the time we came up here and the leaves
that I have been putting on the sores on Kaleimanu's feet
    seem to be doing no good now maybe they were only
for the old sicknesses before the haole came bringing
    all the new things to die from and turned them loose on us
to get rid of us but I keep putting those leaves on him
    the right way with the prayers and still the sores are no better
and yet he never cries about them and that night when we
    went down the stream there I thought his feet would hurt him
and he would cry but he never made a sound and when I
    asked him he told me they did not hurt and I thought maybe
the cold water helped him not to feel it—and she
    stopped and said nothing more and Koʻolau said
—It was true that his feet were not hurting him—and she looked up

and he said—Mine are hurting me less and less now
though the sores seem to be getting worse the way they did
on Kaleimanu's feet before we came to the valley—

33.

When they got back to Limamuku they found him
        out on the level ground across the stream lying
looking up along the cliffs and the cliff top and he said
        he was cold and they felt his hands and feet and he was
cold everywhere and Koʻolau brought a blanket
        and Piʻilani said—do you think we could go
for part of the day down to where it is warmer—and Koʻolau said
        that they should look now for somewhere else and they gathered up
their few things and and he carried Kaleimanu in the blanket
        on top of the rolled bundle and they went down the stream
watching as carefully as ever and crossed a gorge
        where the cliffs almost met above them but opened out
just below there and taro was growing at the base of them
        by the rock face in the reflected sunlight and deep woods
covered the nearby slopes He told her the name of that place
        was Oheoheiki there were cave shelters in the rock
and there was food all around them and it was warmer
        below the gorge and Kaleimanu seemed better again
and they went on every day learning the valley again
        like some place that was new to them as it reappeared
out of what they remembered and what had happened there
        the whole of Kalalau seemed to be empty now
the echoes sounded as though no one else was there
        besides themselves but they knew the places from which
someone could watch from the heights or the side valleys
        or the turns on the trails and they took care not to
show themselves where they could be seen from any of those places
        they made their fires far back by the cliff faces or in caves
when it rained they stayed in caves far up in the gorge
        and in the sunlight they skirted old taro ponds where the weeds
were returning and looked out from bushes at the blackened
        rings and pointed out to each other where the houses had been
Koʻolau took Kaleimanu down into the clearings
        full of sunlight and they would gather food among trees
they had known before and they watched the light change from
        summer and the moon swell and the rains quickened
When Kaleimanu was left by himself he made up
        stories of his own which he told them as though they had happened
and he had seen them and after the chills he would tell them
        where he had been travelling all that time while they
held him and rocked him in the blanket and talked to him

34.

The months of autumn passed and they moved from one sheltered place
    to another sleeping in hollows among the cliffs
the rains were growing heavier toward the end of the year
    all the clothes they had were becoming the same color
the taro ponds were brimming and they worked together
    in the sunlight clearing some of the overflows
pulling weeds and piling them on the banks as they were
    pulling the taro to eat and they found stones for pounding it
wherever they went because there had been houses
    by the ponds for so long and banana groves and fruit trees
sugar cane tamarind and candlenut trees and the stones
    that had been used as tools for generations were lying
by the stone walls and steps and platforms of the houses
    where the grass was fringing the black clearings again
and the three of them had grown used to hearing the empty
    valley as an unbroken sound in which there were no
voices except their own and still they spoke softly
    and close and would hear the note of the valley recede
as they bent among the taro leaves and it was there
    around them again when they stood up One morning
Pi‘ilani was down in the taro pond wearing
    the ragged dress and a pair of trousers she had made
out of some cloth they had found and over them Ko‘olau’s
    jacket and hat to keep the sun off it was a morning
when the sound of the valley was not clear sometimes the sick wind
    did that or rain somewhere or a mist and she stood up
among the leaves listening thinking that she had heard
    something different and then there was nothing and then
a man’s cough and not Ko‘olau and she crouched under
    the broad leaves and stopped breathing and heard men’s voices
and she looked up to where the trail climbed the side of the valley
    and she saw that half-white Wili Kini the cane burner
looking down toward her and she drew back under the leaves
    but she was sure he had seen her and she heard him whistle
and looked out and saw Kelau and Keoki come up
    beside him and she slipped along in the mud under the leaves
and out to where Ko‘olau was sitting with Kaleimanu
    she was breathless telling that there were men there
Wili Kini and others Kelau and Keoki up there
    and he asked—Did they see you—and she said—Yes

when Wili Kini saw me he whistled—and Koʻolau said
    —Come and hide—and he took his gun and they crawled under
the thicket and listened hearing the voices come closer

    and when the talking came to the thicket and stopped outside it
Koʻolau stood up facing them holding the rifle

35.

—Oh it is Koʻolau—Wili Kini said and the others
     came up and said—Koʻolau—and Wili Kini told him
—I am happy to see you we never knew where you were
     we saw somebody down in the taro and we were looking
for one Japanese who has been stealing from houses
     over Hanalei and Haena way and they caught him
but he got away and we thought that was who was down there—
     and all three came over to Koʻolau and held out
their hands and said—Koʻolau—and they embraced and he said
     —Now you all know we are here what does that mean for us—
and Wili Kini said—I am your friend Koʻolau
     I will help you if I can—and the others said the same thing
and Kelau who had long been Koʻolau's friend and whose house
     the soldiers had used for a guard post had tears in his eyes
and they asked how he was and Piʻilani and Kaleimanu
     and Koʻolau called them to come out and they all sat down
and Piʻilani brought food for them to eat together
     and Kelau said how glad they had been to see the soldiers go
and Kini told about the five lepers who had been caught
     and about the ones who had got away and were still hiding
in the cliffs over Hanalei side and they said
     that Koʻolau seemed to have driven the soldiers away
but no one knew what had become of the three of them
     at first people thought they had escaped from the valley
up the cliffs but then the time passed and no one saw them
     in Kekaha or Mānā or anywhere and they wondered
whether they could still be alive and Piʻilani
     saw the men looking at Kaleimanu and at Koʻolau's
feet and Koʻolau said—We are well in spite of them—
     and they told him what had happened to the lepers
from the valley the steamer took them to Honolulu
     they had heard about it and it was in the papers
it took four men to carry the Judge down the gangplank
     in his city suit with his broad hat and the band
of peacock feathers around it and his blue sunglasses
     he told them that in his opinion they were all pirates
and their authority was pirates' authority
     he could not use his hands or his feet and they carted him
to the hospital along with Kaenaku and that
     little girl whose whole face was gone and Kamalinui

and he died there a few weeks later They sat in silence
　　　Tears ran down Pi'ilani's face and Wili Kini said
—If you see any cattle they might be mine you can shoot them
　　　and eat them if you want to—and Ko'olau thanked him
but he said—You know I could never repay you—

36.

The next day they were down there and they heard voices again
    and watched from hiding and saw Kelau and his wife
Keapoulu coming down the same trail and they went out
    and greeted each other in the old way this time
without suspicion crying and embracing each other
    and their friends had brought along clothes for all of them
and matches and a bag of fish caught that night and another
    of dried fish and some cooking pots and knives and gourds
and they cried together and ate together talking
    about friends they all knew and what had happened to each one
since the summer and Kelau and Keapoulu
    sat with them through the middle of the day talking
they were all trying to tell each other everything
    Kelau said that a few people of Kalalau
were talking about moving back and rebuilding their houses
    and Koʻolau nodded and said—You will remember
not to tell anyone that you have seen us here—and they
    promised and promised again as they were saying good-bye
and after they were gone months passed and became years
    in which they spoke with no one else though they saw people
they knew come back into the valley Wahinealoha
    came back with his wife and they built their house again
in the old place and cleaned out their taro ponds and they kept
    chickens a few at first and then there were many of them
and Piʻilani or Koʻolau went every day
    and watched what they were doing but Koʻolau said
that Wahinealoha should not know that they were there
    He said—He is someone who says yes to everybody—
and they agreed that they must let no one in the valley
    know that they were there because then everyone would know
and Kelau had said he had heard that a reward
    had been offered to whoever could catch Koʻolau
so they moved more often than before taking more care
    to leave nothing behind them that would show that they had been there
they watched the Pā family come back and build their house again
    and then one neighbor after another but they never
showed themselves and they saw cattle from time to time
    that must have been Wili Kini's and Koʻolau's rifle
was never far but he said he would not use it again

267

except to protect them and Kaleimanu grew weaker
month by month and his nose shrank away and his mouth puckered
it was hard for him to hold anything and he shivered
more often and for longer and they carried him everywhere

37.

It was summer again and they were in the upper valley
    where it was safer to risk a fire and one morning
they looked down to the bay and saw a whaleboat coming in
    and Koʻolau made his way down the valley to learn
who had arrived and he managed to see from a hiding place
    Wahinealoha walking down to the beach
and loudly greeting twelve young men nine of them haoles
    the other three Hawaiians whom he knew from Kekaha
he thought the whaleboat was the one Knudsen kept at Kekaha
    and as the haoles came closer with Wahinealoha
he saw that Knudsen's sons had come with friends of theirs
    and Wahinealoha was telling them that he could have
chicken for them all to eat and yes he could show them
    where the battlefield had been and Koʻolau's stronghold
and the boy he recognized as Eric was telling his friends
    how this Koʻolau who had worked for his father and this
Louis Stolz had shot it out here a couple of years ago
    it sounded strange to hear it called a couple of years
and Wahinealoha said nobody knew what had happened
    to Koʻolau and whether he and his family
were dead or still living somewhere in the valley but no one
    had seen them and Koʻolau heard Eric tell them
that he had known Koʻolau since he had been a boy
    and they had ridden to Halemanu together and gone out
hunting together and Koʻolau was the best shot
    he had ever seen and he admired him and Koʻolau
as he listened was trying to think what reason Eric
    would have for speaking like that to Wahinealoha
and he watched them go up the trail to the temple platform
    where the soldiers had camped the first night and on up the valley
and he followed and watched them go part way up the stream
    and then go back down and sit eating along the beach
and later swim in the surf and then leave in the whaleboat
    heading toward Nualolo and that night they talked about
Knudsen and Halemanu and Waiawa and Kekaha
    and their friends and then the summer went on and they moved
through the valley like birds as Kaleimanu said once
    when a dark thrush flicked past them among the tree shadows
before evening in the upper valley and then autumn
    was there in the light and they saw how weak he was growing

269

38.

It had been three years since the night they set out from Kekaha
    and they nursed Kaleimanu into the end of the year
and though the upper valley was safer for lighting fires
    it was colder up there and the small clearings where the sun
shone but he could still remain hidden where almost all
    down in the lower valley and Koʻolau's own feet
were growing worse but he said to Piʻilani that it was
    the chills shaking the child that frightened him most and he told her
one night that Knudsen had said about the leper house
    that it was seldom the sickness itself that they died of
but he had said that it weakened a person so deeply
    one way and another that something else at last
would take them down—But he was always thin like that—she said
    —and often cold and his lips would turn blue and he shivered—
—This may have been following him a long way—Koʻolau said
    The next day he climbed the cliffs away from the trail
high up to where he knew the petrels nested the ʻuwaʻu
    that Kaleimanu kept talking about in his story
and he waited and caught one in his hands which were beginning
    to grow numb and to curl and stiffen and as he caught it
he knew that he would not be able to do it again
    and he took it down finding it hard to cling to the rock
with his feet feeling almost nothing though he saw that the sores
    were torn and bleeding and his feet seemed to be shrinking
back into the heels and he thought how hard it would be
    to come up there again but he carried the bird
to Piʻilani and they made a broth of it
    and gave it to Kaleimanu that night telling him
what it was and he drank it saying ʻuwaʻu
    over and over and then he seemed to be better
for a few days and then a few more but they could see
    that he was sinking away from them whatever they did
he was still with them when the year turned at the rising
    of the Pleiades and through the winter almost
to the days when the light changed to spring and one night then
    he grew cold and weak from shivering and he was
too far to hear them and his breathing grew hoarse and then stopped
    and they knew he was gone and they sat with him until morning
and then they took him up to a small cave hidden
    in a buttress at the base of the cliff and they dug
a grave for him inside it and lined it with ferns and buried him

39.

As they laid him in the ferns she began the chanting
　　in a low voice patting her knee she chanted to the water
dripping down to them and past them and below them she chanted
　　to Kane there on the cliff top to the altar of Kane
the water of Kane who listens and to Kane the sound of rain
　　to Kane the light that comes back Kane the silence
Kane the silence of the stones Kane the silence
　　of the face of the child we are waiting for you
for you at the place you know at the foot of the mountain
　　to see whether you are coming back and then they sat there
until it was full daylight and they covered him with ferns
　　and with the earth and set stones on the grave and sat there
all that day and it seemed to Pi'ilani that she had
　　turned into a shadow with no weight and no senses
and when the light began to go from the air she longed
　　to walk down to the shore and into the sea and lie there
floating with the waves moving her and she told Ko'olau
　　that she wanted to go down to the water and let it hold her
but she knew it would be too dangerous someone would see her
　　and he said he had the same wish to go down to the ocean
and walk into it and let it carry him and wash him new
　　and he said that someone might see them but that it was the time
to go and they went carefully down through the safe places
　　and on down the valley after dark and out over the stones
of the shore and out into the waves and rocked there
　　she felt the tears burn on her face and the knowledge
that Kaleimanu had gone was rocking her and turning
　　into her and into knowing that she would lose Ko'olau
and that she was losing him as they rocked in the same waves there
　　looking up at the same night clouds over the deep valley
she knew it that night as they went up through the darkness
　　to the cliffs and the grave and after that night she knew it
as she had known that she was no longer afraid after that time
　　on the ledge when she had agreed that they should all die
together if the moment came now a fear made of hope
　　went out of her and a fear made of none took its place
they left the grave without offerings and went down
　　toward the valley and slept that night in another place

40.

Without Kaleimanu to take care of any more
     and keep warm and carry with them it was easier to move
around the valley and to her it seemed too easy
     as though she had been cut adrift and was floating away
but Koʻolau's feet were much worse after the day
     when he climbed the cliff and after they buried Kaleimanu
the torn sores were deeper and they never stopped bleeding
     and rotten water came out of them and she saw
him walking on the open sores as his feet shrank back
     and when he walked he left prints of blood and fluid and rags
of flesh trailed behind his footsteps then she took pieces
     of clothes that were falling apart and she washed them in the stream
and wrapped them around his feet and he cut a stick to walk with
     —We do not have to travel very far or move very fast
the way we live—she said and it was a summer of plenty
     they watched friends of theirs come and rebuild their houses
and take care of the fruit trees beside their taro ponds
     and there were fruit trees wild or untended up through the valley
fern shoots and shellfish from the streams and he still carried
     the rifle from one sleeping place to the next and it lay
within reach at night but she saw the way he held it now
     distantly absently as though he had forgotten it
the kamani stick that he used for walking was nearer
     to his mind and grasp than the rifle seemed to be
and they had hidden the other guns months before that
     she saw that his hands were curling tighter the fingers
shrivelling until it was awkward for him to eat
     and he picked up more things with the heels of his hands
but he seemed almost well that summer although he was weaker
     than she had ever believed he could be and in
the evenings they would sit in the dark as the coals
     closed themselves in the ashes and they would say nothing
for a long time and then find that they had been thinking
     of the same thing and they would talk of what they remembered
without sadness or it seemed to be without sadness
     and then would be silent again and she would start to chant
under her breath patting a shell or her knee bringing the chant
     out of the darkness around them and offering it
to the darkness ahead of them and she thought of his face

as it was crumbling into itself that summer and autumn
and winter and when they slept to the sound of the rain
some nights she dreamed of white sand and voices along the shore

THE SHORE

1.

The shore was what she had always known but could not see
    she saw nothing clearly except the sands and the footsteps
it was like Kekaha and Mānā and it seemed that it was
    Kekaha and Mānā but it was neither of them
and out to sea it was dark and the voices had just gone
    they had just been there and she was still hearing them but they
were silent again and there was only the breathing
    of the sea and she opened her eyes on the ghost dawn
and saw the owl in the hala root watching her
    where she was lying on his grave under the ferns in the thicket
as she stared at it she was thinking of Kawaluna
    and when she closed her eyes and opened them again the owl
was gone and she lay knowing where she was and she heard
    the trees dripping and the stream whispering below the rock wall
and she remembered the whole of it in a moment
    the last months together four years after they had come
into the valley the winter rains sweeping the cliffs
    the streams roaring at night and rocks crashing and lunging down
through the trees and day by day it was harder for him to move
    with his feet nearly gone and his hands almost useless
and his mouth twisted into itself so that it was hard
    to eat or drink and he talked about what she would do
after he was gone his fear that if they were to find her
    she would be punished for what he had done and for staying
with him and for their life together they saw footprints
    in the mud by the streams as they moved from one shelter
to another and as she went down over the rocks
    to get food for them and they talked of the footprints
whose they might be and who might be trying to find them
    one time as they were moving upstream in the water
they found a bundle tied like an offering sheltered by ferns
    beside the trail and he said they should not touch it
no one must know they were there and at other times
    during those months they found bundles like that by the trails
up near the cliffs and knew someone was looking for them
    either to trap them or try to help them but they never
touched them and she went on getting food from the stream
    and wild fruit from the valley and he talked about how long
it might be after he was gone before it would be safe
    for her to be seen and be recognized and go back
to Kekaha and her mother and her family again

2.

She remembered Kaleimanu saying that he was falling
   asleep before he died and his face was in front of her
all during the days when she could see Koʻolau
   sinking from beside her those months when he was going
the same way the child had gone it was more than seven months
   like that and at the beginning of that time he could
still talk to her as they had always talked and they stayed
   close in their words but later when he tried to talk to her
it sounded as though he were calling from a long way off
   in a hoarse voice though there was a day in one of those long spells
of green sunlight and fragrance and stillness that arrive sometimes
   in the winter with the drops shining at the ends of the leaves
when he spoke to her again from no distance and told her
   that after he was gone he wanted her to bury
his rifle with him because he said she had never been
   the one who had used it and it would stay in the ground with him
afterward and that then she should leave the valley
   and go back to Kekaha and their house and families
and when she was questioned she should tell them the truth
   that she had stayed with him and their child as she had always
said she would do and as she had promised to do
   when they were married and that she had killed no one
but had come with him and stayed with him until the end
   and when she had buried him in that ground where she was lying
and had left him there in the sleep of the seasons
   and gone down the stream through the trees and close to the houses
of people she knew who had come back and had passed by there
   down into the sea and out through the turning of the waves
and had lain there again looking up at the clouds and the stars
   that appeared and vanished between them she stepped out
onto the rocks and went around by the side of the valley
   to leave no trail and went to a spot near a side stream
where there was a thicket of lantana next to the water
   near a path that led along by the taro ponds
a place where she could be hidden from everyone
   but look out and see them and hear what they were saying
and she crawled into the deep thicket and made a bed there
   and slept alone for the first time in the valley
wanting to be near some of the people she knew
   but not wanting to show herself to them not yet not yet

3.

Then for a while she made her home in the thicket
    listening to the voices during the daytime
as they went by on the path and to those who were working
    in the taro ponds recognizing some of them trying
to hear what they said and learn what had been happening
    while she had been up in the cliffs however long that had been
syllables floated past out there like butterflies and she
    tried to catch the sounds of names even her own name
she kept watching for signs of soldiers of the Provisional
    Government or of the police and only after dark
would she come out of the thicket to gather fruit and fern shoots
    after the moon rose and she lived that way until the moon
had returned to where it had been when he died and then when it
    darkened again and before it grew full she crept
out of her hiding place toward the end of one day
    when she had heard them all going home from the taro ponds
and she smelled the smoke rising from the evening cooking fires
    she stood up and watched the last sunlight out on the headland
and when it was gone she moved farther from the houses
    keeping off the trail as she started back toward the cliffs
she had wrapped tightly the few things she still had with her
    the knife the rope the can of matches in her one blanket
and as she climbed along by the stream she put wild fruit
    inside the front of her dress as she passed trees she knew
after dark she paused at one of the places where they had lived
    when there had been three of them and she sat with the moonlight
coming through the 'ohia leaves and the halas
    she looked back down through the valley where she had been
where she had known that pain was ahead of her and she looked
    for that pain as though she might see it but there was
only the moonlight in the valley now where she had stepped past
    the days and where she had lost and hidden and had known
what she was losing and had expected to die
    she looked through the moonlight and thought that perhaps she
had died and was seeing the valley from afterwards
    but she felt it still around her sheltering her
protecting her as it had done through all that time
    and a love for it welled up in her eyes and filled
with moonlight and she stood up and started along the trail
    and climbed to the mountain house where they had first stayed

279

when they came at the beginning the roof had fallen in
    the leaning timbers were deep in moss and she rested there
as the moon was setting and slept until the stars
    were growing faint and then she went on up the trail
with the darkness dropping away around her and came out
    into the cool of the cliffs and she climbed until dawn
and kept on climbing until she came to the cliff top
    as the rays of the sun were reaching down into the valley
and she stepped out on the level brink of Kalou
    and turned to see it all below her in the morning

4.

Time had vanished since she had stood at the top of the cliff
 looking down and out over the valley of Kalalau
seeing it from outside and above and then it had been
 somewhere she had not seen before and now it seemed
as she looked down into it that it was her own life
 out of which she had climbed and the whole valley with the clouds
and the cloud shadows passing over it was closer
 than the night's sleep that was behind her and she knew it
wherever she looked she knew what was under the trees
 what was in each hollow and she stood there seeing again
what had happened in each place then carefully she
 took her leave of a life that she felt was still with her
she spoke to it aloud out of the aching of her body
 calling by name to one part of the cliffs and the valley
after another You Kamaile guarding the darkness
 of Kane you that watch over the sleep of Koʻolau
You Kahalanui that hid us at the beginning
 under your wing You Waimakemake that kept us
safe from the soldiers' bullets I will remember you
 with love until I am nothing but bones in the ground
You Kohco that embraced us and Puneʻe
 where we were never hungry and Limamuku
green hollow above the waterfalls into you
 we had vanished when they could not find us and You curtained
cliffs of Kaʻalaneo with the ridge below
 that kept them from seeing us You rock face of Kalahau
that broke the flights of the bullets everywhere around us
 You Oheoheiki that welcomed us and fed us
and shaded us through the hot days and kept us dry in the winter
 you were like a parent to us and you Kaluamoi
that cradled us when we needed you and hid us from the hunters
 where we saw the clouds blow away and the stars shining
and the waterfalls white far above us you Kalalau
 where I am leaving hands and arms that I love eyes that I love
faces that I love you that hide them and keep them
 I am going away now I will not set eyes on you now
you will be hidden from me now I am cold with a coldness
 that was not there in the night not there until this moment
a coldness in me a coldness all around me spreading out
 the thickets are tangled in Kuhonua the flowers

have fallen onto each other in piles the sea is wild
    under the battering south wind the Waipao wind Kalalau
the wind at the edge shook her and she turned away

5.

She went slowly along the trail that followed the cliff
    from Kilohana to the path down to Kaunuahoa
and the valley of Halemanu and the mountain house
    of the elder Knudsen whom they used to call Father
the house where they had stopped when they were coming over
    those years before when all of them were together
the moment she turned from the cliffs a great weariness
    settled into her the weariness of the climb
caught up with her all at once and the weariness
    of uprooting herself at last from her life of hiding
and from the bare ground a great effort even though the thoughts
    of her mother and of Kekaha and her friends there
had been with her all that time and more closely than ever
    after she had buried Koʻolau and had gone down
to hide through the days so close to people she knew
    hearing their voices and as she lay there in the thicket
listening to their voices sometimes she thought of Kekaha
    and saw it more clearly than the day that she was watching
through the lantana leaves and now as she walked down the trail
    like a shadow in the forest it was not the forest
that she had come to know like a thought of her own
    in which every sound was something she recognized
During those years in the valley sometimes she saw faces
    and houses and moments from long before in Kekaha
and then among them places by the stream and moments
    of light in the valley and when she saw the house
at Halemanu she stopped as the place and her own
    memory of it came together not all at once
but hesitantly and then she walked down watching
    to see whether anyone was there but the house was empty
and she went nearer under the big trees through the running
    sound of the stream and saw the blind stare of the windows
the day was going and she climbed the front steps
    onto the lanai and sat looking down the green slope
as the light lengthened and she took out the last
    of the fruit she had brought with her from Kalalau
and the rain began whispering into the trees around her
    she unrolled the blanket on the lanai and lay down
and when she closed her eyes the stream she went on hearing
    was in Kalalau somewhere and she tried to think of its name

283

6.

In the first light she saw the mist travelling in silence
     under the dark trees and she thought she was in the night world
where there were no faces and she was not sure where she was
     until her hand moved on the cold blanket and she felt
the rough wool that had come with her so far from its first life
     stained and torn through years of hers and then she remembered
Halemanu the house of the birds and she heard them
     all around her beginning the day and she sat up
and rolled up the blanket and walked down with the bundle
     to the Brook of Tears below the house and put her face in it
she remembered where there were guavas along the trail
     and she started down through the mist moving stiffly
slowly after the climb of the day before and she heard
     the forest stirring around her as she had come to hear
the valley around her through the years of hiding
     Where the trail was joined by another she heard something
in dry leaves on the ground and at once she was gone
     among the bushes until she saw that it was a pair
of dark thrushes finding their food and now that she
     was on her way to being among people again
she found that she did not want to be seen by them
     she was not sure what she would do when she was back
in Kekaha before faces she knew or used to know
     but as she went back to the trail she listened as before
and as the mist thinned and wore away into the opal shade
     of the ʻohia trees it seemed to her that the forest
was exposed to the daylight and she moved cautiously
     down the mountain to the broken rim of the canyon
everywhere open and she moved away from there
     out of the sound of the wind through which she could hear
nothing else and she went on past the ghost place that smelled
     of dried fish still and came to the turn where the west slope
of the mountain all lay before her as far as the coast
     Waimea and Kekaha and the broad shore before Mānā
glittering in a crescent and the sea beyond them
     she stopped at each turn watching for signs of anyone
on the trail below her and she stopped at the spring thinking
     of where she was and trying to recall Kekaha
which all at once seemed to be like the other side of a door
     she stopped at a turn and stared over Waimea and where the trail

284

forked she turned toward Kekaha letting the day pass
    approaching it along the back trail past the small valleys
and at dusk she passed like a shadow among the houses
    to the tamarind tree and her mother's back door

7.

There was a fire burning between rocks and her mother
       and Kinoulu were bending over something they were cooking
and she walked toward them slowly until they stood up and saw her
       and burst out with those cries that were sounds both of love
and of grief and they stood with their arms around her
       wailing and crying and she cried with them and Ida
came out of the house so much taller that Pi'ilani
       was sure she must be someone else and then she knew her
and they stood there crying together auwe auwe auwe
       for all that was lost and the pain and the finding again
repeating each others' names and then Ida was gone
       and came back bringing Kepola's parents and went again
and came back with Ko'olau's parents Kukui
       and Kaleimanu and they all stood embracing and crying
by then it was dark and the fire shone on their wet faces
       showing grief and joy and bewilderment and it was long
even before the questions began and longer
       before anyone thought of eating but she told them
that she was thirsty and they brought her water and watched her
       hold it up and drink and they talked to her the whole time
and Kukui could be heard crying above all the rest
       and then they brought soft things and had Pi'ilani sit down
with something to lean back on and something for her feet
       and someone brought her cold sweet potatoes and someone else
fish and taro but before she could eat they wanted her
       to tell them something and then the crying began again
and she told them of the deaths and of the soldiers
       a little at a time and of the houses being burned
and the hiding and the time on the ledge and the bullets
       then someone came bringing Ko'olau's cousin Palila
the one they both called Sister and she cried louder
       than Kukui and told Pi'ilani how the soldiers
had come to her house at night and had taken her
       and her husband and ordered them to come with them
to Kalalau and told them that they had to go up
       and make Ko'olau surrender and said that if they did not
they would be killed and she cried and told them how frightened
       they had been with the soldiers' bayonets in their backs
making them go up onto the ledge and how happy they were
       when they found no one there and Pi'ilani said nothing

286

8.

She woke in the dark again believing that she was nowhere
    a tide without waves a night without leaves or streams
a wooden stillness then she followed the smell of wood
    to her mother's house and knew where she was and heard
her mother stirring in sleep and the next time she looked
    there was enough light for her to let her eyes roam
over the dark boards of the walls in the room where she
    had not slept since before she had gone with Koʻolau
it came back to her from that time through the way it was now
    fishing nets sagging from the pegs for clothes and sacks standing
in the corner then her mother woke on the other side
    and they began their morning together and Kinoulu
and Ida came bringing fruit and Piʻilani said—Now
    tell me while we are here by ourselves how you came back
after you left us that morning—and Kepola said
    —Kala led us along the loose rock into the ferns
where there was a pig tunnel and we crawled after him—
    —With those hooks on the ʻuluhi ferns tearing us—Ida said
—But Kala told us not to widen the tunnel at first—
    Kepola said—or the soldiers might find it and try
to come after us———And then we came out on the other side
    of the rock wall—Ida said—And we started to go up
in a crack of the cliff and I was so frightened
    that I was trying not to shake——Then we heard the shooting—
Kepola said—But the soldiers were on the other side
    of that cliff where it runs out and we even heard bullets
but nowhere near us—And Ida said—Kala told us
    that the soldiers could not see us but I was afraid
that they would see us when we got higher and we would
    not be able to move there in the rock and when I looked down
it was a long way to fall but we kept on climbing
    after Kala hearing the shooting and the echoes
that went on and on around us and then we came up
    into bushes near the top of the rock and the ground
was steep and crumbly but there were places to step and he
    waited for us at every step and then there was a ridge
where he told us the goats ran and we went up that way
    that was steep too but there were aʻaliʻi bushes
but some places it was like walking on top of a wall
    and I never looked down the sides—And Kepola said

287

—At the top we were in the woods with only the goat track
      but we went along and then we were on a trail
and all at once we met Kua up there watching the cliff top—

9.

Kepola said—He had come up from Halemanu
    he told us he had been up there every day since they heard
that Ko'olau had shot Stolz he had watched along the trail
    from Waimea and had seen the boats come into the bay
and he had watched the soldiers come up from Waimea
    and set up their sentry post in the trees above the trail
he went and talked with them none of them friendly at first
    the haoles suspicious asking him who he was
and what he was doing there but the Hawaiians knew him
    and they all knew who Mr Knudsen was and then Kua
went by every day and talked with them and saw the mirrors
    and heard what the soldiers were doing down in the valley
and what they were planning and he saw who the soldiers
    caught at the top of the trail and took away
to Waimea he rode with them part way he warned
    friends bringing things to the valley and told them about
the sentry post he could hear the big gun booming
    from far down in the valley and he kept watching then
to see whether any of us might be coming up
    and he told Kala not to let the soldiers see him
and then Kala left us and it was Kua who brought us down—
    Kepola said it with sadness and disbelief
—It was Kua who brought us to Halemanu and down here
    all the way down but we never told everybody
only family you know and to all the others
    we just said we made it back and what a long way it was
and you know that is true but nothing about Kala
    or Kua and of course we knew nothing about you
what had become of you and that was true it was true—
    Then Kepola cried with her arms around Pi'ilani
and Ko'olau's father Kaleimanu came and Kukui
    and Kawaluna and all the grandparents and they
went over the stories and the questions and Kaleimanu
    said that Palila and others were talking of having
a big feast for Pi'ilani with everyone there
    but Kaleimanu said he thought that would not be wise
and Pi'ilani said that she wanted her homecoming
    to be as quiet as possible with as little talk
as possible and she said she hoped it would be a long time
    before the government people heard that she had come home

10.

Pi'ilani's father Ho'ona came home later from the mill
    and said that he had heard down there that she had come back
and then they went over the whole story again and when
    they stopped for a while Pi'ilani asked her father
who had told him that she was home and he said—You know
    how news travels—and he told her who had told him
then she said—That is why I do not want everybody
    coming now that I am back and asking and asking
going away talking there is too much talk already—
    And they all considered that and agreed with her
and Kepola said—It is not only government
    you know there were always some who said Ko'olau
was too stubborn he went his own way he spoke out—
    —I suppose so—Pi'ilani said and Ho'ona went on—When he told them
he would not go to Moloka'i if they ordered him to go
    even then some said he was a trouble-maker
and they called it a shame—and Pi'ilani said
    —I know some of those—and Kepola said—It is worse now—
And then one day Ho'ona brought news that would make it still worse
    —Dr Smith—he said—But not old Dr Smith in Koloa
whom you remember—and Pi'ilani said—The one
    who sent Niuli away——Not him—Ho'ona said—His son
young Dr Smith everyone liked him he was a kind man
    and he has been killed he was shot in his own house
and by a Hawaiian at night there in Koloa
    his sister was living with him and she had gone to bed
he was writing a letter at a table and there were horses
    in the street and feet on the steps and a knock at the door
and when he opened it this man Kapea shot him
    full in the chest and then rode off but they caught him
he did it because the doctor had seen that Kapea's
    sister and another woman in the family
had leprosy and he had told them that he would
    have to report it and he was a friend of the family
he had taken care of them he had them live in his house
    when the father was sick and everyone knew that he
took care of Hawaiians for nothing when they needed him—
    —When did it happen—Pi'ilani asked—Just now—
Ho'ona said—It was Friday night he was shot—

11.

She learned that all the lepers had been taken away
    from the house in Kekaha where Valdemar Knudsen
had arranged for them to be cared for and that Knudsen
    had been sick recently and seldom left Makaweli
she stayed at home with her family and with Kawaluna
    and she could talk with Kawaluna about the valley
the days and nights in hiding the cold the sickness the dying
    the darkness the sounds in the night the burying
the valley at night when the soldiers had all gone
    the sound of the empty valley it was only to
Kawaluna that she could talk about those things
    and Kawaluna would sit without moving and listen
and when Pi'ilani stopped she would say—Yes—but if
    someone else came they seemed to be talking about nothing
and to those outside the family Pi'ilani
    said little and waited for the questions to stop and she thought
that some day the government would hear that she was back
    and someone would come asking but the months passed and the winter
and Ho'ona came back from the mill one evening and told her
    in a low voice that there was a rumor of someone
from Hanalei finding Ko'olau's grave in Kalalau
    and showing people things that he had taken out of it
and Pi'ilani felt a cold hand tighten around her
    that would not let go of her and she asked Ho'ona
what he knew about the man and the things from the grave
    and who had told him and that night she said nothing
and lay awake and then got up and went out and made her way
    behind the houses to the house of Ko'olau's family
she saw Kawaluna sitting outside and sat beside her
    and after a while told her in a hushed voice all
that she had heard and Kawaluna said that Ho'ona
    had told them and that others had told them the way everyone
tells secrets and Pi'ilani heard that she said it
    with her own laugh and Kawaluna said—And so you
stayed awake—and when Pi'ilani said nothing
    Kawaluna asked her—Are you afraid to know
whether you think the grave this man found was Ko'olau's—
    And Pi'ilani said—I have to see—and Kawaluna
said—Then you have to see—and after a while she said
    his name—You have to see Kalua i Ko'olau—

12.

The next day Pi'ilani said to Ko'olau's father
　　—It was not Ko'olau's grave that the man broke into
I am sure of that but now someone claims to have found it
　　I want to go back to the place where I buried him
and visit his grave—He said—You should have someone with you—
　　—Not to the grave—she said—But maybe part of the way—
Kaleimanu said—I would go myself but my legs
　　I think are too old for the climb down so maybe I will ask
Kuala at Waiawa when I go up there tomorrow
　　he was a good friend of Ko'olau's they used to hunt
together up at Koke'e with Kua and he spoke
　　to Ko'olau as to an elder brother and I know
he went with Kua along the edge there while you were
　　in the valley he used to take things from the ranch
for the lepers in Kalalau he does not talk much
　　and if a stranger asks him questions he says nothing
he has come here with Ko'olau——I remember him—she said
　　and it was Kuala who was waiting for her
in the early light a few mornings later and she
　　mounted the horse that Kaleimanu had saddled for her
and rode up the trail behind Kuala and there were
　　friends of his from the ranch staying at Halemanu
one of them rode with them up to the cliff and the trail head
　　below Kilohana to take back the horses
and she saw Kalalau open again before her
　　with the clouds coming over it telling nothing
and again she started down the trail under Na Iwi
　　stepping into her own memory into the same light
and the air and the rock smells and the cries of white birds
　　wheeling and flashing below her as she went down
and the shadows climbing around her the goats calling
　　on a cliff far away in the white sun and she let Kuala
get ahead of her at the turns until she was
　　going down alone into all of it and when they came
to the stream she told him to go on by himself
　　and told him she would meet him some time later at the house
of Kelau and Keapoulu who were friends of his
　　from the days when he used to come over into Kalalau
with Kua and Ko'olau and hunt in the valley
　　and she watched him go down the trail and stood listening

13.

Then she crept silently down the trail behind him
     and stood again listening and again and stood listening
and waited to be sure that he was not hiding and coming back
     she thought that even he might be turned around by
curiosity and try to see where she was going
     she waited hearing the sounds of the valley the stream
there below her the trees in the late afternoon the birds
     then she stepped back hearing her own footsteps and watching
the forest as she went up the trail and aside
     carefully to the left through the ferns under the trees
breaking nothing and drawing the fronds back together
     behind her and then stopping still as a thrush stops
in the fallen leaves to look around without moving
     she climbed slowly into the long hollow between
the rock walls at the foot of the cliffs and came silently
     through the green shade at each step drawing it shut again
until she stood before the ferns where she had buried him
     and once more she stood listening and heard the whisper
of that place as she knew it in her mind a breath
     a rustling lighter than water and she bent in the ferns
and looked and saw that nothing had been touched and that moss
     had grown back over the stones she had set on his grave
she knelt and the tears came and shook her and when she closed
     her eyes she was there in the time when they were all
still together cold and wet a time with dread running through it
     like an echo at night but it was a time that she
tried to touch in the darkness with her head on her knees
     crying silently and then she stopped and whispered
into the moss—Koʻolau Koʻolau Here I am—
     and then she was still and stood up and looked around her
it was the same place that she knew and had kept in her mind
     when she was not there but it seemed that she had not seen it
before in its own light and age in which she was
     a stranger like a dream that had vanished upon waking
and now the grave was part of the place and its light and age
     it was looking past her at something she could not see
that must be all around her in the daylight and the shadows
     She drew the ferns back and made her way down through the rocks
the way she had come and when she reached the trail again
     the sun had already gone from the top of the cliffs
and she went on to the house of Kelau and Keapoulu

14.

Their house was set in a lap of rock with the cliff behind it
        they were standing outside watching for Pi'ilani
as she climbed toward them and they ran down the path to meet her
        greeting her as at her homecoming in Kekaha
crying and wailing and drawing her back up the slope
        then the questions and fragments of stories tumbling over
each other all that had happened since they had last seen her
        down there by the taro pond with the things they had brought
for all three of them when there had been three of them
        and then nothing and they had not known and no one had heard
and they brought things at other times food and clothing
        cooking pots and knives and tools other friends had sent for them
to bring over but they never knew where to leave them
        where the three of them might be or whether they were alive
but all that winter they left bundles by the upper trail
        hoping some of them would be found and Pi'ilani
sat with her arm around Keapoulu and told her
        —We found some of them and knew they might be from you
but we never knew who might be watching for us
        looking to see whether those things had been taken
and coming to think that we were up there somewhere and hunting
        for us so we never touched them we left them there
to make it seem that we were not here in the valley—
        Then they started telling her which friends had come back
into Kalalau and of their learning that she had
        returned alone to Kekaha and they cried and she said
—Now they tell me that someone is saying he has found
        Ko'olau's grave—and they said to her—Some men came by here
from Hanalei side and said they were hunting goats
        and went down to talk with the Pā family whom one of them
said he knew and they met Wahinealoha
        you know the way he is when any stranger is coming
so they asked about Ko'olau and he said that he could
        show them places they wanted to go and then they went on
by themselves he says and must have been looking for the grave
        and they came down saying they had found it—And Pi'ilani
said nothing at first and then she said—Whatever they
        found it was not Ko'olau—and Kelau said he never
thought it was Ko'olau—We never believed that they
        had found our friend there were always graves up there and we
can guess sometimes whose they were and sometimes nobody can say—

15.

Half waking again knowing that she was in the valley
        but under a roof once more she lay still in the darkness
it seemed to her that she felt nothing and knew no names
        no stories and that she was flying without moving
in a night without stars without end without morning
        or memory and then she thought This is the grave
that is not a grave this is the wind that is not air
        this is where they will never find us and even as
she thought it she knew that she was Pi'ilani
        in the house of their friends Kelau and Keapoulu
her hand was touching the black grass of the wall and she knew
        why she was there with Kuala sleeping outside
and then she slept and woke knowing that it was near day
        and she got up and went out to watch the clouds trailing
their long arms across the sky showing a fragment
        with its stars in their places fading as she looked
and then closing over them again and the dark valley
        under them seemed to her like the sleep of a child
closed in itself then she heard the grass rustle in the door
        and Keapoulu whisper behind her—Sister—
and they stood together at the edge of the rock platform
        with their arms around each other and then sat down
and Keapoulu began to tell her who they should visit
        and Pi'ilani spoke of friends she had seen in the valley
when she was alone and living in the lantana thicket
        listening to them and Keapoulu told her
which taro ponds they were working now and which families
        had rebuilt their houses and had babies and who was fishing
down in the caves and out in the bay and she said
        they were dancing again up on the temple platforms
three of the teachers were back and the children went up there
        almost every day and danced the way they used to
and Kelau came out and joined them and told Pi'ilani
        who was planting new fruit trees beside the ponds there would be
more oranges than before and papayas on the banks
        and mangos in the lower places and tamarinds near the shore
—It is beginning over again—he said as the first
        daylight revealed the valley below them under the trees
and she thought of all of them waking there and of going
        down there herself and them seeing her as she was now

295

16.

She tried to say something about that to Kawaluna
　　　later when Kuala had been to see Wili Kini
and whoever else he had wanted to see over there
　　　and she had guessed that in any case he had come mainly
as a way of paying respect to his friend Koʻolau
　　　and after she had said her good-byes in the valley
as she had never done before and they had climbed together
　　　to the top of the cliff one morning starting before daybreak
and then on along the trail down from Kilohana
　　　to Halemanu and friends and horses and they had ridden
down the far side of the mountain with the light in their eyes
　　　as the day was sinking and she had seen Kekaha below her
with something of the same strangeness the same stillness
　　　and distance the same light of disbelief welling
out of a place so familiar that she had known
　　　on that morning when she walked down into the valley
which she had watched for so long like a face the face of her days
　　　and when she closed her eyes at any hour could see it rock
by rock tree by tree shadow and water and there it was
　　　again and her eyes were open and it looked to her
like the other side of itself and out of reach even when
　　　she touched the cold stream or the moss by the waterfall
and before she came to hear voices and the surprise of friends
　　　one after another welcoming her back to them
from far away far away and all day as they talked
　　　and friends joined them and they cried and ate and began
again and brought her the children to see and asked
　　　the same things over and over and kept telling her
that this was her home too now and they they would build
　　　a house for her in the valley if she would stay there
they said that to her on the first day and they asked her
　　　where she would like it to be and she smiled and talked to them
about her mother and she felt like a cloud in no wind
　　　but she told them that she would come back to the valley
and Kawaluna nodded—You will go there again—
　　　Piʻilani said—When I saw it in the other time
we were together and we were going to be together
　　　as long as we were alive and that was the way I saw
Kalalau then but now it looks like another place
　　　since I am no longer the one who was hiding there—

17.

But now she felt that she was hiding in Kekaha
    she lived in the back of Kepola's house and she listened
to find out who was coming and what was in their voices
    she seldom went far from the house and then she followed
the back lane but she walked as she had always walked
    and she told Kepola that she was not hiding
though she never knew what the officers would do
    if they found her now that she had come back after
what had happened and she did not want people asking
    about Kalalau and Kepola said—They stop asking
after a while but you know they will start again
    if they hear anything—So Pi'ilani stayed at home
and kept house with Kepola and talked with Kawaluna
    who listened to her but never seemed to ask questions
waiting for whatever Pi'ilani wanted to tell her
    and it was still that same summer when Naea came up
from a whaleboat to say to Kepola that someone else
    was saying he had found Ko'olau's grave and his rifle
Pi'ilani thought they will always say they found his rifle
    and she listened to Naea and all she said
was —Thank you—but a few days later Penekila
    the same Penekila from the old days disturbed the dogs
to tell them the same thing and Pi'ilani asked him
    what he had found out and who had told him and he answered
so that she was startled to see that he had not changed at all
    he was always on the other foot it was like trying
to pick up a roach with two fingers and she watched him
    while he was talking and thought that she would never
be able to tell the truth of it by listening
    to Penekila and then he said he was going
into Kalalau the day after next and he told her
    that if she wanted to go he would bring a horse for her
and she said yes she would go and as he was leaving
    she saw the way Kepola was staring after him
and she said to her mother—Do you want to come too—
    and Kepola shook her head slowly and Pi'ilani
told Kawaluna that she was going again
    and with Penekila this time and Kawaluna said
—Why do you think Penekila came to tell you—

18.

He said nothing as they rode up out of Kekaha
     and then when the trail narrowed toward the ridge and the brink
of the canyon and they went one behind the other
     they could not talk and she looked ahead at his shoulders
that seemed to her to tell everything about him
     and it occurred to her that he could never see them himself
she was looking at something about him that he
     could never see and she felt a touch of embarrassment
and kept her eyes from his back and when they stopped at the spring
     she asked him again what he had learned and he told her
about meeting a man in Waimea a haole name
     she had never heard and this man said that he travelled
to dig up things to sell and he told Penekila
     who he had dug up and what he had found in the graves
and where he had sold things and to whom and for how much
     —He must be rich—Pi‘ilani said—He did not seem rich—
Penekila said—But maybe he has all the money
     buried away somewhere——Did he ask you to help him—
Pi‘ilani asked—He said he had been told that I might
     know things that would be of interest to him—Penekila said
—And did you—Pi‘ilani asked and she listened
     to the way he did not answer her and began
to tell her how he had come to be working for Stolz
     who had said he needed a native able to talk
to the natives and Penekila laughed—How did he know
     you could do that—Pi‘ilani asked—After I was
working for him and he got to know me I heard how he
     talked about natives nothing new only the way
he said it he told me that if they betrayed him he would
     skin them alive and things like that and he told me
over in Kalalau that if I did not do
     as he ordered he would shoot me he would shoot anyone
who betrayed him and he told me to tell Ko‘olau
     that he had gone to Hanalei that afternoon
when he went looking for Paoa and what could I do—
     Pi‘ilani said—We thought it was like that—and she stood up
and they rode on to a camp at Kilohana
     where they left the horses with friends but in Kalalau
after they parted she followed him a long way
     down the trail watching him before she turned back to the grave

19.

No one had been there since she had left it months before
 she stood listening to the place in its own sound
with the grave part of it now and she heard only
 the hour at the end of summer as she remembered it
at last she lay down on the moss listening to the ground
 under the ferns but this time she did not stay long
with Penekila in the valley and she sat up
 with the old caution and listened and when she slipped out
did not go back to the trail but down to the stream
 and to the way they had come that night when they left the ledge
at Waimakemake and she climbed out at the old camp
 below the ledge all overgrown now with guava
and the creeping barbed uluhe ferns and she could see
 that someone had been there but not for months and ferns
were closing in over what she remembered there
 as though she had never been there and she skirted the clearing
and went down through the trees to the fork in the stream
 and on to the house of Kelau and Keapoulu
and their greetings and the evening of talking together
 and she told them why she had come and with whom and said
that the grave had not been found and they told her that this time
 they had seen the man who came asking questions and Kelau
had listened to him and had gone after them when
 Wahinealoha led the haole up the trail
and had watched when the man went on alone and had followed him
 —He never found anything up there—Kelau said
—except in Naoheiki's old mountain house all fallen down now
 he fished out one old rifle only part of it
you remember it was always there never worked
 he picked that up and took it away and a few more things
I never saw little things that was all the grave he found—
 Then they talked about Penekila and what they thought
he had come over for and Pi'ilani said
 that he was staying down with Wahinealoha
and the next morning they all went visiting and her friends
 begged her again to stay in Kalalau and she did stay
longer than before waiting to see what Penekila
 was doing over there and he said he was going
to Hanalei and was gone for days but it was Kelau
 who said—When Penekila tells me he is going
to Hanalei I begin to ask myself where he might be—

20.

Friends down near the bay said they had seen Penikila
    on the trail to Hanalei and some who had family there
and went there often said they had noticed him going
    into the old sheriff's house and there were those who wondered
whether Penekila might still be working for the police
    in one way or another but no one knew for certain
and they talked about the new sheriff named John Coney
    whom they had heard was not so bad and Keapoulu
urged Pi'ilani to stay on with them and friends there
    talked again about building a house for her and she stayed
to watch for Penekila though she was wary
    about going back to the grave again for fear
of making a trail and being followed but she climbed
    toward the cliffs every few days and followed the paths
in the upper valley looking for signs that someone
    had been through there and she told Kelau and Keapoulu
that she would not leave the valley as long as Penekila
    was on that side of the mountain and Kelau told that
to Wahinealoha who told everyone
    that she was waiting for Penekila and they talked about that
until one afternoon when she was down at the shore
    watching the fishing in the deep cave and the children
at the edge of the water and helping to load taro
    into the whaleboat for Ni'ihau her friend Keke
next to her turned and said—There he is—and they stood up
    and watched Penekila come down the trail and Pi'ilani
could tell from the way they were looking that some of them
    must have thought that Penekila was her lover
and her shoulders burned with shame as she turned back to the taro
    and that evening when Kelau told her that Penekila
was back she asked whether he had talked about leaving
    for Waimea and Kelau said he would ask him
but the next morning Penekila came up to the house
    to tell them that he was going and when and to ask
whether Pi'ilani wanted to go with him
    then the next day were the good-byes and the stepping back
and the morning after that the climb before daybreak
    there was a turn in the trail where he had gone ahead
and she stopped and looked back at the valley she had left
    it looked new and shining in an age that never changed
and farther away than she had ever seen it

21.

Even Kepola had heard that she had been waiting
    for Penekila this time and that she had stayed so long
because of Penekila and had come back part of the way
    with Penekila and Pi'ilani said—Nobody
has found the grave—and for a while that was all she said
    but she stayed at home as before and she told Kawaluna
and Kepola of her suspicions of Penekila
    and Kawaluna nodded and then laughed and Pi'ilani
looked at her and then began to laugh and Kepola laughed
    they all laughed all the women in the family
thinking of Penekila and what some people thought
    That winter they learned of the death of Valdemar Knudsen
and Ho'ona and Kaleimanu went to the funeral
    and they mourned him in Kekaha and said he was a good haole
and wondered what would come after him and then in the spring
    two men came to the house asking for Pi'ilani
one of them was the new High Sheriff John Coney
    and the other his assistant named Kaumeheiwa
and Kepola said she would try to find Pi'ilani
    and went and whispered to her but Pi'ilani said
—It is time to talk to them—and she walked into the house
    and greeted them and asked them to sit down and she looked
closely at Kaumeheiwa whom she had not seen
    since he had gone off with the soldiers in the whaleboat
she sat facing them both and the sheriff said—I was
    going to tell you not to be frightened but I think
that is not necessary—and Pi'ilani said nothing
    —Will you tell me what happened as you remember it
after you left here with your husband and son and went
    into Kalalau until you came back here alone—
and Pi'ilani said—My mother was with me
    part of that time and she can sit here and listen—
and she reached her hand to Kepola who sat down next to her
    —Yes I will tell you—Pi'ilani said and she answered
his questions and told him about it all from the night
    they left until she climbed back out of the valley
Kepola was crying but Pi'ilani's voice
    was steady as she stared past them and when she had stopped
they could hear the children playing down along the beach

dogs barking and the evening cries of the stilts and the sheriff
told her he believed her and that she would not be blamed
or made to suffer for anything that had been done

22.

So it seemed to have come to a kind of resting place
    at least in the government records but after the summer
one day Kaumeheiwa rode up to the house with a paper
    for Pi‘ilani it was a note from the sheriff
enclosing a report that he had made of finding
    a grave in upper Kalalau that he believed
to be that of the leper Ko‘olau he told of the rocks
    on top and the rotting boards and the raincoat and the rifle
and the note said the report had gone to the papers
    but he was sending this copy in case she had
anything of her own to say and she thanked Kaumeheiwa
    and told him she would send a message to the sheriff
and when he was out of sight she took the report and note
    to Kawaluna and read them to her and they sat
in silence and then Kawaluna asked—What will you do—
    Pi‘ilani said—You know it is not Ko‘olau's grave—
Kawaluna said—Yes I know—and Pi‘ilani
    said—This time I know too and maybe the next time
I will know it the way you do but this time there were no boards
    there was no raincoat and it is the wrong rifle
I can even guess whose grave it might be but it cannot
    be Ko‘olau's——Is that the message you will send
to the sheriff—Kawaluna asked her—Yes but I must
    go back to his grave myself before I send it
and tell him that I have been there and no one has found it
    I want to be able to say to him that I have seen it—
—Maybe after this time you will know—Kawaluna said
    —This time I will go by myself—Pi‘ilani said
—I will tell only you and Kepola that I am going—
    and she put her head down in Kawaluna's lap
and felt Kawaluna's hand on her head and the tears ran
    and she forgot how long she stayed there but she remembered it
when she opened her eyes and saw the owl watching her
    from the hala root close to the foot of the grave
all of it came back at once and she could still feel
    Kawaluna's hand on her head though the tears on her face
were cold and she closed her eyes feeling the hand there
    and when she opened them again the owl was gone
she put her face down onto the moss of the grave
    —Ko‘olau—she said—Kalua i Ko‘olau
It is Pi‘ilani I am here Kawaluna was here—

303

23.

The stream was swollen and loud as she picked her way
    down through the first gray light to the trail and then climbed
the path to the house of Kelau and Keapoulu
    and they greeted her and she told them why she had come
told of the sheriff's visit and what he had said to her
    —And this time—she said—I will stay only today
and rest and start back tomorrow—and as she said it
    she felt a sinking coldness in her breast at the thought
of Kawaluna feeling that Kawaluna might be gone
    Keapoulu was pregnant and they sat talking
while the sun rose and Kelau went down to the taro pond
    and after a while Keapoulu and Pi'ilani
walked down the valley meeting friends and they asked her
    the same questions and she told the story over
and over and then went back with Keapoulu
    and Kelau came up from the taro and they spent the day
together and friends came in the evening and she said
    good-bye to them all that night and before daybreak
she was on the trail up out of the valley and it seemed
    that she was still asleep and was climbing in endless
silence then a stone turned under her foot and the fright
    woke through her and she went carefully to the summit
it was late morning and she had been climbing for hours
    and she turned at the top and in her weariness
looked back one more time over Kalalau and saw it
    moving away from her like a vessel without a sound
toward the horizon and then she was walking under the trees
    on the trail to Halemanu and no one was there now
and she slept again and slept the whole of that day
    and that night and in the morning went on to Kekaha
Kawaluna had died and had wanted to be buried
    in the old way she had kept to but Kukui had wanted
a Christian service and Ho'ona had taken her part
    and by that time there was a young Hawaiian minister
there in Kekaha who had come and read from his book
    the grave was behind the house on the side toward the mountain
Kepola showed her the wilted flowers in the moonlight
    and Pi'ilani stared down and saw only the moonlight

24.

The life with her mother the old life of Kekaha
    closed around her the months passed over her like clouds
she lived as before like anyone in the families
    hers and Koʻolau's she was no different no different
but the life she had thought of as her own was past
    it was gone and she woke into what was not there
even the dread in the valley the nearness of death
    day after day the pain and helplessness and the anguish
of losing and of watching the light fade in those faces
    it had been there with her and awake in her even
the age alone in the lantana grove after they
    were in the ground they were there in the valley with her
it was part of what had drawn her back when she heard
    those first claims that someone had found his grave it was
what she still knew of that time and what she had had to touch
    and see and have around her again just as it had been
but she saw now that when she went back it was already gone
    and now she had come into Kawaluna's certainty
that no one would find Koʻolau's grave and with that she knew
    that her life there was gone and that it had been her life
and here she was in a before and after that she had
    always known and could never have foreseen and she knew
that she was older she was the same but older
    it seemed to have happened while she was somewhere else
and to keep happening when she was somewhere that she
    could not remember and she saw how the others were growing
old around her her mother and Koʻolau's family
    as though they did not notice it happening and it
was already past but when they would draw the nets in
    at daybreak she would go down to the shore with them
and haul on the rope and as the net crawled through the shallows
    with the fish flashing and shining in the clench of death
wrung in their lives and shuddering against her there
    in the same waves there was nothing else and then it would
be afterward and years had passed and she was sure
    that it all must have been forgotten now and they must think
that it was somebody else they had heard about somebody
    they used to see and she thought that now there was only
what she remembered of that life that had been there with her

25.

Ho'ona had been living much of the time in Waimea
        for years and everyone knew of his other family there
and his grown daughter but he came back to Kekaha
        almost every week for a night or two and one day
several years after Kawaluna died he told
        Pi'ilani that the Hon William Sheldon in Waimea
had left a message for him and when Ho'ona
        had called at the Sheldons' house he had been shown in
by Mrs Sheldon who was Hawaiian and they had
        gone into the parlor and she had asked him to sit down
and they talked for a while about the church in Waimea
        and the work of Pastor Rowell and then Mr Sheldon
had come in and said that his brother John had asked him
        to find out whether Pi'ilani would be willing
to meet him and talk with him about what had happened
        in Kalalau and Mr Sheldon said—Our father
as perhaps you know was a newspaper editor
        who founded one of the first newspapers on the island
of Hawaii over a half a century ago
        our mother was Hawaiian and my brother has suffered
at the hands of the Provisional Government
        because of his loyalty to the deposed Queen
Liliuokalani and no doubt because of his
        writings in defense of Hawaiian causes for John too
is a newspaper man like our father and in both
        languages and he is a man of deep Christian zeal
which I know matters to you and if your daughter
        would consent to talk with him about her own life
so that he could write it down in Hawaiian and publish it
        for Hawaiians to read my wife and I would be happy
to have her stay with us here as our guest for as long
        as it takes her to recall the events and for him
to write them down and prepare the story for publication—
        and Ho'ona said to her—I think Mr Sheldon
is a fine man and you know he is in the legislature—
        but Pi'ilani said nothing at first and went and sat
on the doorstep and Ho'ona talked to Kepola
        about the Sheldon house and how he had known Mr Sheldon
in the church and Pi'ilani sat looking toward the mountain
        and then she stood up and said—I can talk with him—

26.

Ho‘ona came back two days later and told her
       when to be ready and Pi‘ilani and Kepola
washed and packed her best clothes in a box and made three
       new dresses and Kukui gave her a new straw hat
with a band of feathers and Ho‘ona was anxious
       for her to take shoes they got her shoes out of their wrapping
and cleaned them up and Pi‘ilani asked him where
       she would have to wear shoes and he did not answer at first
but he said she should have them with her and he told her
       to be sure to take the Bible that Reverend Rowell
had given her when she finished going to his school
       and they got that out and put a new cloth around it
—Do you remember your Bible—he asked her and she could hear
       that he was trying to sound like Reverend Rowell
—I remember it—she said—Because in the Sheldon house
       I am sure they read the Bible every day—he told her
and on the day before she was to go she and Kepola
       made leis for her to wear and the Sheldon carriage came
driven by a young man who had worked at Waiawa
       with Kaleimanu and he and Ho‘ona put the box
of Pi‘ilani's belongings into the carriage
       and she said good-bye to Kepola and all the friends
who had gathered like a flock of birds to stand watching
       and Pi‘ilani said—Waimea Waimea
you would think it was the moon and I used to walk there to school
       every day and back—and she laughed and said—I will be home
before the moon is new—and then they drove off and her face
       darkened as Ho‘ona began talking to her as though
she were at school and she watched the road where she used to walk
       but she had not been to Waimea since Kaleimanu
was a child and the last time she had come with Ko‘olau
       they had been on horses and Kaleimanu was riding with him
and now that she was in the carriage she felt naked
       without him and as they came closer to Waimea
it was all familiar but it looked strange like someone
       who has been waked up suddenly and there were new houses
in place of some of the old ones there were many of them
       that she did not recognize and many were painted
and there were many people whom she did not know and they came
       to a big new house painted gray and stopped at the door

307

27.

Ho'ona got down and reached back to take her hand
    but he was in her way and she stepped down without him
and when she looked up she saw them coming out of the door
    onto the lanai at the top of the steps first there was
a Hawaiian woman maybe as old as Kepola
    and then two haole men with white hair and moustaches
and as Ho'ona raised a hand toward Pi'ilani
    and was about to say something the woman said
—You must be Pi'ilani come in come in I am
    Becky Keaonaueole Sheldon and this is my husband
William Sheldon and his brother John Sheldon and you
    are welcome to our house and are among friends here
and she held out both hands to Pi'ilani and drew her
    up the stairs and kissed her on both cheeks in the Hawaiian manner
and then turned to her husband and he and his brother
    repeated the greeting and Pi'ilani saw with relief
that they were not wearing shoes but when they led her
    into the cool house she saw shoes lined up in pairs
inside the front door and Pi'ilani looked at the stairs
    and the hatstand where she saw herself in the mirror
looking like a stranger with her hat on—I will show you
    your room—Mrs Sheldon said—And then you must be thirsty—
and she led Pi'ilani up the stairs saying—Nalu
    will bring your trunk up for you and you will meet Mele
who helps in the house—and she showed Pi'ilani
    the washstand and the chamber pot in its cupboard
and then she straightened in the middle of the room and said
    —John has talked about you for a long time wanting to meet you
he has prayed that you would come we all pray in the evenings
    together I hope you will pray with us—and Pi'ilani
nodded slowly—Come down and join us when you are ready—
    Mrs Sheldon said and she left Pi'ilani
looking at the walls painted sky blue and the picture
    of Jesus over the table the pegs for clothes
the open window with white curtains blowing and she
    could look down to a white fence and a garden plot
with a barn beyond it and then the dry pasture
    along the beach and suddenly to her surprise
she heard someone behind her and turned to see a boy
    holding the old box with all of the things from Kekaha

28.

Mrs Sheldon came and helped her to do the right things
    and it was true what Ho'ona had told her about
the Bible because when they came down to supper
    they prayed and when they were standing at the table
Mr Sheldon prayed for them and then John Sheldon prayed for them
    and thanked the Lord for bringing them Pi'ilani
to show them that He did not forsake his children
    and when they sat down to supper and Mele came in
with the soup John asked Pi'ilani whether she had
    brought her Bible with her and when she said—Yes—Mr Sheldon
told her that they read the Bible every morning
    before breakfast and would be happy if she would join them
it was like being back at school at Reverend Rowell's
    but was easier in a way because they all spoke
Hawaiian in the house and prayed in Hawaiian
    and read from the Hawaiian Bible though Mr Sheldon
spoke of the government's plan to get rid of the language
    and of Thurston boasting every year about how many
schools there were now in which not a word of Hawaiian
    was ever heard—A pity—Mr Sheldon said
in English—But we will tell your story in Hawaiian—
    John Sheldon reassured Pi'ilani—And can we begin
tomorrow morning——Yes—Pi'ilani answered
    and the passage of the Bible that they read before breakfast
was from the Book of Exodus and they each read in turn
    about the deliverance of the people of Israel
the crossing of the Red Sea and the Lord holding back
    the waters and drowning the army of Pharaoh
and when they finished reading Pi'ilani saw
    that they were all looking at her as they said Amen
and after breakfast she went into the parlor
    with John Sheldon and he opened a notebook on the table
and said—From what I have read and heard I believe
    that the cliff below Kilohana which I must confess
I have never seen is the place from which warriors
    used to hurl torches far out over the valley
and watched them sink like stars falling have you heard of that—
    —I have heard about it—Pi'ilani answered
—Because I think that might be part of our title—he said
    —The Firebrands Flung from The Heights of Kamaile and The Hero
of the Cliffs of Kalalau or something like that—

309

29.

He asked her about things that happened before she was born
    and he asked her about Koʻolau and when they were children
and about times that she had forgotten and she answered him
    as well as she could and when she told him about
Koʻolau's baptism she could see that he was pleased
    and he said he was sure that their faith and baptism
had sustained them in the trials they had endured
    but when he read back to her what he had written about them
it sounded like a story about somebody else
    more than like what she remembered of what happened
but she could not think how to tell him that it had been
    not like that and would never have belonged in those words
that came from church but she could see that he wanted it
    to be true and down under all those words it was true
and he thought the words made it true but she kept thinking
    of the time when Sheriff Concy asked her about
what happened in Kalalau and all he had wanted
    was for her to say what she remembered about it
and she thought how much easier that had been and how
    Mr Sheldon always seemed to be hoping to hear
something better but she thought he was a kind man and she liked him
    and his sister-in-law Mrs Sheldon told her
that his wife too was Hawaiian and that he spoke often
    of his Hawaiian mother and she said that he was
a real scholar and talked of Abraham Fornander
    who had befriended their father and of Fornander's
collection of the stories of the Hawaiians
    and his comparison of their customs and beliefs
with those of peoples who had lived in other places
    a long time ago and he told her that Fornander
had believed that the Hawaiians were the lost tribes
    of Israel and Mr Sheldon had said that
it might be true but he said that too was a story
    and he said that Fornander's wife was also Hawaiian
and Mrs Sheldon said I love to hear him talk
    about his mother and father and Mr Fornander
and their newspapers and Mr Fornander said
    that the story is all that we have when things are over
the story begins as an echo of what went before
    but then it is only the story we are listening to

30.

In the afternoon Ho'ona came to the house
    to ask whether Pi'ilani would like to go out
for a walk through Waimea with him and he had brought her
    a parasol and a lei to wear and they went
past the courthouse and the churches and he said he could show her
    the Kauai family house but before they went so far
he asked whether she would like to stop at a friend's
    for a glass of juice and a piece of watermelon
and he led her behind the Rowells' house and along the lane
    by the river bank to a house under a mango tree
in the doorway stood a woman about her own age
    and Ho'ona said—Pi'ilani this is Kealia—
and for a moment the two women stared at each other
    then Ho'ona said to Pi'ilani—This is your half sister—
—Come in come in Pi'ilani—Kealia said
    and Pi'ilani went up the steps slowly and stood
looking at Kealia and then she kissed her
    on both cheeks and Kealia kissed her in return
and then they embraced and Kealia began to cry
    —I have wanted to meet you for a long time—she said
—and ever since I was small I have been afraid of you
    I heard everything about you I saw you when you came
to church I heard how beautiful you were and I thought
    when I saw you how beautiful you looked and all the time
when you were gone and we heard what was happening
    I kept praying for you—and she stopped and covered her face
and took Pi'ilani's hand and Pi'ilani said
    —A long time ago when we were small I saw you once
in church I remember and I tried to see what you looked like—
    and they both laughed and a child appeared in the doorway
—This is my daughter—Kealia said—This is Shirley
    Come and meet your Aunt Pi'ilani—she said to the child
who inched forward and Pi'ilani knelt and said
    —How are you Shirley—and the child said—I am very well—
and they kissed—Come in—Kealia said—and meet—
    but an older woman had appeared behind her
and when Pi'ilani turned to her she said—I am her
    mother Malukauai Kaiwi welcome Pi'ilani—
and she led her into a room where a table was set
    with plates and melons and a pair of candlesticks

311

31.

Most afternoons after that while Pi'ilani
    was staying at the Sheldons' she would meet Kealia
and they would walk around Waimea or sit in the shade
    and talk while Shirley and her friends played nearby
they sat talking for hours and Pi'ilani said
    that she had never talked so much in her whole life
they talked about Ho'ona and about when they were children
    and about everyone they knew and Waimea and the mill
and Kekaha and Makaweli but they did not talk
    about Kalalau at first nor about Ko'olau
and all that she was telling John Sheldon about
    in the mornings and hearing him read back to her
but they talked about the Sheldons and Kealia said
    how different from each other the brothers seemed to be
and both of them married to Hawaiian women
    and she said—In their family they have no trouble with that
but some haoles do I can tell you my aunt my mother's
    sister used to work for Charles Gay a few years ago
before he moved to Lanai you know Mr Gay
    he was Mr Knudsen's brother-in-law one of the grandsons
of Eliza Sinclair who bought Ni'ihau and died
    at Makaweli in the time when you were away
Mr Gay took care of the ranch and people liked him I hear
    but when he married a Hawaiian woman my aunt says
his mother disowned him and cut him out of her will
    and that was when he took what was his and went over
to the island of Lanai and they never spoke after that
    she told me his daughter went once to see her grandmother
just so they could have met one time before the old woman
    died and my aunt says her grandmother sat up straight
in her chair and would not say one word to the girl
    so many families with people not speaking
to each other haole families Hawaiian families
    do you think I would ever be able to meet your mother—
And Pi'ilani said—It might happen some day
    after she hears about you—and it seemed a strange thing
to be saying as though both of them were children
    but then everything in those days seemed as though it had
come out of hiding and strangest of all was the Sheldons'
    parlor in the mornings and telling John Sheldon

about the years in Kalalau and whether she had prayed
    on the ledge at Waimakemake and trying to say
the words she had chanted that day when she left the valley

32.

One evening Mrs Sheldon led Pi'ilani
    into the parlor after dinner and showed her
an album of old pictures of the family
    and of the islands years before and portraits of people
from still earlier times and to Pi'ilani
    they were familiar and untouchable as dreams
or as the story about herself as Mr Sheldon
    read back to her the parts that he had written down
then he and his brother came into the parlor and joined
    in the conversation over the photographs
and John Sheldon said to Pi'ilani—I hope that you
    will agree to have your picture taken to be published
along with the story of Kalalau I have taken
    the liberty of speaking with a photographer
here in Waimea who makes studio portraits
    and would be happy to oblige us—and Mrs Sheldon
said—I would love to have a picture of you for the album—
    and Pi'ilani agreed to it but she said—I look
more angry in pictures—and they laughed and Mrs Sheldon said
    —That is because they tell you to hold still and you become
very serious—And Mr Sheldon asked—Are there
    other pictures of you—And Pi'ilani said
—A few—And then he asked about pictures of Ko'olau
    and the house and she said there were a few of those
—Bad ones—she said—Some you can hardly see anything—
    —I would like to look at them—Mr Sheldon said—And perhaps
publish them too—and when he said it she did not
    want anyone but her family to see them
but then she thought that if she was telling the story
    showing the pictures was part of it and they seemed
as far away from the faces and days she remembered
    or almost as far as pictures in the album
of places she had never seen and so one afternoon
    Mrs Sheldon and Mele came and helped her to dress
and hung a lei around her neck and they took a big Bible
    and a bouquet of flowers from the garden and Mrs Sheldon
and John and Pi'ilani went down to the studio
    where Pi'ilani sat in a straight chair clutching
the flowers by the neck in her right hand and the Bible
    in her left and held still looking angry for her picture

33.

Mr Sheldon said that his story was complete
      except for what he called finishing touches and he wrote it
all over again and when that was done he read it
      to all of them that evening and Mrs Sheldon cried
and the next day they took a lunch out toward Koloa
      and Mr Sheldon said he would like to see Kekaha
and asked Pi'ilani whether she would show it to him
      and she looked at them all and then nodded and he said
that there might be those who would challenge the facts of their story
      and so he had decided to swear to the truth of it
before a notary public and he asked her
      whether she would add her name to his and she looked
at Mrs Sheldon and the others and she nodded
      and later he told her that he and the photographer
would like a picture of her standing high among rocks
      holding a rifle and he said they could find a place
at the mouth of Waimea canyon that would provide
      a setting that would look like Kalalau and she said
they must not say it was Kalalau and he told her
      it was the picture of her that mattered and they went
the next day and rode up the canyon and the photographer
      kept her standing up in the rocks with an old rifle
while he crouched under his black sheet behind the camera
      and she looked down at him with the sun in her eyes
and none of it seemed to have anything to do
      with Kalalau and then they were saying good-bye
in front of the Sheldon house as though she were going away
      forever and thanking each other and John Sheldon
and Ho'ona were with her in the Sheldon carriage
      on the way back to Kekaha and Kepola
got out the pictures for them to look at and Ho'ona led
      Mr Sheldon around Kekaha and they came back
and sat talking and eating watermelon and then
      Mr Sheldon stood up and promised to bring back the pictures
and was gone and Kepola and Pi'ilani sat talking
      about Kealia and Malukauai and the house
by the Waimea river and when Ho'ona
      was out of the house Kepola said she thought
it was time for all of them to know each other

34.

One day a man and a boy rode up to the house
     at Kekaha and the man leaned over the pommel
and said—Pi'ilani—and she looked up and it was Kala
     and he jumped down and embraced her and—This is my son
Iwa—he said and the child bent for her to kiss him
     —Is your mother at home—Kala asked and Kepola came out
and kissed him and he said—It has been ten years ten years
     and I wanted to see you and Ida I have
thought of you many times after that day when we went
     up like smoke into the cliff in Kalalau—and he laughed
They went into the house and the family gathered
     to celebrate and he told them that he had hidden
in the cliffs for weeks and then gone down to his friends
     at Wili Kini's ranch and worked there for a while
and then along the coast toward Kilauea and there
     he had started a family—And Kua is married too—
he said—A few years back after I heard that you
     were home in Kekaha he married a widow
over near Hanalei and I go to see him
     he has a few horses and a garden out that way—
and he said he remembered how brave Ida had been
     when they were climbing out that morning and now she was
grown up and beautiful and as he talked Pi'ilani
     felt how far away Kalalau seemed to have become
and how her telling about it at the Sheldons' house
     seemed to have drawn a shadow across it blurring
and fading it like the pictures and Kala looked
     so much older that she would scarcely have recognized him
but when he spoke of Kalalau it seemed as fresh and clear
     in his words as ever and she saw then that it was
the terrible moments there that she did not want to forget
     the time on the ledge with the sound of the bullets
and the cannon echoing and that night when they went down
     through the stream with Kaleimanu and the voices
of the soldiers were so close that she had been sure
     they could hear her and she could still smell the smoke of their
cigarettes through the smoke of their campfire and then
     the sickness of Kaleimanu day by day she did not
want it to slip through her fingers now and be gone
     or his dying and their burying him she wanted

to keep even the pain of it and she felt that it was
    slipping away from her and what she saw in her mind
was the long sand at Mānā when the tide had gone out

35.

When Mr Sheldon's book was published Nalu came from Waimea
    to invite Pi'ilani and Kepola and Ho'ona
and Ko'olau's parents Kukui and Kaleimanu
    to Waimea to celebrate it and he said
he would be back the next day with the carriage for them
    At the Sheldon house there was food on a long table
in the back garden and they all prayed and gave thanks
    for the Lord's mercy and this work well done and Mr Sheldon
read from the psalms He that dwelleth in the secret place
    of the Most High shall abide under the shadow
of the Almighty and he read it first in Hawaiian
    and then in English while Kukui cried and Mrs Sheldon
cried but Pi'ilani seemed to be looking at something
    out past them and they said Amen and began to talk
as though they had wanted to know each other for years
    Mr Sheldon's other brother Henry was there with his wife
and they started to talk of their brother John all the places
    where he had lived and his newspapers and the time
when he was a fisherman and his loyalty to the Queen
    which had led the government to seize his possessions
and to put out a warrant for his arrest—He should
    have been here to read that psalm—his brother William said
And then they were all eating shellfish and Kepola
    said to Pi'ilani—Do you think this would be
a good day to meet Malukauai and Kealia
    since we are here in Waimea and it is a kind
of family time only how could we do it
    without Ho'ona because he cannot be there
when we meet—and Pi'ilani looked at Ho'ona
    talking with Henry Sheldon and she said—The Sheldons
have arranged to have Nalu take us home in the carriage
    but I will tell Mrs Sheldon that we have friends
here in Waimea to whom we want to show the book
    and let Nalu take Kukui and Kaleimanu
you can tell Ho'ona that I am going to see Kealia
    and that you want to meet her but not with him there
and I will ask them whether they want to see us today
    and will come to the church and tell you—and both of them laughed
behind their hands like children making up a new game

36.

Malukauai said she wanted to meet Kepola
    but she was embarrassed to have her see the house as it was
and she wanted to be sure that Ho'ona was not
    anywhere around and she thought about it and they agreed
to meet under the mango tree beside the Rowells' house
    and Pi'ilani went to the church and found her mother
standing out in front of it in the shade and Ho'ona
    had gone—When I told him he looked frightened—she said
—I wonder who he could be afraid of—and she walked
    with Pi'ilani past the Rowells' big house and they all
met shyly with small voices under the old tree
    and stood talking about nothing with those same voices
and then Kealia said to Pi'ilani—
    —Do you have the book—and Pi'ilani showed it to them
and said—That copy is for you—and Kealia
    showed it to Malukauai and they opened it
to Pi'ilani's picture and they all stood looking at it
    and Pi'ilani put her hands to her face and suddenly
Malukauai was crying and Kepola embraced her
    and then they all embraced and Malukauai said
—It is silly for us to be standing out here
    as though we had no place of our own to go to
but you must promise not to pay attention to the house
    I never thought we would have somebody coming today—
and she led them along the river lane to her house
    and Kealia brought Shirley back from the neighbors
for them to meet and kept finding things for them to eat
    as they sat talking and in a moment when they were
silent Malukauai looked at Pi'ilani
    and said—Are you glad he wrote the book—and Pi'ilani
did not answer for a long time they waited
    and finally she said—Yes—and Kealia
picked it up and looked at the title page—She will
    read it to me—Malukauai said—And we will
keep it there with the Bible on that table—
    —And will you come to see us in Kekaha—Kepola asked

37.

So they arranged for a visit to Kekaha
        —Maybe only women—Kepola said and Malukauai
said—I think he would be ashamed but you know how families
        crowd in and get curious it will be all right—
And Kepola Kukui Kinau Ida and Pi'ilani
        started getting food ready days before and then
Kaleimanu and his friends saw that they were making
        a banquet and they brought more fish and they took it
for granted that the whole family would be there
        and they asked which day it would be and that morning
they brought crabs and sea urchins shellfish and seaweed
        reef fish and eels and mangos papayas and melons
it was all piled up before Kaleimanu asked
        Kepola what the occasion was that they were
celebrating and when she told him he told his old father
        and they all began laughing and Kaleimanu said
Ho'ona has to be here even if we have to bring him
        tied hand and foot like a sacrifice and we will go
and get him and say—Ho'ona are you not coming
        to the feast——What feast is that—he will ask——You never
heard—we will ask—Everybody in Kekaha will be there—
        —Malukauai would be embarrassed—Kepola said—
—We will bring him later—Kaleimanu said—And you can
        warn her after she knows everybody and this time
the laugh will be on Ho'ona—And Kepola
        and the rest of the family made the first visit
of Malukauai and Kealia and Shirley
        a great feast and Kinau played the ukelele
as she had not done for years and the chants and dancing
        began and were well under way when the men came back
with Ho'ona and he stood speechless and they told him
        to eat and make himself at home and went on singing
all the neighbors were there and when the dancing was over
        and they were standing and sitting in twos and threes
eating and talking Ho'ona went over to where
        Kepola and Malukauai were sitting and he stood
looking at them not knowing what to say and Kepola
        put up her hand and said—Not one word not one word
go have something to eat and pay no attention to us
        as you see we are able to entertain ourselves—

38.

By the time the neighbors had left and the fire had died down
    and the talk had sunk to low voices from under the trees
Kepola looked up and said to Malukauai
    —It is too late for you to go back to Waimea
please stay here with us tonight if you do not mind
    not much room there will be plenty to eat in the morning—
Malukauai said—You are inviting me now
    to sleep in this house—and Kepola said—Yes I am—
and they went on clearing up after the banquet
    while there was still daylight they put away the food
and Piʻilani fed the dogs as the sun went down
    Shirley was falling asleep and Ida put her to bed
and at last there were only Kepola and Piʻilani
    and Malukauai and Kealia sitting
on the front steps looking out at the sea rustling
    along the sand and the stars over the black shell
of Niʻihau and for a while no one said anything
    and then Malukauai said—I told you I have a sister
she used to work out at Makaweli and she knew
    the Knudsens and now for years she has been working
for a family on the other side of the island
    up near Kilauea by the name of Ewart they have
a big farm and pastures up that way and dairy cattle
    up on the hills she says it is very beautiful
and they are good to her and she likes it there and keeps
    telling me to come and see her but it is a long trip
and she does not get to Waimea very often
    but she came to see me last week and Kealia
showed her your book and my sister was trying to read it
    and Kealia read some parts of it to her and later
she told us something that had happened up the coast there
    she used to say that one of the things she liked there
was the way the Ewarts played music she said they all
    had their houses near each other and the families
and their children would all get together in the evening
    several times a week and every one of them played
some instrument and so after the milking and dinner
    they would sit and play music for hours with the candles
burning she says they have a piano and they have
    violins and even a harp and one night when they stopped
they heard a flute playing all by itself out in the dark—

39.

—They listened and then the flute stopped and they waited
    and then they went back to playing but listening
and did not hear it again but a few nights later
    when they stopped what they were playing to play it over
they heard the flute again and it went on playing
    where they had stopped and Mr Ewart put down his violin
and opened the door onto the long lanai and the flute
    stopped right there and they all sat listening and one
of the Ewart girls who had been to college said
    that it must be a ghost but they sat there with the door open
and after a while went back to playing the same music
    and listening and then Mr Ewart said I know
that flute playing and they looked at him when he said it
    but then he went back to playing and a few nights later
they heard the flute music coming from the pastures again
    when they had finished playing and Mr Ewart opened the door
and picked up a lantern that he had ready there
    and they followed him out toward where the sound seemed to be
coming from but the playing had stopped when the door
    opened and they were frightened and held up lanterns
staying close behind Mr Ewart that night they found
    nothing and then the next day Mr Ewart found hoofprints
under a tree and hoofprints leading toward the farm
    of a neighbor who had been there longer than they had
a family from Germany named Bertelmann
    with a dairy farm like their own and they all remembered
Christian Bertelmann who had been a child when they came there
    and had grown up into a tall young man who loved
music and sang and who used to come for a time
    and play the flute with them in the evenings and he had
represented Kauai in the legislature but that
    had been years before and then they had not seen him
for a long time and the family said he was sick
    and then that he was away in a hospital
but only last month Mr Ewart had heard that the sickness
    was leprosy and that they had dressed up Christian
as somebody else and sent him away to Japan
    where there was supposed to be a cure for that now
but they never cured him and to get him back this time
    they had him dressed up as a tall woman in mourning

322

who had come from Germany in response to a bid
        for a German wife that one of the Bertelmanns
was said to have published in a German newspaper—

40.

—Their house is built around a courtyard she told me
    which nobody can see from outside and they built him
a room of his own inside the courtyard and in there
    he could take off those clothes and only the family
ever saw him and to console himself he would play
    the flute or he would go out at night and ride his horse
across the pastures and then he would go and listen
    to the music from the Ewarts' where he used to play
and then he began to take his flute out with him
    and play when he heard them and then they heard him and he
stopped doing that and they thought the ghost had gone but he
    still played farther out where they could not hear him or could not
be sure they were hearing anything and then he
    died my sister told me and she said that happened
not long ago and she said that only the family
    knows where he is buried—And she stopped and they sat
hearing the long low wave ending on the shore—A flute—
    Pi'ilani said—There was a man in Kalalau
down by the stream who played the flute and when I heard it
    I would go on thinking I heard it all the next day—
Later that summer at Hofgaard's store in Waimea
    some of them who had seen Sheldon's book were talking
about Ko'olau and some remembered him and Judge Kauai
    and the shooting of Stolz and what Coney had said
after he talked with Pi'ilani and they spoke of those
    pictures of her somebody had heard she was beautiful
but said you would never think so from those photographs
    they agreed she looked plain and they talked about the lepers
still being shipped off to Moloka'i in the same way
    Hofgaard was an old man by then and he said to them
—Those things happened a long time ago but I went to see her
    she told me that she does not regret anything
she said Stolz came to kill her husband and the soldiers came
    to kill her husband and that if her life came to her
again the way it did the first time she would live it
    all the same way—And when Hofgaard had left Pi'ilani
had said to her mother—Why do you think that man came
    to see me Did he think I would tell him something else
after all of the others he has listened to

what does he know now about what I remember
maybe he only wanted to see for himself
    whether I was the one in the book he had been reading
where he told me that some of the words were too crooked for him—

CHARACTERS

Archer—Early, unsuccessful farmer at Kekaha, before Knudsen.

Gibson—Walter Murray Gibson, King David Kalākaua's premier and secretary of state during the 1880's.

Hofgaard—Christopher B. Hofgaard. Storekeeper in Waimea, where his emporium was a local gathering place for decades.

Ho'ona—Pi'ilani's father, born on the island of Hawai'i.

Ida—a younger cousin of Pi'ilani's.

Kaleimanu—son of Ko'olau and Pi'ilani. Named for his grandfather.

Kanaloa—One of the great origin gods of Hawai'i and probably the oldest of them. God of death, of the sea, and of the west.

Kane—Another of the principal gods of Hawai'i. God of origins, the east, life, humankind. High on the summit of Waialeale a huge stone formation comprises the altar of Kane. The number forty was his, representing the forty forms of life. Kane and Kanaloa, in myth, are often in each other's company. Here they are the mountain and the sea.

Kanemahuka—Ko'olau's paternal grandfather.

Kapahu—Pi'ilani's maternal grandfather.

Deborah Kapule—1798–1853 Kauai chief, daughter of ruling chief Kahckili, favorite wife of chief Kaumuali'i. She endured many losses during her lifetime, opposed and survived the Lauai rebellion and massacre, and lived to be one of the most revered and beloved of the Hawaiian elders on the island, and one of the few surviving representatives of the Kauai nobility.

Judge Kauai—A prominent figure in Waimea in the latter part of the nineteenth century. Native Hawaiian, landowner, member of the legislature for several terms.

Kawaluna—Ko'olau's grandmother, Kukui's mother.

Keawe—Ko'olau's paternal grandfather.

Keiwi—Older friend of Pi'ilani's.

Kekiele—Ko'olau's maternal great-grandfather.

Kepahu—Cowboy friend of Kua's.

Kepola—Pi'ilani's mother, born in Kekaha.

Kinoulu—One of Pi'ilani's aunts, a sister of her mother's.

Anne Sinclair Knudsen—1839–1922. Born in Stirling, Scotland, daughter of a distinguished officer in the British Navy. After an interval in New Zealand her family settled in Hawai'i where her mother bought the island of

327

Ni'ihau and land on Kauai near Waimea. Anne married Valdemar
Knudsen, Ko'olau's employer.

Valdemar Knudsen—Anne Sinclair's husband, born in Norway, 1819. Rancher
and planter on west Kauai. Botanist, ornithologist, archaeologist, linguist,
writer in correspondence with many scientists of his time. Married Anne
1867. Died 1898.Pohaku-o-Kauai—mythological personage, the Rock of
Kauai, referred to by Pele as her grandfather.

Ko'olau—Kaluaiko'olau. Pi'ilani's husband, a cowboy, born in Kekaha in 1862.

Kū—Fourth of the chief Hawaiian gods. The war god.

Kukui—Ko'olau's mother.

Prince Kunuiakea—1851–1903. Known by those sympathetic to him as "The
Last Kamehameha," Albert Kukailimoku Kunuiakea was the natural son
of King Kamehameha III and a high chief, Jane Lehilani Kaeo. Albert,
who was brought up as a Catholic, helped teach Father Damien Hawaiian.
He served in the legislature after 1880, and in 1895 was a delegate to the
Constitutional Convention. When he died he was accorded a state funeral,
partly as a way of mourning the end of a dynasty.

Lono—Another of the principal gods. God of the rain and of the cycle of
returning life.

Maka'e—Hawaiian woman, a housekeeper and cook in the Knudsen household.

Me'eawa—Cowboy, employed by Knudsen.

Naea—A neighbor of Pi'ilani's in Kekaha.

Nahola—Pi'ilani's maternal grandmother.

Nakaula—Ko'olau's maternal grandfather.

Palemanō—A point of the coast of Hawai'i.

Kua Papiohuli—elder friend of Ko'olau's. Cowboy.

Pi'ilani—Hawaiian woman born in Kekaha, 1864.

Pohaku-o-Kauai—mythological personage, the Rock of Kauai, referred to by
Pele as her grandfather.

Puako—A purveyor of Hawaiian lore, west Kauai, mid-century. Cooperative
and unreliable.

Reverend Rowell—George Berkeley Rowell, born 1815, Cornish, New Hamp-
shire. Missionary. Sailed to Kauai in 1842. Settled in Waimea. Built a
stone church, then a smaller church and a school.

Umi—An ancient chief of Hawai'i.

Father Whitney—The Whitneys were missionaries at Waimea before George
Rowell.

GLOSSARY

amakihi—the Amakihis—Latin *Hemignathus*—are a group of small honey-creepers with yellow markings. Some were specific to single islands. A number of them have become extinct in this century.

'awa—Kava; *Piper methysticum*. The root is the source of a narcotic sedative drink.

'elepaio—*Chasiempis sandwichensis*—a small indigenous flycatcher, the Kauai form brownish gray with orange breast.

hala—The "screw pine". Indigenous *Pandanus odoratissimus*, whose long leaves are used for matting and thatch.

haole—Hawaiian word for caucasians—and by extension for foreign and introduced things. Its overtones pejorative.

hau—*Hibiscus tiliaceous.* A spreading, thicket-forming lowland tree, its bark used for making rope and its light wood for the outriggers of canoes.

Hilinama—on Kauai, the month corresponding to November.

hilu fish—name for several kinds of Hawaiian reef fish.

Hiva—is what the Marquesans called the place they had come from. The main island of the Marquesas, the northernmost of that archipelago, is Nuku Hiva.

Hua—thirteenth night of the lunar month.

Huna—the name for the eleventh night of the Hawaiian lunar month.

kahuna—a word whose range of meanings refers to mastery of an art, from medicine to divination to black sorcery.

kamani—Alexandrian laurel. A noble tree, to 60' tall. Blunt, magnolia-like leaves, fragrant flowers. The nuts yield medicinal oil that is also used in lamps. Hard, dark wood. Sacred in some parts of Polynesia.

Kao'ea—star, planet (perhaps Jupiter) or constellation believed to preside over Hanalei on the north coast of Kauai.

kapu—Proscribed. Forbidden. The word that has become familiar in English as "taboo." A system of protocol which sustained the war chiefs. Infractions incurred the death penalty.

koa—the *Acacia koa;* Hawaiian acacia. It is a principal tree of the Hawaiian forests and one of the most beautiful. War canoes were traditionally made from the koa.

kopiko—any of the *Straussias,* small Hawaiian trees of the coffee and gardenia family, growing as understory plants, generally up to 4500 feet altitude.

kukui—candlenut tree, *Eleurites moluccana.* A large tree with maple-shaped

329

leaves. The nuts, the size of walnuts, yield an oil used in cooking and for light.

lantana—The common invasive bush, *Lantana camara*, native to the American tropics, now established in many parts of the warm latitudes.

makua—father

makuahine—mother

Manahunes—a name with a devious history, at one time designating a people of Tahiti, and later evolving (with the spelling *menehune*) to mean the semi-legendary archaic settlers of Kauai.

milo—A tree, *Thespesia populnea*, found on coasts in the Pacific tropics. It is a shade tree with hibiscus-like flowers and dark, heavy wood used in making bowls and carving. The tree is revered in some places.

mountain apples—*Eugenia malaccensis*. Malay apple—'ohi'a 'ai in Hawaiian. A tropical fruit somewhat resembling certain apples in appearance and taste.

'ohia—*Metrosideros polymorpha* or *M. collinia*. Another of the principal trees of the Hawaiian forest and mythology. A beautiful tree, sacred to the fire goddess Pele and used in her rituals.

olokele—a brilliant scarlet honey-creeper, the Kauai name for the i'iwi, the *Vestiaria coccinea*, with a distinct, ringing call and a gift for mimicry.

Pele—the fire goddess, a central, varying, and extremely important figure in Hawaiian mythology.

Pohaku—the word means rock. Pohaku o Kauai, the Rock of Kauai, is both a place and a mythological character in the legend of Pele, who refers to the rock as her grandfather.

poi—Taro root pounded to a smooth paste. A staple of Hawaiian diet.

tapa—a cloth, often very fine and durable, made by pounding the paper mulberry or one of several other plants.

taro—*Colocasia esculenta*. An aroid, the staple vegetable of the Hawaiian diet, both root and leaves cooked and eaten. The plant has an important place in Hawaiian mythology, somewhat analogous to that of maize among the indigenous peoples of the Americas.

ti—is *Cordyline terminalis*, a plant common in Hawai'i, in lowland forests and gardens, and of great importance in the culture of the Hawaiians. The long, broad shining leaves have been used for ceremonial purposes, for dancers' skirts, for wrapping offerings of food, and for cooking food wrapped in it as tamales are wrapped in corn leaves.

'ulei—native shrub, *Osteomele anthyllidifolia*, with small white flowers, edible white berries. A member of the Rosaceae related to the hawthorn. Sacred to the goddess Hiʻiaka.

uluhe—any of the so-called false staghorn ferns. Native, creeping, barbed growth in a variety of habitats.

ʻuwaʻu—or ʻua ʻu, or uuau in various texts. The Hawaiian petrel, *Pterodroma phaeopygia,* a bird of the open seas, breeding in burrows on barren mountain slopes, coming and going at night. It is now a rare, endangered, declining species. The Hawaiian name mimics the bird's cry.

A NOTE ABOUT THE AUTHOR

W.S. MERWIN was born in New York City in 1927 and grew up in Union City, New Jersey, and in Scranton, Pennsylvania. From 1949 to 1951 he worked as a tutor in France, Portugal and Majorca. He has since lived in many parts of the world, most recently on Maui in the Hawaiian Islands. His many books of poems, prose and translations are listed at the beginning of this volume. He has been the recipient of many awards and prizes including the Fellowship of the Academy of American Poets (of which he is now a Chancellor), the Pulitzer Prize in Poetry, and the Bollingen Prize in Poetry; most recently he has received the Governor's Award for Literature of the state of Hawai'i, the Tanning Prize for mastery in the art of poetry, a Lila Wallace-Reader's Digest Writers' Award, and the Ruth Lilly Poetry Prize.

A NOTE ON THE TYPE

THIS BOOK is set throughout in a digitized version of *Ehrhardt*, a type face deriving its name from the Ehrhardt type foundry in Frankfurt (Germany). The original design of the face was the work of Nicholas Kis, a Hungarian punch cutter known to have worked in Amsterdam from 1680 to 1689. The modern version of Ehrhardt was cut by The Monotype Corporation of London in 1937.

Composition by NK Graphics, Keene, New Hampshire
Printed and bound by Berryville Graphics, Berryville, Virginia
Designed by Harry Ford
Maps by Manoa Mapworks, Inc., Honolulu, Hawaii